Return to the Place

The Magic, Meditation, and Mystery of *Sefer Yetzirah*

Rabbi Jill Hammer, Ph.D.

Ben Yehuda Press
Teaneck, New Jersey

Return to the Place: The Magic, Meditation, and Mystery of Sefer Yetzirah ©2020 Jill Hammer. All rights reserved. No part of this book may be used or reproduced in any manner whatsoever without written permission except in the case of brief quotations embodied in critical articles and reviews.

>Published by Ben Yehuda Press
>122 Ayers Court #1B
>Teaneck, NJ 07666

http://www.BenYehudaPress.com

To subscribe to our monthly book club and support independent Jewish publishing, visit https://www.patreon.com/BenYehudaPress

Ben Yehuda Press books may be purchased at a discount by synagogues, book clubs, and other institutions buying in bulk. For information, please email markets@BenYehudaPress.com

Permissions and Acknowledgements: Interior design and illustrations by Shir Yaakov Feit. Cover illustration, "The Three Mothers," by Tamuz Shiran. The meditation on page p. 118, "A Palmful of Merit, A Palmful of Guilt" is used by permission of Catherine Shainberg.

ISBN13 978-1-934730-06-5

Advance praise for *Return to the Place*

Sefer Yetzirah has been called the foundational text of Jewish mysticism, but despite many scholarly attempts to explain it, readers still find its language baffling and its message indecipherable. Now Rabbi Jill Hammer has clarified the text for us all. Without ruining its mystery, she reveals its cosmic vision of "space, time, and body-soul." Beyond this, she has created a new-ancient meditative practice based on this mystical masterpiece. Her superb achievement is a gift for all of us!

Dr. Daniel Matt, author of *The Essential Kabbalah: The Heart of Jewish Mysticism*

Rabbi Jill Hammer's new opus, *Return to the Place*, is a tour de force—at once scholarly, whimsical, deeply poetic, and eminently accessible. In it Hammer combines translation, commentary, and meditations with her uniquely seasoned sensibility, one that balances feminine and masculine, sensual and philosophical. Calling the Book of Creation an incantation, Hammer takes on a difficult assignment. She pushes back the heavy curtain that has kept this cryptic text hidden and impenetrable, and invites us into its cosmic landscapes. Hammer does this with graceful intelligence and without ever disavowing the physical body of the reader, or our capacity to embrace the body of the world. This volume is a rare gift that comes—*echad ba-dor*, once in a generation.

Rabbi Tirzah Firestone, author of *The Receiving: Reclaiming Jewish Women's Wisdom*

Rabbi Jill Hammer's *Return to the Place* is a major event—both for the Jewish world and far beyond it. As in all her writing, teaching, and spiritual leadership, Rabbi Hammer here displays her unique combination of scholarly rigor, spiritual depth, ritual innovation, and poetic virtuosity. Rabbi Hammer, one of the most original religious guides of our time, opens up for us a text that has fascinated mystics and philosophers for more than a millennium—and yet has remained deeply mysterious. *Return to the Place* shows us that the *Sefer Yetzirah* is a "doorway into the deep structure of creation"—with the power to transform the cosmos as well as each person's most intimate experience. She writes that her discovery of the *Sefer Yetzirah* made her feel she had "come home"; but her readers will feel that it is she who has given them a new "home" within the age-old traditions of Jewish and world spirituality.

Dr. Nathaniel Berman, author of *Divine and Demonic in the Poetic Mythology of the Zohar*

Advance praise for *Return to the Place*

Like its subject, the mysterious Book of Creation, *Return to the Place* brilliantly defies categorization. It is a detailed commentary, a bold spirit-guide, and a valuable work of scholarship. It is both audacious and perspicacious. And no one could have written it but Rabbi Dr. Jill Hammer.

Rabbi Dr. Jay Michaelson, author of *Everything is God: The Radical Path of Non-Dual Judaism*

Rabbi Jill Hammer has restored a seemingly arcane ancient text, the *Sefer Yetzirah*, or Book of Creation, into what it was always meant to be: a manual for ritual and meditative practices. In simple prose she returns each verse to its organic experience in the body, using focused visualizations that carry us directly into the 'knowing' offered by the text. This is a book to peruse and experience over time and one that will endure as an important commentary on kabbalists' profound wisdom of inner states of being. Rabbi Hammer's voice is one you can trust and with her gentle prodding the Book of Creation will bring you back to the Place at your core where divinity awaits. I highly recommend it to all seekers of the Truth.

Dr. Catherine Shainberg, author of *Kabbalah and the Power of Dreaming: Awakening the Visionary Life*

The *Sefer Yetsirah*, the Book of Creation, is both appreciated for its mystery, and respected for its difficulty. Rabbi Hammer's Return to the Place takes giant strides in clarifying the work for contemporary practitioners and scholars. The introduction is both precise and heartfelt, a combination that is as wonderful as it is rare. Her translation is supple, while her commentary is clear and meaningful. *Return to the Place* brings the fascination of this ancient work into the present.

Dr. Marla Segol, author of *Word and Image in Medieval Kabbalah: The Texts, Commentaries, and Diagrams of the Sefer Yetsirah*

Dedicated to

Kohenet Alumah Terri Schuster

who made this book and its pathways possible

and to my beloved family

Shoshana and Raya

who are the place to whom I return.

> My name and yours, and the true name of the sun, or a spring of water, or an unborn child, all are syllables of the great word that is very slowly spoken by the shining of the stars.
>
> Ursula LeGuin
> *A Wizard of Earthsea*

> It is the animate earth that speaks; human speech is but a part of that vaster discourse.
>
> David Abram
> *Spell of the Sensuous:*
> *Perception and Language*
> *in a More-than-Human World*

Acknowledgements

This book is one of the most ambitious writing projects I have ever undertaken. I could not have done this work without scholars who gave me assistance and advice along the way. I particularly want to thank Rabbi Shir Yaakov Feit, Dr. Nathaniel Berman, Rabbi Jeff Hoffman, DHL, Dr. Lorelai Kude, Rabbi Simcha Raphael, Dr. Alan Brill, Dr. Daniel Matt, Rabbi Leah Novick, and Rabbi Jay Michaelson for their generous help in researching, writing, and discussing these ideas over the year. I want to thank Dr. Joy Ladin and Dr. Peter Pitzele for their comments on drafts of the material. Gratitude goes to Dr. Catherine Shainberg, a visualization adept who has taught me so much about how to bring these texts into the present.

This book could also not have been written without the extensive time I spent learning *Sefer Yetzirah* with students and workshop participants. I have deepest gratitude for the students in my classes at the Academy for Jewish Religion, the Kohenet Hebrew Priestess Institute, the Isabella Freedman Jewish Retreat Center, Congregation Romemu, the Rowe Center, Starr King School for the Ministry, and elsewhere.

Thank you to the staff of the Kohenet Hebrew Priestess Institute—Rav Kohenet Taya Shere, Kohenet Keshira haLev Fife, and all the rest, for tirelessly supporting this work and research. Thank you also to the staff of Congregation Romemu for their warm support of this work—Rabbi David Ingber, Cantor Basya Schechter, Rabbi Jessica Kate Meyer, Larry Schwartz, Rabbi Dianne Cohler-Esses, Betsy Shevey, Miriam Rubin, Kohenet Sarah Shamirah Chandler, and more.

My deepest gratitude goes to Kohenet Alumah Schuster for her generous support of the writing of this book and for being a fellow traveler on the journey. Thank you also to Dr. Ora Horn Prouser and the staff of the Academy for Jewish Religion for doing without me for a year so I could write this book.

So many thanks are due to Larry Yudelson for his work to publish this book, and to the editing staff of Ben Yehuda Press for all their help. Thank you to Rabbi Shir Yaakov Feit for his extraordinary vision in laying out the book. Thank you to Tamuz Shiran for the beautiful elemental art she created for the manuscript.

Appreciation and love also go to my late father Leonard Hammer, who always expressed interest in my work even when it seemed esoteric to him, and to my mother Erna Hammer for her support of my writing. Much gratitude to the trees and creatures of Central Park, the Isabella Freedman Jewish Retreat Center in Falls Village, CT, and the whole planet—they have sustained me when I needed contemplation and rest during the writing process.

From the bottom of my heart, I thank Shoshana Jedwab, my beloved spouse, and Raya Jedwab-Hammer, my cherished daughter. Your love and presence in my life makes everything possible. Thank you, Raya, for taking the Three Mothers of *Sefer Yetzirah* into your own heart and practice. It means more than I can say.

Introduction	viii
Visualization and Sacred Practice	xxxviii
Chapter 1	2
Chapter 2	88
Chapter 3	113
Chapter 4	162
Chapter 5	195
Table of Letter Correspondences	224
Chapter 6	226
Appendix I Correspondences with Other Translations	265
Appendix II Translation without Commentary	267
Appendix III The Two Hundred and Thirty-One Gates Meditation	282
Appendix IV Index of Practices	292
Endnotes	294
References	327

Sefer Yetzirah: An Introduction

Whenever I begin to teach about the Book of Creation, I feel a kind of anticipatory energy crackling in the air. The book does its magic, and I witness a kind of surprised excitement on the faces of the people who are present. They don't expect ancient words to speak to them so directly. The text we are reading together is a work of uncanny wisdom. It teaches that we are a tiny part of a vast unfolding cosmos. Yet it also teaches that we can create worlds. We can have the peace of a connection to the larger universe, and the power to access that connection for good. In these moments, I share the excitement of the people around me and reflect it back to them. That is why such energy arises when I teach the Book of Creation.

The Book of Creation, or *Sefer Yetzirah* in Hebrew, stands out from most of ancient Jewish literature. Its central focus is a tale of creation: the making of a unified yet multiple reality. *Sefer Yetzirah*, in its poetic, cryptic, carefully structured words, proposes that the many aspects of our world stem from one creative force. This mystical work probes divine unity, yet is entirely focused on this world—on water, wind, fire, sky, and earth. *Sefer Yetzirah* is at home in the natural world; it is a celebration of the Place, the sacred universe in which we live.

Sefer Yetzirah's fundamental claim is that God creates the world through the Hebrew letters. God engraves each letter as a channel for a particular energy: the energy of water, say, or of breath, or of the left eye. Moving through these letters and their energies, the book describes, step by careful step, the diverse mystery that is creation.

But the book does not only offer a story. *Sefer Yetzirah* directly addresses its readers, expecting them to become active participants in the book's imaginal incantations, channeling God's creative energy into the world. How do we do this? By sounding the letters, by imagining the images, we tune ourselves to the energies of creation. We become the network of channels through which divine energy flows into the world.

Two transformative images bind the text of *Sefer Yetzirah* together. The first is the image of engraved letters, which appears again and again throughout the book. *Sefer Yetzirah* names this network of pathways Wisdom—an intermediary web of forces through which God creates and directs the universe. This web of engraved letters becomes a mysterious sacred text that is no text, but rather the sum total of all that is.

The second image is the Temple. The Temple (in Hebrew, *Beit haMikdash*) refers to the central shrine in Jerusalem—a very specific place, built by the Israelite kings and then destroyed (in 586 BCE and then again in 70 CE). Yet the Temple in *Sefer Yetzirah* is not a building, or any "place" in the usual sense of that word. It is a sacred architecture of the universe, a cosmic cube structure, composed of directions and elements. This Temple contains and protects all creation.

Both of these images, letter-web and cosmic Temple, convey a single message, which is multiplicity-within-unity, or unity-within-multiplicity.[1] The unfolding text relates that there is a single Creator dwelling within existence, whose creative intention underlies all of the cosmos. This single Creator acts through a multiplicity of forces, some of which are in tension with one another. These forces are natural yet also divine: they are intermediaries, or channels, between the Creator and the creation. This multiplicity of forces includes the twenty-two Hebrew letters and the ten *sefirot* or cosmic dimensions, and is structured in the shape of a Temple—a cube with opposing walls. In this cosmic Temple, the many forces combine to create a textured, multi-voiced oneness.

A Return from Exile:
Sefer Yetzirah Embraces the Cosmos

That these two images, letters and Temple, appear as equally important throughout *Sefer Yetzirah* is profound. These two intertwined images are a reconciliation of two conflicting Jewish themes: sacred text and sacred space.

In biblical Israel, Israelites used the Temple and other shrines as places to worship God. Later, the Jews who evolved from the exiled Israelites and returned from exile, faced with displacement from their land and the destruction of their Temple, turned to sacred text in order to keep their faith and identity. Having lost their sacred shrine twice, they focused on Torah as a portable gateway to holiness. Sanctity came to dwell in books and commentaries rather than in embodied places. Yet there continued to be a longing for a sacred place. Sometimes this longing was contained in prayers for the restoration of the Temple in messianic times, poems lamenting the Temple's loss, or mystical visions in which a heavenly Temple still existed.

Whoever wrote and/or edited *Sefer Yetzirah* chose an expansive way to relate to the Temple: they re-imagined the Temple as the entire world. They were not alone in seeing the Temple as a physical echo of the world:

Midrash Tadshe, a Talmud-era collection of writing, sees the pillars, washbasin, and altar of the Temple as representations of the mountains, the sea, and the earth.[2] But *Sefer Yetzirah* went one step further: it hinted at the Temple not as a symbol of the cosmos but as the cosmos itself. The Temple was not and could not be lost. It was all around, always. The Temple that had stood in Jerusalem was only one manifestation of a Temple created at the beginning of time and present throughout all of human experience and history. Kabbalah scholar Elliot Wolfson describes the Temple imagery in *Sefer Yetzirah* as "a way to depict the topography of the divine realm precisely in the absence of an earthly Temple."[3]

Yet *Sefer Yetzirah* did not reject the Torah as a vehicle for holiness. Like other rabbinic texts in which Torah is a cosmic document and a pattern for the world, *Sefer Yetzirah* understood text as a way for God to write the world. *Sefer Yetzirah* departed from the usual rabbinic narrative in which Torah was the world's pattern. Instead, the texts within the book focused on the individual Hebrew letters as dynamic elemental forces. Thus, *Sefer Yetzirah* stayed bound to text while also binding itself to a holy physical world.

Scholar A. Peter Hayman (hereafter called Peter Hayman) believes that in its essence *Sefer Yetzirah* is trying to move away from the image of the Temple toward the alphabet as the defining source of Jewish spiritual wisdom. The alphabet cannot be taken away by the conquerors, and therefore it is preferable to the Temple as a source of holiness. In Hayman's view, *Sefer Yetzirah* insists that the Temple was never important. Hayman writes: "...the author is deliberately exchanging an old, worn-out symbol for one which he thinks has greater durability." [4]

But *Sefer Yetzirah* is not rejecting the Temple per se. Rather, the text enacts the belief that the physical Temple was always a microcosm of something larger: the universe. The destroyed Temple is only one face of a Temple that is as huge as the world and can never be destroyed. The book does not reject the Temple but rather enlarges it. In fact, scholar Rachel Elior believes that it was precisely Jewish priests, expelled from service in a physical Temple, who disseminated the idea of the cosmic Temple throughout the exiled Jewish communities.[5] It is this cosmic Temple that *Sefer Yetzirah* pairs with the sacred *aleph-bet* as the two primary images of divine creation.

By weaving together sacred text with sacred world, *Sefer Yetzirah* offers a healing for the rift between the Jewish people and the earth that began when Jews went into exile. This ancient work rejects the duality of text and world. Instead, the book joins the two together, combining the power of word with the power of matter. For *Sefer Yetzirah*, the primary way for humans to relate to the world is not through revealed law or story, but through wonder at the intricacies of the universe.

What could be more relevant to today's world than an active practice of knowing ourselves as part of the diversity of creation? What could be more in sync with ancient mysticism and current science than an understanding of creation as a network of intertwined energies of which we are a necessary component? What could be more relevant to us than a path to value our literacy while also reconnecting to body experience as a primary form of human knowing? *Sefer Yetzirah* offers us, too, a return from exile: a return from our twenty-first century exile from the earth, the body, and physical experience. Ecofeminist thinker Lachelle Schilling writes: "The earth never runs out of messages. But humans as a species have lost touch with this reality. The majority of the human population lives in urban areas where we consume and live processed lives... How can we think of what we do not encounter?" But *Sefer Yetzirah* gives us a way to encounter the world.[6]

Sefer Yetzirah as Ritual Script

As a teacher of *Sefer Yetzirah* for over fifteen years, I have taught it as a text and also engaged it as a discipline. Using the letters of the Hebrew alphabet, *Sefer Yetzirah* creates a language to orient the practitioner to the architecture of creation. This architecture then becomes a frame within which individuals can transcend their ordinary consciousness and tune into the cosmic reality. That is, the book is not primarily a source of ideas. It is primarily a sacred practice. As kabbalah scholar Marla Segol writes, it is a "ritual script."[7]

Sefer Yetzirah offers brief, poetic statements, some of which tell a story, some of which describe the cosmic architecture, and some of which invite us into practice. The ritual script alternates between descriptions of God's actions (e.g., "God engraved"), descriptions of the multiple categories of letters and/or creation ("three mothers, seven doubles, and twelve simples"), and instructions to the reader ("restrain your mouth from speaking"). The descriptions and instructions sometimes interweave, suggesting that the narrative must be punctuated—or enacted—by action from the reader. The book appears to define a space within which the reader-participants can have a sacred experience in which they encounter "their society, their cosmos, and the powers that generate and sustain them," which, according to anthropologist Victor Turner, is one of the functions of ritual.[8]

Folklorist Lauri Honko has written that ritual "implies the defense of the world order…by imitating sacred exemplars, the world is prevented from being brought to chaos."[9] The ritual of *Sefer Yetzirah*, using God the Creator as a sacred exemplar, is a defense of the world. By frequently focusing on the "seals" and "boundaries" of the cosmic Temple, the reader reifies and thus strengthens the protective boundaries of creation. And, by learning God's language for creation, readers/participants in the text learn a language for our own creative desires.

Finally, the book seeks to create resonance between human and divine. Bobby Alexander, a scholar of ritual, suggests that "a ritual is a planned or improvised performance that effects a transition from everyday life to an alternative framework within which the everyday is transformed."[10] The text of *Sefer Yetzirah* seeks to move the reader from an "everyday" state to a state in which all is connected through a web of divine energies.

In service to the practice that is *Sefer Yetzirah*, the text invokes the infinity of space and time, the majesty of lightning, the fecundity of water, the ephemerality of breath, the shape of the human hand, the power of a single syllable. These images are meant to reveal and illuminate. Throughout this commentary, we will explore these images, relate them to the larger picture of the book, and engage them as practices to transform our consciousness.

Where the Book Comes From and Where It is Going

The book that has come down to us as *Sefer Yetzirah* is difficult to place in space or time. This is partly because of how unusual it is. Scholar Itamar Gruenwald writes that "The book occupies a kind of spiritual isolation that is positively unique in the history of Hebrew literature."[11] There is very little literary context to help us establish the book's milieu.

Scholars have argued considerably about the book's date and about who wrote it and why. Legend attributes the book to Abraham, the patriarch of Genesis.[12] Yehudah Liebes dates it to the first century CE, immediately after the Temple's destruction.[13] Some Jewish commentators, such as Shlomo Pines, believe the original version was written in the second century CE, at the time of the Mishnah.[14] Still others, such as Gershom Scholem, place the date in the third to sixth century,[15] noting that the Hilchot Yetzirah or Laws of Creation, an otherwise unknown magical text, is mentioned in the Talmud:

> What magic is permissible? The kind performed by Rabbi Hanina and Rabbi Oshaya, who spent every Sabbath eve studying the Hilchot Yetzirah, and by means of which they created a third-year calf and ate it. [16]

This text refers to a book with a title similar to *Sefer Yetzirah*, a book that instructs sages in magical creativity. Some believe the book of magic mentioned in the Talmud is the same as *Sefer Yetzirah*. Others believe the two are not connected. Still others believe that some core material from the Mishnaic period might have made its way into later versions of the book.

However, many scholars convincingly date the book from somewhere between the sixth and ninth century. Marla Segol proposes a fifth to seventh century date, observing that the Hebrew poet Eliezer ben Kallir of seventh century Palestine seems to mention *Sefer Yetzirah* or a similar text in his poetry.[17] The date Segol proposes is also the same period during which the Jewish magical items known as incantation bowls were produced in Mesopotamia. The language of *Sefer Yetzirah* has something in common with these bowls, as a number of scholars have noted and as will be discussed in later sections of this commentary.[18] I find Segol's theory compelling and tend to believe the dating she proposes is correct. However, still other scholars, such as Peter Hayman and Elliot Wolfson, date *Sefer Yetzirah* to the ninth century, just prior to Saadya Gaon's writing of a commentary on it.[19] Some cite parallels with Arab Muslim science as support for this theory.[20]

To place the book in space is also difficult. Scholars have placed the writing of *Sefer Yetzirah* in the land of Israel, in Egypt, or in north Mesopotamia.[21] Tzahi Weiss, in his recent book *Sefer Yesirah and Its Contexts*, identifies a Mesopotamian/Syriac origin for *Sefer Yetzirah*, citing textual parallels with Christian Syriac texts. Weiss believes the book was written not by the same Jews who wrote the Talmud, but by Jews more distant from rabbinic Jewish life (that is, Jews whose lives were not guided by Talmudic law and discourse). Weiss writes: "*Sefer Yetzirah* is not similar to rabbinic literature with regard to its style, makes no mention of rabbinical figures, differs completely in its method of presentation, and makes minimal use of biblical sources as prooftexts... *Sefer Yetzirah* does not express an attraction, acceptance, rejection, or opposition toward rabbinic literature, and as such, it is a non-rabbinic Jewish composition."[22]

It does appear that *Sefer Yetzirah* has little in common with rabbinic works such as the Talmud. Though its texts cite the Bible, the book pays little attention to the art of interpretation so beloved by rabbinic Judaism. It also seems to reject the notion that rabbinic law is a cosmic institution that supersedes natural realities, proposing its own cosmic realities instead.[23]

Texts in *Sefer Yetzirah* do occasionally make reference to rabbinic stories. For example, we see in one Talmud text a story about creation through letters. In this story, the artist Betzalel uses letters to create the Tabernacle, echoing God's process of creating the world through letters: "Betzalel understood how to combine the letters by which the heavens and earth were created."[24] An identical method of creating by combining letters is at the core of *Sefer Yetzirah*'s claims.

Yet the book's main concerns are not rabbinic. *Sefer Yetzirah* is uninterested in Torah commentary, rabbinic prayer, law, or parables. As Peter Hayman writes, "[The author] never mentions Moses or his Torah, has no interest in ethics or apparently in the national dimension of Judaism, and hardly ever quotes Scripture. His is a Judaism with no historical dimension."[25] Joseph Dan concurs: "There is in this book no mention of the uniqueness of the Jewish people... there is not one judgment in the book that divides between Jew and non-Jew."[26]

Nor does the book present itself as a journey through the heavens, as some Jewish mystical literature does; it is a text anchored in physical reality. *Sefer Yetzirah*'s way of communicating is poetic and incantational rather than narrative-based or law-based. Its text offers us a direct transmission of a sacred practice. This type of communication is unheard of in rabbinic Jewish life. We are dealing with a text that is an outlier, from an author or authors with an unusual perspective on Jewish tradition.

No one can even agree on the genre of the text. Jewish sages of previous generations—Saadya Gaon most notable among them—read the book as a work of philosophy and science. Some recent scholars, such as Gershom Scholem, Peter Hayman and Marla Segol, have seen it at least partly as a work of magic, noting the parallels between the structure and content of *Sefer Yetzirah* and magical rituals in the ancient world.[27] It has even been presented as a work of linguistics. Still others claim that *Sefer Yetzirah* is the forerunner of classical kabbalah, and attempt to harmonize its teaching with the teachings of the Zohar. Aryeh Kaplan is most notable among contemporary scholars who take this approach, and his book *Sefer Yetzirah: The Book of Creation in Theory and Practice* has inspired many modern readers.[28]

To create this translation, I have had to take a position on many of these issues. Yet I am less a scholar of *Sefer Yetzirah* than a lover of it. I read *Sefer Yetzirah* in my own context as a ritualist and poet. The moment I encountered this text, I knew I had come home. To me, the book offers a sacred experience of the elements that make up our planet and our bodies. It has a powerful Jewish perspective on universal mysteries, a perspective that references Jewish ideas and also reaches beyond them. The text brings together the Bible and Hebrew language with an attitude that embraces the world and all of its multiplicity and wonder. This is exactly the way I want to be addressed as a spiritual person: not only as a member of a tribe, but as a person in need of transformation.

While I'll refer often to scholarship in working with the book's text, my intention is not to provide a critical commentary but to explore *Sefer Yetzirah* as a vehicle for spiritual experience, theological depth, and creative expression. My experience, after seeing the excitement the book generates in those who encounter it, is that the ideas and practices this book holds can transform the lives of others as it has transformed mine.

Sefer Yetzirah as a Composite and Changing Text

In order to translate any text, a translator has to choose what text to translate. In this case, that's not an easy choice.

There are three basic versions or "recensions" of *Sefer Yetzirah*, and each one has a different text. These versions are known as the Short Recension, the Long Recension, and the Saadyan Recension (named for the commentator that offers it, the tenth century CE Jewish philosopher Saadya Gaon). Even within these versions, there are variations.

All of these texts may not be the "original" *Sefer Yetzirah*. The Long Recension has significant material that is not in either of the other two recensions and it is clear that this version contains added materials from later generations. Scholars debate the extent to which the Short and Saadyan Recensions were altered by scribes, editors, and commentators. Scholars often use the manuscripts of the three tenth-century commentators on *Sefer Yetzirah*—Saadya Gaon, Dunash ben Tamim, and Shabbetai Donnolo—to compare the versions of the text that the commentators had before them.[29] These medieval commentators also were aware of differences in various manuscripts, which they attributed to faulty transmission of the original text.[30]

Many contemporary critical scholars believe that *Sefer Yetzirah*, even in the earliest form we can discover, is a composite of several texts. Kabbalah scholar Gershom Scholem, for example, believes that Chapter 1 was appended to the book, and is from a different author than much of the rest of the book. Scholar Ronit Meroz identifies three different texts from different authors, edited together by the author of the third text.[31] Others, like Elliot Wolfson and Peter Hayman, suggest that we cannot confidently separate the text into its original strands, as there likely was significant editing of the book prior to the first manuscript we have available. The differences in early manuscripts compound the problem of fixing an actual text. For these reasons, Elliot Wolfson memorably has referred to *Sefer Yetzirah* as "textual chaos."[32] Wolfson adds: "It is not accurate, in my opinion, to speak of a date of composition of this work, nor is it particularly helpful to speak of an author."[33]

In spite of these controversies, readers should not despair. It is still true that there are core images and ideas that carry through the entire text. The Hebrew letters, elements, directions, and "realms" of space, time, and soul appear over and over again, structuring our perceptions and addressing our imaginations. While the variant manuscripts can make interpretation of the text somewhat difficult, ideas in the text still come through with bracing clarity.

Peter Hayman, a translator of and commentator on *Sefer Yetzirah*, has made an effort to determine the "earliest recoverable text"—though he states that the earliest/original text is not recoverable, given the layers of additions and edits that seem to have occurred prior to the first manuscripts of *Sefer Yetzirah* that we have.[34] Hayman writes: "The manuscript tradition of *Sefer Yetzirah* is too varied and inconstant for anything like a definitive edition to be produced."[35] Hayman analyzes all of the existing manuscripts to arrive at this earliest recoverable text. In this commentary, we will mostly work with Hayman's "earliest recoverable text" as our version of *Sefer Yetzirah*. We will take this route to avoid some of the later additions to the text, and to keep *Sefer Yetzirah* as simple and close to its origins as possible.[36] (Where I have diverged from Hayman's "earliest recoverable manuscript" to include material from the Short Recension, this has been noted in the commentary.)

That being said, we cannot fully put ourselves in the original context of the book. Tzahi Weiss has noted that the book is hard to read precisely because we have so little indication of its cultural context.[37] Our only option is to read it, not as the authors would have read it, but as we are able to read it, with our own set of perspectives and concerns. This book has much to say to the modern reader; I encourage you, the reader, to read it as if the book is speaking to you. The book is in fact speaking to you—inviting you on a spiritual journey.

The Structure of *Sefer Yetzirah*

Sefer Yetzirah has six chapters.[38] Each chapter focuses on a particular element within the web of channels that create the world. The first chapter offers an introduction and also deals with the *sefirot*, ten dimensions of reality that structure the universe. The second, third, fourth, and fifth chapters deal with the Hebrew letters. Chapter 2 deals with the letters as a whole; Chapter 3 with the three "mother letters" *Aleph, Mem,* and *Shin;* Chapter 4 with the seven "double letters;" and Chapter 5 with the twelve "single letters." Chapter 6 provides a conclusion, with a few new twists, including the announcement that Abraham used the spiritual methods of *Sefer Yetzirah* in order to come close to God.

Sefer Yetzirah is written in short paragraphs that contain poetic and often cryptic language. Each chapter (except Chapter 6) has a particular phrase that marks the sections of that chapter. In addition, various catch phrases such as "God engraved and carved…," sprinkled throughout the text, serve to unify the language and ideas of the chapters. There are also many lists: of letters, attributes, directions, etc. These lists serve to emphasize the structured diversity of God's world. Some chapters also contain comments that address the reader, inviting engagement with the book's mysteries.

Marla Segol has suggested that the taglines of *Sefer Yetzirah*—the phrases that mark each paragraph as part of a particular chapter—create a ring structure: the book begins with a prologue, moves to the center of the ring, then circles back to the beginning of the ring—the whole structure ending with an epilogue.[39] The ring structure "instructs the reader to visualize the structure of a narrative."[40] Segol suggests that this ring structure indicates the book has a magical purpose: "a mythological narrative describing a cosmology and providing instructions for acting on it." [41]

The Realms, Elements, and Directions

Sefer Yetzirah's fundamental guiding image is unity within multiplicity, multiplicity within unity. While dualities (such as good and evil, beginning and end) do appear within the text, ultimately all dualities are part of a larger multiplicity generated by God's unified creative power. *Sefer Yetzirah* has a language for this multiplicity within unity, and the language is that of realms, elements, and directions. These categories, which are intertwined with the Hebrew letters and the *sefirot* or cosmic dimensions, are a way of depicting how multiplicity, structured by unity, is the architecture of the cosmos. *Sefer Yetzirah* explains with precision the diversity of forces in the world and how they work together to achieve God's intended creation. There are three categories that we see over and over again as *Sefer Yetzirah* lays out a diagram of creation for us.

THE REALMS

Sefer Yetzirah divides reality into the three basic realms of existence: space, time, and body-soul (*olam*, *shanah*, and *nefesh*). (Although *nefesh* is often understood to mean soul, in *Sefer Yetzirah* it appears to mean the entire human being, especially the body—just as it does in certain places in the Bible. We will discuss this further in Chapter 1.) *Sefer Yetzirah* refers to these three realms as "books" or "witnesses." These three realms of the universe—space, time, and human experience—provide the fundamental playing field on which creation can unfold.

In Chapter 1:7, the ten *sefirot* or cosmic dimensions of beginning/end, good/evil, up/down/east/west/north/south, combine to create the three realms of time, person, and space. The *sefirot* are divinely emanated forces that seem like rays or fields, moving out from the sacred center and structuring the universe into its component parts. Each pair of *sefirot* combines to create one of the realms—beginning and end joining to make time, for example. In the commentary on Chapter 1, we will discuss how kabbalists in later Jewish generations will use the language of *sefirot* to speak about their own cosmological system. However, for now, we will focus on the role of *sefirot* in creating the realms of the cosmos.

We also see references to the three realms in other parts of the text. In Chapter 3:9, the three mother-letters manifest in different ways in the realms of space, time, and body; in Chapter 4:3 and 5:3, the seven double letters and twelve simple letters also manifest in the three realms. In Chapter 4:6 and 6:2, the three realms are called three "witnesses," each set aside by itself, yet each part of one mysterious cosmic fabric.

This threefold nature of reality is a kind of space-time-person continuum. Chapter 1:1 names these realms *sefer*, *sfar*, and *sippur*. *Sefer*, "book," is space; *sfar* is number, which is time; and *sippur* is story, or human experience. The three realms are all named for variations on the single root *saper* (to tell). This suggests that a unity underlies them all even though they are different. Einstein, who theorized the space-time continuum, would have been proud (and the modern quantum physicists who include experience as an underlying determinant of reality would be even more proud).[42] Ultimately, God is the one who weaves the realms together into a perceivable world. These realms are the "books" God writes. The text/world is an "engraving" of God's intention into the fabric of existence.

THE ELEMENTS

Reality also manifests in elements: air, water, and fire (sometimes joined by a fourth element: divine breath). In Chapter 1, the elements are another manifestation of the *sefirot*. These elements proceed directly from the Divine. Divine breath breathes out air, which in turn gives rise to water and fire. The elements are a division of God's energy into primary forces that interact dynamically with one another to produce diversity within the physical world. Scholar Ronit Meroz writes: "It would appear that the incorporation of various elements, both primary and secondary, is responsible for the functioning of this world."[43]

In Chapter 3, the elements are "mothers" or matrices for the substances of the world. The mother-letters *Aleph*, *Mem*, and *Shin* are identified with air, water, and fire. The elements provide fundamental structures within the larger realms of space, time, and body. They manifest as sky, earth, and atmosphere; the days, months, and seasons; and the limbs and organs of the human body.

In *Sefer Yetzirah*, as we shall see when we delve into the texts, the elements are not symbols or abstract ideas. Water is water. Fire is fire. These entities are building blocks for a natural world that is in intimate dialogue with the Divine. *Sefer Yetzirah* means for us to see divine creative presence in the physical substance of our world.

THE DIRECTIONS

The six directions—up, down, east, west, north, and south—appear three times in *Sefer Yetzirah*. In Chapter 1:8, the directions appear as the six *sefirot* that define space. In Chapter 1:13, they appear as the six walls (including the floor and ceiling) of the cosmic Temple. In Chapter 4:2, the directions appear as six of the seven double letters, marking the walls of the cosmos (the seventh letter is the sacred center). For *Sefer Yetzirah*, the directions are an expression of unity-within-multiplicity. A building cannot exist without its walls, and the unified world cannot exist without its multiple directions.

The text's focus on the elements and directions invites us to concentrate on nature as a site of sacred experience. To contemplate ourselves and our world as made of water, fire, and wind is to give spiritual power to the physical landscape.

The System of Elements and Directions

The elements and directions are so important to *Sefer Yetzirah* that it duplicates them in its thought-system. [44]

Consider that there are two versions of the *sefirot*:

DIMENSIONAL VERSION (1:7)
Beginning	End
Good	Evil
Above	Below
East	West
North	South

ELEMENTAL VERSION (1:13-1:16)
Divine Breath	Breath
Water	Fire
Above	Below
East	West
North	South

Each of these versions includes the directions. One of the versions contains the elements, while the other contains the components of time (beginning/end) and body-soul (good/evil). To state what centuries of kabbalistic commentary have obscured: the two versions don't match.

Now we have to also note that in Chapter 3, the three mothers (*Aleph, Mem,* and *Shin*) denote the three elements of air, water, and fire. Thus, they overlap with the elemental version of the *sefirot*. Further, in Chapter 4, the seven double letters (*bet, gimel, dalet, kaf, peh, reish, taf*) are identified with the seven directions. Thus, they overlap with the dimensional version of the *sefirot*. So, we have further inconsistency in the text.

The conflicting versions of the *sefirot* stem from the earliest manuscripts of the text that we have.[45] So it seems that the multiple renditions of the *sefirot* are a feature of the older versions of the text rather than a later addition or commentary. It seems that *Sefer Yetzirah* is integrating elemental/directional systems that differ slightly: one has four elements (divine breath, air, water, fire) and one has three (air, water, fire). The book also does not agree on a directional system: in Chapter 1 there are six directions (north, south, east, west, up, down) and in Chapter 4 there are seven (the first six plus the center). Further, one system names the elements as *sefirot* and one names the elements as mother letters; one names the directions as *sefirot* and one names the directions as double letters. Why all this confusion?

Contemporary scholars agree *Sefer Yetzirah* is a composite text, bringing together passages from different writers at some point before the text we now have. This suggests that several Jewish writers, writing at a similar time and place, are similar enough in their outlook to be working on the same problem: the nature and identity of the dimensions and elements of creation. This may hint at a group of Jewish practitioners in Mesopotamia who used dimensional, directional, and/or elemental language to express their view of the cosmos and whose views could be edited together to produce *Sefer Yetzirah*. One wonders if multiple ideas about the dimensions and elements of the universe could have become the multiple versions of the *sefirot* that exist in *Sefer Yetzirah*.

What seems to matter to the authors/editors of *Sefer Yetzirah* is not complete consistency, but rather that the elements and directions have an important role in divine creation. By emphasizing the elements and directions as part of God's world, *Sefer Yetzirah* telegraphs its sense that the world is a diverse yet ordered place, and an adept can understand the world via a knowledge of these component parts.

The language of elements and directions may seem foreign to the Jewish mythos. However, Jews, like others in the ancient world of the Mediterranean, spoke of four elements. The Book of Ecclesiastes lists the four elements of earth, sun, wind, and water in its opening chapter:

> One generation goes and another comes,
> but the earth remains the same forever.
> The sun rises and the sun sets

> And returns Shining to where it rises.
> Blowing northward, turning southward,
> Ever turning blows the wind,
> The wind returns on its whirlings.
> The rivers run to the sea, but the sea is never full.
> To the place from which the rivers flow,
> There they return again.[46]

Much later, in the tenth century CE, the philosopher Maimonides explicates the elements as the building blocks of matter: "There are four bodies, and they are fire, air, water, and earth. They are the foundation of all that is created beneath the sky."[47] Yet rather than four elements, *Sefer Yetzirah* has three elements (air, water, fire) and sometimes includes divine breath as a fourth rather than earth.

The reason for this departure from the four-element system is unclear. One possibility is that for *Sefer Yetzirah*, the mobility of the elements is fundamental: "God's word in them is running and returning." Earth may have been eliminated from the taxonomy of elements because it seems solid, not mobile. The elements need to be able to "flow" through the channels of the letters so they can act in the world. Perhaps for the author(s) of the text, air, water, and fire feel more in sync with this "channeling" than earth. *Sefer Yetzirah* likes its elements fluid, able to move through the engraved channels God has made for them.

Or, it may be that the three-element ayurvedic system from Hindu thought somehow influenced the writing and practice of *Sefer Yetzirah*. In the Hindu medicine system known as Ayurveda, *vata* (air), *pitta* (fire), and *kapha* (water, which has an earthy quality) are the primary energies, or *doshas*. There are obvious similarities to *Sefer Yetzirah*, since the element of water (as embodied in the letter *Mem*) also includes earth. There has been speculation that ideas from India made their way into *Sefer Yetzirah*, and this could also explain the three-element system.[48]

Yehuda Liebes notes that Chapter 1 of *Sefer Yetzirah* seems to try to square a three-element system (air, water, fire) with the more common four-element system. The passage does this by dividing air into two: *ruach hakodesh* (holy spirit or holy wind) and *ruach meruach* (wind from wind or breath from breath). Thus, air has a human and a divine element.[49] The text preserves the fluidity of the elements while adding a fourth element to satisfy those who want a four-element system.

Sefer Yetzirah: An Introduction

Later, the kabbalah comes to use the language of elements and directions to talk about multiple, dynamic aspects of God—and reverts to the idea of four elements. For example, the Zohar describes the four elements of earth, water, air, and fire, in addition to the four directions, as divine forces:

> Fire, air, earth, and water are the sources and roots of all things above and below, and on them are all things grounded. In each of the four winds these elements are found: fire in the north, air in the east, water in the south, earth in the west...[50]

The kabbalistic use of elements and directions to name divine forces at least partly derives from the language of *Sefer Yetzirah*. Indeed, the later kabbalistic texts incorporate *Sefer Yetzirah*'s specific teachings around the elements. This beautiful passage from the Zohar describes God's creative process and includes the three elements.

> The world did not come into being until God took a certain stone that is called the foundation stone and cast it into the abyss so that it held fast there, and from it the world was planted. This is the central point of the universe, and on this point stands the holy of holies... The stone is compounded of fire, water, and air, and rests on the abyss. Sometimes water flows from it and fills the deep. The stone is set as a sign in the center of the world.[51]

In this thirteenth century kabbalistic text, we see the three-element structure as well as the notion that there is a sacred center to the cosmos. As we will see in Chapter 1, the story of the stone that seals the cosmos is relevant to *Sefer Yetzirah* in more ways than one.

A Single Master Rules Them: How The Letters Build the Temple

We have said early in this introduction that one of the foci of *Sefer Yetzirah* is the letters as engraved channels for divine creation, and the other is the cosmic Temple constructed by God via the realms, elements, and directions. These two foci do not remain as separate strands, but come together at various points throughout the book. We can therefore say that

Sefer Yetzirah has one integrated theme: a cosmic Temple constructed of engraved letters.

In the various chapters of *Sefer Yetzirah*, each of the Hebrew letters has a "primary" manifestation. For the mother letters *Aleph*, *Mem*, and *Shin*, the primary manifestation is the elements (air, water, and fire). For the double letters, the primary manifestation is the states of being described in Chapter 4: life/death, wisdom/foolishness, sovereignty/slavery, etc. For the simple letters, the primary manifestation is a human faculty: sight, hearing, speech, etc. The letters are also channels for a variety of forms in space, time, and the human body.

In addition to these primary and secondary manifestations, each of the Hebrew letters also occupies a specific place in the cube-shaped cosmic Temple. The simple letters provide the "borders" or lines of the cube. The double letters provide the faces of the cube, identified with the directions of north, south, east, west, up, down, and the center. Thus, these letters manifest as components of the Temple that is the universe.

In 3:3, a brief poetic text describes the mother letters as follows: "Fire above, water below, and wind in the middle." We could read this as a description of the basic components of the cosmic Temple: three horizontal sections: above, below, and middle. The mother letters provide the inner layers of the Temple, with the double letters and simple letters providing the cube that surrounds these inner components.

Thus, the entire *aleph-bet* (a system of writing/meaning) is also a building (the cosmic Temple). Temple and sacred text are not, in the view of *Sefer Yetzirah*, a tension between two kinds of sacred practice. They are one and the same.

Sefer Yetzirah and Magic

In my view, when I envision the Book of Creation, I see it as a mysterious tome that, when one opens it, reveals a portal to another dimension. *Sefer Yetzirah* doesn't mean to be a "book" as we understand books. It means to be a doorway into the deep structure of creation. It names the ingredients God uses to build the world, and the way in which those ingredients are to be combined. Gershom Scholem writes that *Sefer Yetzirah* "may conceivably have been intended as a manual of magical practices, or at least as a statement of general principles" of Jewish magic.[52]

The use of the term "magic" is difficult because "magic" is partly a political term, often used to marginalize those whose ritual work is not affiliated with societal authority or norms. Contemporary anthropologists have noted that what is called "religion" and what is called "magic" are not as distinct as once thought; these terms are often used to reify societal authority (e.g., a clergyperson, a representative of religious hierarchy, performs "ritual" or "prayer," but a witch, a marginalized spirit worker, performs "magic.")[53]

Yet some have tried to specify traits associated with magic. Emile Durkheim understands religion as service to the group, while magic serves the individual.[54] Or it may be that magic arises in response to a specific situation, individual or communal. Yuval Harari cites Misha Titiev as claiming that "religion serves the entire community," while magic is "critical ritual activity that follows from crises or concrete and actual needs. It serves those who experience such needs; the entire community, or as is usually the case, individuals in it."[55]

Magic may also implicate the spiritual power of human beings. Dorothy Hammond writes that "Magic represents the human power to act in order to influence and change reality."[56] Rebecca Lesses defines magic as a ritual performance used to gain power. This definition too is relevant, as *Sefer Yetzirah* includes ritual "performances" meant to align with God's creative power.[57] *Sefer Yetzirah* does seem to offer the possibility that individual humans can act to create, just as God has created. That *Sefer Yetzirah* addresses a single active reader (rather than a collective nation or tribe) is consistent with a magical outlook.

Marla Segol writes: "The texts of *Sefer Yetzirah* prescribe meaningful action."[58] Each letter in the book has a specific power that God uses to channel particular creative events. The book directly invites the reader to also make use of these specific powers, prescribing the letters as creative forces. The combination of letters, described in Chapter 2:4, seems to be a creative act: a ritual that grants creative and protective power to human beings. This apparent magical purpose of the book feeds the later Jewish lore that claims the book can be used to make a golem, an artificial person.[59]

One clear reference to magic in *Sefer Yetzirah* has to do with an act called "sealing." God "seals" the universe using the letters of the divine name, and God also seals various aspects of the universe using letters. We will discuss this sealing activity in depth as we dig into Chapter 1, but for now, let us note that sealing is a term that means "to activate a magical spell or protect it from interference or disruption."[60] The term "sealed" is used frequently in the corpus of Mesopotamian Jewish incantation bowls: magical items, texts inscribed into bowls, which are created for the purpose of protecting a home or individual from evil forces.

God's sealing of the world, as Hayman has pointed out, identifies God as a magician.[61] According to *Sefer Yetzirah*, God is using a magical technology to protect the universe and keep out chaotic disruptions. It makes sense that the reader is also supposed to take the book as a primer on how to seal spaces and protect them. This suggests that the authors of *Sefer Yetzirah* who introduced this imagery of thought themselves as magicians just as much as scholars.

But the greatest "magical" act of the book is returning the Creator to the proper place. We might understand this "return" as the full connection between the multiplicity of creation and the Creator's oneness. In other words, the Creator is in the right place when the Creation is fully (and in the human case, consciously) in connection with the One.

How is the book's magic relevant to us? David Abram writes: "What is magic? In the deepest sense, magic is an experience. It's the experience of finding oneself alive within a world that is alive."[62] It is this kind of magic that resides within *Sefer Yetzirah*. As the book describes the mysteries of the cosmos, it invites us to be alive within a living world.

Sefer Yetzirah and Contemplation

The magical premise of *Sefer Yetzirah* is complicated by its equal focus on contemplation. Much of the practice *Sefer Yetzirah* offers the reader has to do with disciplining the consciousness. Aryeh Kaplan writes: "*Sefer Yetzirah* appears to be an instructional manual, describing certain meditative exercises."[63] Perhaps the most obvious example of this is in 1:5, where the text says:

> Stop your mouth from speaking
> and your heart from murmuring
> and if your heart runs
> return to the place...

Anyone who meditates can relate to the way that the mind runs away from the meditative focus (whether the breath, an image, a chant, etc.) and pursues its own mundane line of thinking. The work of meditation is to interrupt this obsessive inner monologue, pull the mind back and attend to the meditative focus. For most of us, this push-and-pull will occur many times during the course of a meditation sit.

Sefer Yetzirah seems to know all about this. In order to contemplate the images and ideas of the book, the passage seems to suggest, we must become accustomed to returning our focus when the mind chatters. The Buddhist concept of "mindfulness" has something in common with this idea.[64]

The phrase "return to the place" is particularly poignant, since the word "Place" in rabbinic Hebrew can also refer to God. To return to the place is to return to the Divine, who is the ultimate focus of attention. And, to return to the place is to return to where we left off—to come back to what we had intended to do. Finally, to return to the place is to become at home in the universe: to be situated in space, time, and body.

Other passages in the book relate to contemplative practice, such as the instruction to combine all twenty-two letters in a "revolving wheel," reciting all of their possible combinations. This process is similar to meditation techniques in which a complicated and repetitive thought activity (such as a mantra) provides a focus for the mind so that the practitioner can reach a meditative state. The combination of letters that *Sefer Yetzirah* uses as a core practice also has a meditative component.

These meditative techniques may be related to Jewish mystical practices such as *Hekhalot* mysticism, a second- to fifth-century practice of "ascent" which involved intense visualization.[65] Like *Sefer Yetzirah*, *Hekhalot* mysticism involved the visualization of a divine building (though in that case the building was otherworldly rather than this-worldly). Some scholars are convinced that *Sefer Yetzirah* was partly influenced by meditative ideas and practices from India,[66] so it is possible that some of the book's texts may resonate with Hindu meditative practice as well.

Once we understand that meditation is also a focus of the book, we can see that many passages in the book are images to contemplate. For example, in 2:5, a passage relates that God "formed great pillars out of air that cannot be grasped." This profound image makes a connection between the intangibility of air and the solidity of matter. Images like this can serve as a focus for contemplative practice, and this commentary has used the text's images in that way.

Sefer Yetzirah is so relevant today partly because it offers a unique Jewish entry into meditation. The meditation that *Sefer Yetzirah* offers is a clearing of the mind, followed by allowing the book's sacred images to pour into the consciousness. We might say that the "engraving" or "hollow" aspect of *Sefer Yetzirah* is particularly associated with meditative practice, which requires "hollowness."

Ronit Meroz, in supporting her theory regarding multiple authors of *Sefer Yetzirah*, identifies two voices in the text, one with a "magical and activistic spirit" and one with a "visionary and meditative spirit."[67] These two spirits indeed seem to be intertwined within the book. We therefore cannot speak of the work as being either meditative or magical, but must expand its genre to include both at the same time.

Why *Sefer Yetzirah* Is Not the Same as the Later Kabbalah

The reader may be thinking that *Sefer Yetzirah* is a work of kabbalah and has the same philosophy as other books of kabbalah. However, this commentary, unlike some others, departs from the notion that *Sefer Yetzirah* and the later kabbalah contain the same ideas. *Sefer Yetzirah* has its own version of Jewish mysticism, which is both similar to and different from the kabbalah, which came centuries later.

The kabbalah is exemplified by the composite work known as the Zohar, written in thirteenth-century Spain, and by later writers and thinkers who built on the Zohar's ideas. The kabbalah has a vision of God in which the Divine has many diverse components from utter transcendence to complete immanence, from masculine to feminine, from generous love to severe judgment. The kabbalah also has a view of the cosmos in which humans play a role in redeeming a broken universe. Like *Sefer Yetzirah*, the kabbalah understands God and the world as a continuum of being rather than completely separate entities. The Zohar, the *Sefer haBahir*, and other kabbalistic works frequently refer to terms used in *Sefer Yetzirah*, such as the *sefirot* or divine dimensions. Indeed, scholar Yehuda Liebes asserts that the kabbalah began in commentaries on *Sefer Yetzirah*.[68]

The most popular contemporary translator of *Sefer Yetzirah*, Aryeh Kaplan, has presented *Sefer Yetzirah* as many have understood it: as a work of kabbalah. Kaplan works hard to identify all of the concepts of *Sefer Yetzirah* as kabbalistic concepts. Already by his second page, Kaplan is referring to the Zoharic *sefirot* (*chesed*/love, *gevurah*/judgment, etc.) as identical to the *sefirot* of *Sefer Yetzirah*.[69] For Kaplan, there is little distinction between the ideas of *Sefer Yetzirah* and the ideas of the classical kabbalists. Kaplan's reading is consistent with much of Jewish mystical tradition, which assumes that the thought of *Sefer Yetzirah* is the same as the thought of the Zohar and beyond.

However, if one looks at the plain text, *Sefer Yetzirah* isn't consistent with later kabbalah. For example, the *sefirot* of *Sefer Yetzirah* are dimensional and/or elemental aspects of the universe: north, south, beginning, end, air, fire, water, etc. The *sefirot* of the Zohar (which doesn't mention the word *sefirah* though it uses the concept) are anthropomorphic: love, rigor, compassion, etc. They are dimensions of the universe, but they are personified in ways the *sefirot* of *Sefer Yetzirah* are not.

The Zoharic *sefirot* can manifest physically (as water, fire, etc.) but they are primarily located in the hidden worlds; the physical world is a veil for the true reality. This is not true in *Sefer Yetzirah*. When *Sefer Yetzirah* speaks about the *sefirot* as water or air or time or space, it means to address actual water, air, time, and space—the *sefirot* are physical entities, and there is no veil between them and us. These two ways of understanding the *sefirot*, while they have some similarities, are fundamentally different. When we force *Sefer Yetzirah* into the categories of later kabbalah, we miss some of its message.

Even the kabbalistic commentaries on *Sefer Yetzirah* have trouble identifying the terms of *Sefer Yetzirah* with the terms of the Zohar. For example, Isaac Luria posited that the kabbalistic *sefirot* of *Keter* (crown, or divine will) and *Malkhut* (sovereignty, or divine presence/sacred feminine) corresponded to *Sefer Yetzirah*'s *sefirot* called Good and Evil. Rabbi Moses Cordovero believed that *Chochmah* (wisdom, or male principle) and *Binah* (understanding, or female principle) correspond to Good and Evil, and Rabbi Abraham ben David of Posquieres suggested that *Chesed* (love) and *Gevurah* (judgment) were Good and Evil.[70] The lack of consensus suggests that the two sefirotic maps don't match easily at all.

And the similarities matter, too. Many ideas from *Sefer Yetzirah* did enter the later kabbalah. *Sefer Yetzirah* situates God at the center of the universe, not outside it. The kabbalists would absolutely agree: they see the divine in the world, and often use natural images (such as tree, earth, ocean) to speak about aspects of God. The Zohar, like *Sefer Yetzirah*, speaks of dualities and tensions that are resolved into oneness. *Sefer Yetzirah*'s imagery of God as male and Wisdom as female, Divine Artist as masculine and Mother elements as feminine, finds a new expression in the later kabbalah: the Zohar describes a full-blown relational drama between the Holy One and the feminine Divine Presence, or Shekhinah, who is the Holy One's creative partner. The kabbalah surely resonates with the dance between unity and multiplicity that *Sefer Yetzirah* describes—

kabbalists speak of God and the world as multiple and unified at the same time.

Centuries of kabbalists drew diagrams and wrote commentaries to explicate *Sefer Yetzirah* in the light of kabbalistic understanding.[71] This history matters—and it largely won't be surveyed here. There are many other books that detail how to fit *Sefer Yetzirah* into kabbalistic thought. This commentary will explore *Sefer Yetzirah* as a unique spiritual worldview and practice, different from Jewish texts composed in later times and places. We'll note some similarities to kabbalah, but we won't dwell on them.

Sefer Yetzirah and Gender

We've just noted that the male-female dance hinted at in the pages of *Sefer Yetzirah* had a significant impact on later Jewish mystics. One of the unusual facets of this ancient text is its inclusive and positive view regarding feminine entities. While *Sefer Yetzirah* doesn't have any "women" in a personalized sense, its female elemental beings are a surprising and fascinating addition to Jewish tradition. In this paradigm, the masculine offers the One and the feminine the Many.

Sefer Yetzirah genders God as male (the verbs and nouns referring to God are masculine). In order to create the world, God interacts with Chochmah/Wisdom, an entity that embodies the pathways of creation. Biblically speaking, Chochmah is a female-gendered entity, as we'll discuss when we get to the commentary on 1:1. In *Sefer Yetzirah*, Wisdom is also a multiple entity, composed of many paths. God and Wisdom partner to create reality. Ronit Meroz too has noted that in *Sefer Yetzirah*, God uses an intermediate feminine entity to aid in the creative process.[72] Meroz calls this view "binitarian." She elaborates that Understanding, or Binah, is the mediatrix of creation, the second power in the universe.

But God's collaboration with the feminine doesn't stop there. God also interacts with the female elements of air, water, and fire: "Three Mothers, *Aleph, Mem, Shin*: the Divine engraved them, carved them, permuted them, weighed them, transformed them, and with them depicted..."[73] The three mothers act as a whole to build the primary systems of space, time, and body. They are a set of creatrix powers, acting together to produce the world. Like Wisdom, they are a feminine, multiple force. The phrase "three mothers" (*shalosh imot*) echoes the Talmudic phrase "four mothers" (*arba'ah imahot*) referring to Sarah, Rebekah, Rachel, and Leah. Thus, the elements are identified with the matriarchs of the people. The "mothers" are God's partners in creating the space-time continuum and bringing the world into being.

In the section of Chapter 1 where the first four *sefirot* are described as elements, they too are feminine, grammatically speaking. The *ruach Elohim chayyim* or "breath of the living God" takes a feminine gender, as do the *arba ruchot* or four winds. The "waters" are feminine plural, which is even more striking since "waters" in Hebrew are masculine. And the fire too is feminine. So it is not only the mother letters that are feminized, but the elements as a whole. And all of these elements are vehicles for divine creation.

The female elements exist in relationship to one another, combining to create the diversity of reality. They remind one of the *matronae* in Northwestern European mythology: ancestral mothers depicted in groups of three, whose feminine powers manifest in a group, never by themselves.[74] The feminine is multiple; the masculine singular. The Artist partners with the multiplicity of the elements to make the world. Throughout the narrative, the male Creator and female elemental mediatrix-powers have no apparent conflicts. The One and the Many cooperate.

At no point in the corpus of *Sefer Yetzirah* is the female demonized. God "engraves" and "carves" these entities, which might render them passive (and maybe eroticized). Yet the feminine entities also create and form, which makes them active as well. We could view the elemental mediatrix-powers as subordinate to God, but we could also view them as partners with or even aspects of the Divine, since it is said of the *sefirot* that "their end is imbedded in their beginning" (i.e., the *sefirot* have their source in God).

This gender cooperation seems to extend into the human realm. In 3:9, the human aspects of male and female are mentioned in connection with the human body. It is striking that one gender is not prioritized or elevated over another, nor are the genders presented as adversaries. *Sefer Yetzirah*'s earliest strata are comparatively free of the misogyny that often besets rabbinic text.

We should note that there are three male entities mentioned in a few places in *Sefer Yetzirah*, called the fathers. One version of the beginning of Chapter 6 reads:

> These are the Three Mothers, *Aleph Mem Shin*, and from them were born Three Fathers, and they are air, water, and fire, and from the Fathers, descendants.

Scholar Peter Hayman notes that the place of the "fathers" in the cosmology in *Sefer Yetzirah* is secondary and inconsistent. In most places in the book, the mothers are synonymous with the elements; yet in Chapter 6, it is the fathers who hold the powers of air, water, and fire.[75] Hayman's research suggests that the father letters are a later addition.[76] They may well be an editorial product of discomfort with the book's focus on mothers as primary cosmic forces. Yet the original gender dualism of *Sefer Yetzirah* seems not to be between "mothers" and "fathers" but rather between God and the elements.

This creative dialogue between a single male creator and a multiple elemental mother-web clearly influences later kabbalah. The *Ein Sof* (God's infinite transcendence) is generally described as singular and masculine. *Shekhinah*, the immanent divine feminine, is sometimes described as singular and sometimes as an embodiment of multiple entities—one of Her names is *Keneset Yisrael* (the community of Israel).[77] The *Shekhinah's* nature is close to the physical world, and in that sense. She is similar to the "elements" in *Sefer Yetzirah*. In one Zohar text, *Shekhinah* distributes divine radiance to all of God's creation, and in this way she is similar to Wisdom in *Sefer Yetzirah*, who distributes God's creative powers among the multiple entities that exist. [78]

Other sacred systems depict the feminine as a multiplicity, or multiplicity as feminine. For example, while Hindu gods like Vishnu and Shiva are generally understood as separate personalities, the goddesses (Kali, Durga, Lakshmi, etc.) are often understood to overlap.[79] We have already mentioned the *matronae* of Central Europe, and can also include the *disir* (Norse female ancestor spirits), who always act in a group rather than singly.[80] The Iyaami of Yoruba tradition are creatrix goddesses and female ancestors, honored as a group. [81]

The multiplying done by many female bodies as they give birth, and the erotic entering of female bodies which also implies multiplicity, must be some of the underpinning for this way of thinking. Philosopher Luce Irigaray has identified similar themes in the understanding of the feminine, suggesting that the feminine, as it manifests in European thought and experience, is in the state of "never simply being one."[82] Irigaray adds, in response to a questioner who asks if she is a woman: "'I' am not I, I am not, I am not one..."[83]

The multiple feminine gives us, perhaps, another way of perceiving the Divine and the cosmos. While we wouldn't want to reify this view of the feminine in a gender essentialist way (i.e., men are "one" and women are "many"), we might in fact learn from *Sefer Yetzirah* about how to think about God as an organic many-faceted Being in addition to a singular Person. In this view, all of the elements we encounter in the world around us are a necessary part of the divine whole.

The reader in *Sefer Yetzirah* is grammatically gendered male (and, like God, engages in a dance with the feminine letters and elements). However, in several places, *Sefer Yetzirah* matter-of-factly acknowledges that humans come in a variety of genders, as when 3:2 states that human forms come in "male and female." Given that Jewish magical practitioners of the time were indeed male and female (the Talmud, for example, makes the negatively charged statement that "most women are witches" and records the actions of sorceresses), it is not impossible that *Sefer Yetzirah* imagined readers of different genders exploring the book. *Sefer Yetzirah*'s comfort with the feminine is an intrinsic part of its worldview.[84] It is not impossible, given the magical culture the book seems to arise from, that women contributed to the culture out of which the book was written, or even the content itself, in some way.

This exciting possibility is part of what makes the book so fresh and relevant in our own day.

Tome and Tale: The Structure of this Book

The translation offered here is meant to highlight the poetic, magical, incantational nature of the text. Finally, this book will offer visualization practices that explore the text on an imaginal level.

The current commentary will have four basic parts:

1. A Hebrew text, largely based on Hayman's "earliest recoverable version"
2. A translation of that text
3. A commentary, using the traditional Jewish method of singling out certain phrases within the text to explain and discuss
4. Visualization practices for each passage

The intention is for readers to be able to move at will between reading the text on their own, exploring and understanding the various aspects of that text, and finding images within the text to work with as consciousness-changing practices. Thus, the current commentary invites readers on a journey that is imaginal rather than solely intellectual. As Yehuda Liebes writes: "Human creation... is not just catharsis in the creator's soul. It returns and participates in the creation of the world."[85] The commentary and practices offered here attempts to capture *Sefer Yetzirah*'s way of seeing: that we and everything around us are channels for creative forces much larger than ourselves.

Pillars carved in air, divine dwellings floating in space, elements entwining to make worlds—these are healing images. Our society as a whole is so disconnected from the cosmos, and *Sefer Yetzirah* is a vehicle for reconnection. Physicist Karen Barad writes: "What makes us think that matter is lifeless to begin with?"[86] In *Sefer Yetzirah*, all substance is alive, dynamic, and filled with holiness. The world becomes a book to be opened.

A Note on the Translation

I have attempted to understand the language of *Sefer Yetzirah* in the context of the concepts it appears to be describing. That has meant making careful choices about words—sometimes choices that depart from how the book has usually been translated. These choices have been a conscious process over time as I have read, taught, and worked with the book.

For example, I have rendered the word *nefesh* as "body-soul." Most translators choose "soul" which is generally what *nefesh* means in much of Jewish literature. Yet *Sefer Yetzirah* describes the *nefesh* as having limbs and organs, and is clearly referring to the body. "Soul" doesn't seem to convey the plain meaning of the text. And, biblically speaking, the word *nefesh* often means "body" as well as life-force or spirit.[87] However, *Sefer Yetzirah* likely doesn't mean to exclude the meaning of "soul"—especially since the dimensions associated with *nefesh* are "good" and "evil," terms which have ethical as well as experiential components. So I have chosen this unusual translation of *nefesh* to reflect the full implications of the word in its context in *Sefer Yetzirah*.

I also have made some language choices in order to try to convey the evocative wordplays of the Hebrew, such as "tome, tally, and tale" to echo the relation between the words *sefer*, *sfar*, and *sipur*/book, number, and story; or "engraved law," to convey the Hebrew *chok*—which means "law" but comes from the word for "to engrave." While the sound and meaning plays in the Hebrew are hard to convey in English, I've made some effort to do so where it seems particularly important.

In other places, it's been impossible to find English that will convey the polysemy of the text. So I have sometimes used italics to indicate a second meaning of a word. For example, *b'milah* is translated "in word/in the genitals" to indicate that *milah* means both word, and circumcision (implying the phallus). Similarly, I've translated *boryo* (its clarity) as "its clarity/its absence" to include both of the meanings I understand in that word.

I've also tried to keep the translation close to nature rather than abstract. In service to my understanding that *Sefer Yetzirah* is attempting a spiritual exploration of the physical world, I have used "sky" (instead of "heaven") for *shamayim*, and "air" or "wind" (instead of "spirit") for ruach. I've used "void" for *blimah* instead of something more abstract like "nothingness."

I have made other translation choices in order to accommodate the sensibilities of contemporary readers. For example, I have attempted to render many depictions of God gender-neutral. Sometimes this has meant using "God" in place of He or His, and sometimes it has meant using a gender-neutral Their. This is not entirely at odds with the text itself. Although *Sefer Yetzirah* does refer to God with masculine verbs, often the masculine pronoun (He, or the Hebrew *Hu*) is missing. This skipping of the pronoun is grammatically correct and not uncommon in Hebrew, but the complete absence of the word *Hu* to describe God is striking. My conclusion is that gender is somewhat de-centered in *Sefer Yetzirah*, and so I have de-centered it in my text as well.

However, in Chapter 1:9-12, I have kept the male and female genders as they appear in the Hebrew, in order to make clear the relationship the book posits between the (male) creator and the (female) elements. There is a subtle erotic relationship being implied between these entities, and their gender specificity is part of this erotic relationship.

And, in Chapter 1:9-12, I have chosen to capitalize the pronouns of both the divine creator and the elements. Since in the Book of Creation the Divine and the universe are interwoven, the elements are also aspects of the Divine. It could be said that the God of *Sefer Yetzirah*, who is both the creator and the created world, has a composite gender—we might say that the "She" that describes the elements is as sacred as the "He" that describes the divine artist. So, in that section, I have capitalized the *Shes* and *Hers* as well as the *Hes* and *Hims* in order to emphasize this. This is particularly appropriate since in 1:9, the text foregrounds "the holy spirit/breath," (*ruach hakodesh*) which in Hebrew is a feminine term for the Divine.

In general, my intention is a poetic translation that is accurate to the Hebrew and gives imaginal opportunities to the reader. I have tried to explain the more unusual translation choices in the commentary so that readers will understand (if not always agree with) what I have done. My hope is that the translation will convey the feeling as well as the meaning of *Sefer Yetzirah*.

Sefer Yetzirah and the Contemporary Mystic

My experience of reading and working with *Sefer Yetzirah* is that it awakens my inner knowing in profound ways. As I have offered practices based in *Sefer Yetzirah* to others, I have seen how it affects them as well. This translation and commentary arises not only from intellectual interest, but my experience that the book heals and transforms.

When I offer visualizations that arise from the imagery of the book, people have powerful experiences. For example, when contemplating the text "The One formed matter out of void... and carved great pillars of air from air that cannot be grasped," one person reported seeing the multiplying of the structures of creation until they became the whole world. When contemplating the phrase "the transformation of life is death" one person saw life arising out of death and death arising out of life: the two forces sustaining one another.

The three mothers—*Aleph*, *Mem*, and *Shin*, or air, water, and fire—have become an important part of my personal practice. Breathing air into the chest, water into the belly, and fire into the head is a way I center myself and find peace. Sometimes the *Aleph*, *Mem*, and *Shin* look like elements, sometimes like people, and sometimes like letters. The three mothers have become a way I access divine presence wherever I happen to be.

Often, when I lead a simple meditation that invites people to locate themselves in space, in time, and in their bodies, people report feeling grounded and calm in a way that surprises them. And when, in a group, we practice intoning the six combinations of the divine name that seal the six directions, people find themselves feeling more comfortable and connected in the space we are in. Even reading a passage aloud together creates a tangible impact on whatever group I'm in.

My experience is that, put simply, *Sefer Yetzirah* works. It connects people to themselves and to the cosmos, just as it claims. One of my students has said: "This book got inside me." I hope you, readers, will find voices in this text that speak to you and awaken your vital powers.

Visualization Practice Using *Sefer Yetzirah*

Visualization of divine mysteries—the ten dimensions, the wheel of twenty-two letters, the pillars made of air—seems to be a fundamental part of the texts of *Sefer Yetzirah*. Within its cryptic verses, the book invites not merely study, but contemplation. This commentary therefore attempts to treat the book as a visualization practice as well as a text.

The practice of visualization—opening to internal imagery as part of a meditative state or trance—is already present in biblical narratives. In the Bible we see prophets having visions. Examples of this are as diverse as Jacob's dream of the ladder between heaven and earth in Genesis 28; Moses seeing God's back in Exodus 33; Elijah's vision of the earthquake, fire, and wind in I Kings 19; Isaiah's vision of an angel bearing a coal in Isaiah 6; or Ezekiel's vision of the divine chariot borne by angelic creatures in Ezekiel 1. Israelite contact with deity is often surrounded by powerful imagery, despite the disembodiment of the Hebrew God. Even as the transmission and study of sacred texts became a primary way to encounter the Divine, there continued to be a strong element of visionary prophecy in biblical sources.

Post-biblical Jews continued to develop a visionary practice and literature. At the turn of the millennium (100 BCE-1000 CE), Merkabah (chariot) mystical texts, based on Ezekiel's vision of the chariot, detailed journeys to hidden worlds. The sub-genre of Hekhalot literature—a genre of Jewish texts in which the narrator takes journeys to heavenly realms—is part of this literary and spiritual phenomenon. Consider the apocryphal book of Enoch, in which a human has the opportunity to walk through heavenly storehouses and palaces of angels. The Talmud too contains moments where sages have visions, as when Rabbi Chananya ben Teradyon, tortured and martyred by the Romans, sees the letters of the Torah flying off the burning parchment.[1]

Sefer Yetzirah, while its imaginal vocabulary is different than the elaborate heavenly visions of Merkabah literature, also participates in this visionary tradition. Chapter 1 offers us diverse images from the ten *sefirot* rushing like a whirlwind to the flame imbedded in a fiery coal to the engraving of the four winds of heaven. The images in 2:3 of letters fixed within a turning wheel, or the fiery pillars of air in 2:5, seem meant to be envisioned. These images not only mean something, they offer an experience, a way of coming close to mystery. We might say that these images are healing: they integrate us, transcend our contradictions, open us to a deeper vision of ourselves and the world.

The imaginal world of *Sefer Yetzirah* later becomes part of the image-vocabulary of the kabbalists of the twelfth and thirteenth centuries and beyond. Images of Hebrew letters, of sacred elements and directions forming a cosmic architecture, and of divine energies surging along multiple pathways spill over from *Sefer Yetzirah* and into the kabbalistic works called *Sefer haBahir* (twelfth-century Provence) and the Zohar (thirteenth-century Spain).

The Zohar in particular is filled with powerful dreamlike images that invite the reader to see concrete visions of the sacred: roses, birds, towers, gazelles, mirrors, moons, and a whole host of ways of seeing the hidden world. Melila Hellner-Eshed has discussed how the practice of visualizing is at the heart of the Zohar: the initiate is characterized by an "ability to employ a special kind of seeing... The *maskil* [initiate] knows how to look within the Bible in such a way as to gain access to the mysterious secret world."[2]

Later kabbalistic texts and practices also offer entry into this mysterious world. The circle of Isaac Luria (1534-1572) in Safed in the sixteenth century engaged in visualization as part of their approach to kabbalah (for example, by seeing a verse of Scripture shining on someone's forehead).[3] Luria's student, Hayyim Vital, reports visits to female visionaries like Francesca Sarah who could assure him of the state of his soul based on their dreams and inner sight.[4] Hasidic masters like the Baal Shem Tov also engaged in meditation and visioning. Jonathan Garb's book *Shamanic Trance in Modern Kabbalah* notes the ways that kabbalistic and Hasidic visionaries are similar to indigenous shamans in their understanding of vision as a way to enter the spirit realm.[5]

Much Jewish visualization practice was lost in the vast cultural disruptions of the twentieth century: the Holocaust, Jewish migrations from Europe, North Africa, and the Middle East, immigration to America, etc. In more recent times, Jewish meditation teachers, sometimes influenced by the meditation traditions of the East, have done a great deal to revive these practices of visualization. Recent authors who offer such practices include Jay Michaelson, Tirzah Firestone, Leah Novick, Jeff Roth, and many others.[6]

Colette Aboulker-Muscat (1909-2005), a kabbalist born in Algeria who lived most of her life in Jerusalem, was adept at kabbalistic visualization techniques and has deeply influenced modern Jewish visualization practice. Catherine Shainberg, Madame Colette's student, still teaches visualization in Colette's lineage, and the visualizations in this book are partly inspired by her teaching, particularly her development of brief, clear, sensuous images and her use of the outbreath to stimulate focus and inner vision.[7] Shainberg's method of breathing out before and after visualization has been used consistently here. Aryeh Kaplan, through his translation, commentary, and meditative practices, did much to bring *Sefer Yetzirah* and other Jewish visionary texts into the contemporary practice of Jewish meditation.[8] His influence can also be felt in this book, which attempts a fresh approach to the meditative aspects of *Sefer Yetzirah* by offering clear and simple images that arise out of the text, for readers to contemplate.

The Intent of Visualization

As we have noted in the introduction, *Sefer Yetzirah* focuses not simply on the enlightenment of the seeker, but on aligning with the cosmos. The book even seems to imply that the practitioner can affect creation as a whole. Thus, the intent of the imaginal practice of *Sefer Yetzirah* is somewhat different than "mindfulness," inner calm, or the other internal benefits we usually associate with meditation—though these benefits do also accrue when we work with these images.

How are we to evaluate the claim that generating internal imagery will have an impact on the world? Here, I can only offer my own experience of the impact these images make. The imaginal world of the *Sefer Yetzirah* echoes a cosmic whole: it describes a soup of elements, dimensions, directions, and channels which, when they come together, manifest a single Creator's intent. When I know myself as part of that whole, my thoughts, feelings, actions, and relationships are transformed. For centuries, Jews believed that *Sefer Yetzirah* could be used to create a golem, a living being summoned by the powers of the letters. If there is a golem I am trying to create, it is myself—myself in deeper connection to the universe. If Dorothy Hammond is correct that "magic represents the human power to act to influence and change reality,"[9] then my experience of *Sefer Yetzirah* is magical: I have a greater ability to influence my reality when I work with the images in this ancient book.

One practice *Sefer Yetzirah* asks of the reader is extensive letter permutation—I have placed the instructions for this practice in an appendix, since it is time-consuming, and challenging for non-Hebrew speakers. Instead, I have created a kind of midrash, an interpretive take, on the images that arise throughout the book. I have tried to illuminate the incantational, ritual, magical nature of *Sefer Yetzirah*, and tap into its extraordinary power to open the consciousness. My hope is that these imaginal practices capture some of the spirit of this enchanting, wise and poetic text.*

Engaging the Practice

Imaginal practice is not the same as fantasizing or daydreaming. When we allow imagery to arise using a visioning practice, we are attempting to discover what is real and true for us, using our imagination as a lens. Some believe this imagery comes from God, or Spirit, or the ancestors. Some understand the imagery as coming from the depths of our own knowing. It doesn't matter so much where you think the imagery comes from as long as you are able to trust the process.

West African shaman Malidoma Some has pointed out that Western analytical education makes it difficult to engage in visionary practice.[10] We aren't accustomed to thinking that what we experience on the inside is "real." Some people don't trust their imaginations, or think they are "making things up"—and therefore have trouble entering the world of spirit in a meaningful way. Others find internal images to be destabilizing or scary and thus shy away from them. Doing this work is relatively easy for some, and very hard for others. Go at your own pace and trust yourself about what you need in order to make the practice work for you.

How to Visualize

First, one has to disengage the conscious mind from its usual function. We do this by withdrawing attention from external stimuli, and from the internal monologue to which most of us are accustomed. In this way, we make space for powerful images and experiences to arise. We encourage the mind to make this shift via a meditational focus: breath, chant, an image, etc.

Paying careful attention to the physical sensation of breath is a way to shift the mind away from its usual concerns. Traditions around the world use breathwork as a way to enter a meditative state. The visualizations in this book begin and end with an invitation to focus on the breath. Some readers may only need to pay attention to a few breaths before dropping into a deeper state. Others may wish to concentrate on the breath for a

---

* Please visit ReturnToThePlace.com for more resources.

longer time before engaging the visualization. This is a matter of personal preference and need.

When you are ready to do the imaginal work, you can read the visualization first, close your eyes, and then recall its different steps to yourself. Or, you can head to the website associated with this book, and listen to the recorded visualizations as you meditate with your eyes closed. Don't worry too much if your inner vision starts to diverge from the offered imaginal practice. The goal here is for you to interact with the images of *Sefer Yetzirah* in your own way.

Engaging the visualization relatively quickly allows for spontaneous generation of images rather than a process in which the rational mind gets involved. In other words, one wants to be surprised by what one sees, feels, hears, etc., rather than consciously inventing what one experiences. "Making it up" (i.e., listening to your imagination) is fine, but don't edit: the first image you experience is probably the thing you should stick with, even if it seems strange or silly at first.

When you are finished with the visualization, it's good to focus on the breath for a few moments to take in what you've experienced. Afterward, you may want to journal, record your impressions, or talk with someone about what happened. Like dreams, visualizations can be hard to remember unless you record them in some way.

These journeys depend on the imagistic language of Sefer Yetzirah so they often use the language of seeing, looking, etc. If the visual isn't your best meditative mode, or you're not a sighted person, please feel free to revise the journeys accordingly to focus on the senses that are right for you. And, there are many journeys that invite the use of other senses as well.

If you find an image-journey that you like, you may want to make it a daily practice. For example, every night my daughter and I visualize breathing the three mothers, *Aleph, Mem,* and *Shin,* into our bodies. We imagine the personas of air, water, and fire entering our lungs, bellies, and minds, offering us healing, grounding, and inspiration. We do this just before sleep, as a calming practice. It's been an important part of her childhood; she says she's going to teach it to her children.

You can also create your own visualization journey. You can read one of the passages of *Sefer Yetzirah* aloud to yourself and then meditate on it in a freeform way. Or you can listen to a recording of your favorite passage and meditate as you listen. The words of the book are rich and deep, and you can generate many powerful inner images just by listening to it.

In the contemporary world, there is too little that enchants us. You are invited to open the *Book of Creation* just as one would begin an adventure: with commitment, excitement and curiosity. May you be transformed by the journey.

Chapter 1:1 · The Three Books

שלשים ושתים נתיבות פלאות חכמה
חקק יה
יהוה צבאות
בשלש ספרים
בספר וספר וסיפור

Wisdom's thirty-two marvelous paths
Yah engraved—
the Becoming One who holds many—
within three books:
tome, tally, and tale.

At the beginning of the story, we come upon a mysterious scene: God as engraver. The image evokes the engraved letters in the stone tablets of the Ten Commandments. But the tablets here aren't stone, and the letters aren't merely letters. Rather, the divine Artist forms a universe by engraving "marvelous paths" into the substance of reality. We might imagine looking down each of these paths, and getting a glimpse of the diversity of God's creation.

These paths exist within three books. This implies that the paths are words—though of course, the words aren't merely words, and the books aren't merely books. The books, it turns out, are dimensions of the cosmos: space, time, and body/soul. Each book helps to define and order the world that God creates.

If we open these three books that God engraves, multiple paths beckon like trails in a secret garden. We peer down these wondrous engraved paths, wondering what we might find there. Whole worlds unfold from the paths God has engraved. This is, in some way, similar to the process by which imaginal worlds unfold from the words we read on a page. At the same time, it is similar to the worlds that unfold from the turns we take on a forest trail. We discover, to our astonishment, that we are reading and journeying at the same time.

Sefer Yetzirah, the *Book of Creation*, tells a story about God. Yet it also assumes a reader. It seems this reader is a traveler of worlds, a seeker who wants to understand the mysteries of creation. The book invites this reader to trace the energies that enliven all of the cosmos, and thereby become a creator as well. The reader is us—the book will soon make that very clear, by addressing us directly.

Wisdom's Thirty-Two Marvelous Paths

שלשים ושתים נתיבות
פלאות חכמה

The first passage of *Sefer Yetzirah* lays out before us a network of paths: the thirty-two "paths" by which the Divine creates the world. Thirty-two indicates the twenty-two Hebrew letters—each one a channel for divine creation—plus the ten *sefirot* or cosmic dimensions.[1] Each of these paths is engraved within one or more of the three books of space, time, and body/soul.

The thirty-two engraved paths, by definition, have a hollowness to them. They are meant to channel a force from the Creator: call it intention, energy, or will. The thirty-two channels for this divine energy are "Wisdom's marvelous paths" or "wondrous paths of Wisdom." But who is Wisdom, and why do these engraved paths belong to Her?

To a reader of the Bible, Wisdom is a familiar character. In the Book of Proverbs, Wisdom (*Chochmah*) is a mysterious feminine figure, God's witness at the dawn of creation:

> God created me at the beginning of his path,
> as the first of God's doings of old.
> At the world's beginning, I was formed:
> before the beginning, older than the first things...
> I was there when God fixed the skies in place
> And inscribed the horizon on the face of the depths,
> When God set the firmament above,
> and strengthened the fountains of the deep...
> I was with God as a nursling,
> a daily delight,
> rejoicing before him at all times,
> rejoicing in the globe of his world,
> and humankind was my delight...
> Now, children, listen to me:
> happy are those who keep my ways.[2]

Wisdom is "a tree of life to those who hold on to her, and all who take hold of her are happy" (Proverbs 3:16-17). As "tree of life," Wisdom is one of the sacred trees of the ancient Near East, akin to the Tree of Life in the Garden of Eden. She is related to the long line of tree goddesses of the region—particularly the goddess Asherah, often depicted as a tree.[3] Wisdom is nurturer and lifegiver. She is also God's consultant on the process of creation. And she is a guide to humankind: "Through me kings reign and rulers decree just laws… happy is the one who listens to me, for the one who finds me finds life…"[4]

Wisdom's paths wind throughout the book of Proverbs. "Her ways are pleasant ways, and all her paths (*netivoteha*) are peace." Wisdom stands at the crossroads, "the house of paths" (*beit netivot*).[5] This word, *netivot* or paths, is the same word *Sefer Yetzirah* uses to speak of the thirty-two paths that God engraves. The paths, the *netivot*, are the many interwoven aspects of Wisdom. The world is a "house of paths," a place of Wisdom's ways. *Sefer Yetzirah* borrows this image from the ancient text of Proverbs to build its own model of divine creation.

Of course, the word Wisdom has significant baggage. For centuries, Jews have understood Wisdom to signify Torah.[6] In Christianity, Sophia or Wisdom is the divine *Logos* (Word), often identified with Christ.[7] In Gnosticism, Sophia is an aeon or divine emanation.[8] Later, in the kabbalah, Wisdom (*Chochmah*) comes to mean a divine aspect.[9]

Yet here in *Sefer Yetzirah*, Wisdom seems to be not a single being, but a multiple entity: a web or network. There is a mycelial feel to this entity, because, as we will learn, every path in the web connects to every other path. Wisdom is a labyrinth that God's creative intention must traverse to find its way into expression.

Scholar Ronit Meroz calls *Sefer Yetzirah*'s approach "binitarian," from the kabbalistic term Binah (God's aspect of feminine Wisdom). Meroz understands Wisdom as the mediating entity between God and the world. She suggests that one of the primary ideas of *Sefer Yetzirah* is that God creates with the aid of this secondary mediating entity, Wisdom.[10] Meroz posits that this intermediary figure manifests in different ways: concrete (as an angel) and abstract (as a concept).

Yet Wisdom, as depicted in the pages of the Book of Creation, is not a single angel or concept.[11] Wisdom is (or more properly, are) a multiplicitous womb within which God creates the infinitely varied substances of our world. Wisdom comprises a web of channels by which divine creative energy becomes created beings. *Sefer Yetzirah* invites us to explore Wisdom's paths as they reach between the Creator and each and every creation.

In the Bible, "wondrous" (*pele*) means "pertaining to the divine realm." "In post-biblical literature this word assumes the meaning of that which is hidden, concealed, secret."[12] The "wondrous paths" are mysterious, ethereal, supernal. Yet the book offers the possibility that we humans might acquire experience of these wondrous ways. The images that flow over us as the book unfolds bring the reader on an imaginal journey through the divine creative process, and thus awaken the reader's own creative imagination.

Yah Engraved   חקק יה

God carves channels through which physicality can come into being. These channels are a kind of engraved writing, yet they also have the aspect of waymaking—providing a path from heaven to earth. *Sefer Yetzirah*'s use of "engraving" for God's creative work implies that the Divine is working with primordial material that must be hollowed out.

This brings us back to the first passage of Genesis, where the Divine spirit hovers on the face of primordial waters.[13] In Genesis, the Divine must separate the primordial material—the waters above from the waters below—in order to fashion a world. Similarly, in *Sefer Yetzirah*, divine creativity must seep through Wisdom's channels into some kind of primordial mass (whatever substance God engraves the paths of Wisdom into)—in order to turn an undifferentiated oneness into the many things of the world.

That is, divine creativity must start by making empty space. This way of understanding God's activity blossomed again much later in the work of the kabbalist Isaac Luria (1534-1572), who famously originated the doctrine of *tzimtzum*: divine contraction, which created an empty space within which the physical world could come into being. His student, Hayyim Vital, later wrote:

> A supernal, simple light filled all of existence. There was no empty place, no empty space or void, but everything was filled by that simple, infinite light... then the Infinite contracted itself in its center... and after God contracted that light and withdrew from the center to the sides that surrounded it, there was a vacant space—an empty, hollow void."[14]

While *Sefer Yetzirah* doesn't posit a divine contraction, it does imagine hollowness—engraving—as a space for possibility, a means by which the Creator can create.

We are never told exactly what substance God engraves—the phrase *chakak Yah* (God engraved) has no direct object. It is as if the substance engraved by God is too mysterious, or too infinite to describe. *Sefer Yetzirah* is also never exactly clear about what comes through the channels that God engraves. How does God's creative essence or intention move through the hollowed-out shapes of the letters to create the diverse phenomena of creation? What is the nature of that essence or intention? This, *Sefer Yetzirah* leaves to our imagination—but there are hints of an answer, as when in 1:8 we hear that "God's word in them [the *sefirot* or cosmic dimensions] is running and returning." What runs through the channels of the letters is highly mobile and full of meaning: sound, word, fire, breath.

Scholar Marla Segol suggests that we could read *chakak Yah* (God engraved) as "engraved out of God"—in other words, the primordial material into which the paths are engraved is God.[15] If so, then God is the Creator and also the substance of world—as the later kabbalah will assert. This panentheist view of creation does indeed seem to permeate many of the passages in *Sefer Yetzirah*.

A question now arises: Are the hollow paths through which God structures the world separate from the Divine—are the writings separate from the Writer? Or, are these paths extensions of the Divine—lines of godly energy extending through the engraved letters and into our reality? As we encounter the texts of the book, the answer to this question seems to be "yes"—both things are true.

This also raises the question of whether we ourselves as "writings" are separate from God, or extensions of the divine, or both. In implying "both," *Sefer Yetzirah* may be inviting us to shift our egoic awareness to a consciousness in which we are channels for divine energy. The term "engrave" does not only teach about creation—it informs practitioners what they must do in order to become vessels for divine creative potency.

Yah, The Becoming One Who Holds Many יהוה צבאות

Sefer Yetzirah names the Divine as Yah—a biblical name for God (as in Hallelu-yah), and also as YHWH (the most common biblical proper name for God). Yah is a shortened version of YHWH, which has the meaning of being or becoming (from the root *heh-vav-heh*, to be or become).[16]

YHWH is here translated "Becoming One" because in the context of *Sefer Yetzirah*, God is the agent for creation's becoming. We might even say God "becomes" creation, since the substance of creation seems to arise directly from the Divine. It is this divine substance (never named in the book, but alluded to in many passages) that travels along the marvelous paths and into the world.

The many variant texts of *Sefer Yetzirah* expand God's name to as many as ten divine names; for example:

> With thirty-two mystical paths of wisdom engraved Yah YHVH of Hosts, the God of Israel, the living God, King of the Universe, Almighty God, Merciful and gracious, high and exalted, dwelling in eternity, whose name is holy, he is lofty and holy...[17]

Yet scholar Peter Hayman suggests that most of these divine names were added by later editors and copyists. Only one of these pseudonyms of Yah manifests in all of the ancient manuscripts: YHWH Tzevaot, or "Lord of Hosts."[18] This name is telling. The "hosts," often understood as the angels or the stars, here may signify the vast multitude of creation. God, the singular, constantly gives rise to what is multiple.

Indeed, the divine energetic pathways themselves appear multiple: letters, inscriptions, channels, engravings. Scholar Yehuda Liebes says: "The essence of the *netivot* (pathways) is multiplicity, but they serve unity."[19] The One holds the Many. So, too, the single human mind holds a plethora of multiplying images, images that offer a new world at every turn.

Three Books: Tome, Tally, and Tale

בשלש ספרים
בספר וספר וסיפור

The Hebrew reads *b'sefer vsfar vesippur*—with book, number, and story. Here, those words are translated as "tome, tally, and tale," to try to convey that in the Hebrew, the three words are linked in sound and meaning. The book repeats the same root (*samech-peh-reish*, to tell) three times, with slightly varying forms that alter the root's meaning. There is magic in this: a musical repetition, a threefold spell.

The three books are not defined anywhere in the text; indeed, the phrase "three books" is never mentioned again. However, there is a threefold division of the cosmos in *Sefer Yetzirah*: *olam*, *shanah*, and *nefesh*:

olam, or world (space); *shanah*, or year (time); and *nefesh*, or body/soul. The word *nefesh* is often translated as soul, but biblically speaking, a *nefesh* means a person or other creature, or the life-force of that person or creature.[20] The *nefesh* in *Sefer Yetzirah* has organs and senses as well as intimations of good and evil, and clearly refers to a body, not only a soul. *Nefesh* refers to the human perspective—the ability to experience the world.

These three dimensions of space, time, and body-soul are very possibly the three books. The book is a concrete physical object, like space. Number implies counting, and thus is closely related to time, which progresses forward. And "story" or "tale" can apply to human experience. Contemporary kabbalist and scholar Aryeh Kaplan favors this reading.[21]

However, because of the lack of vowels in the original text, there is another reading of the three books: *sefer vesefer vesefer*—a book and a book and a book. Yehuda Liebes assumes this is the correct reading, and suggests the three books refer to the three divisions of the Hebrew letters found in *Sefer Yetzirah*: the imot or mother letters, the *kefulot* or double letters, and the *pshutot* or simple letters.[22] Each of these three categories of letters could be one of the three books with which the Divine created the world. This is a very plausible alternative. However, in order to be in sync with much of later Jewish tradition about *Sefer Yetzirah*, we're going to proceed with the reading that invokes space, time, and body/soul.

That three words *sefer*, *sfar*, and *sippur*—book, number, story—are all forms of the Hebrew root *samech-pei-reish* implies that these dimensions of space, time, and body are aspects of a single reality. The contemporary phrase "space-time continuum" comes to mind. Yehudah haLevi, the poet and philosopher, wrote: "The *sefer*, *sfar*, and *sippur* are one from God's perspective and three from the perspective of the human being."[23]

What does it mean to call these dimensions of reality "books?" The image of the cosmic books interweaves the spoken/written word with the physical world. The books that God inscribes are composed of language, but they are also composed of existence itself. They are not books but *Books*.

And where did the author(s) of *Sefer Yetzirah* get this idea of cosmic books? Interestingly, there is a talmudic tale that at the new year, God inscribes the names of humankind in three books: one for the righteous, one for the wicked, and one for the in-between:

> Rabbi Yochanan said: Three books are opened on Rosh haShanah: one of the completely wicked, one of the completely righteous, and one of the in-between people. The righteous are written and sealed for life, the wicked are written and sealed for death, and those in the middle—their sentence is suspended from Rosh haShanah until Yom Kippur..."[24]

Notice that the books in the Talmud passage are "sealed" after they are used. "Sealing" also occurs in *Sefer Yetzirah*. "Sealing" means that an element of the cosmos is fixed in place—that it becomes real, solid, and activated for use. Sealing can also refer to keeping out negative forces so that what has been "sealed" can exist in peace. In speaking of three books, *Sefer Yetzirah* may be referencing a Jewish tradition of sealed cosmic "books" that hold the fate of humankind.

Ecophilosopher David Abram has written of the ways that the art of writing changed human experience, pulling us out of our bodies and into words on a page. As this transition occurred, civilizations went from being image-based to being text-based. Human beings identified more with the stories that words told them, and less with their bodily experiences. This had a profound impact on our consciousness.[25] *Sefer Yetzirah*, with its three books of space, time, and being, provides a kind of bridge between writing and seeing, between text and thing. The writing that *Sefer Yetzirah* describes is the body of the world, a cosmic alphabet that brings meaning and the senses together. By traversing this bridge, we can enlarge our consciousness to hold both narrative and sensation.

Practice: Opening The Book

Close your eyes and breathe out.

There is a book in front of you.
Notice all the details of the book.
Reach out to the book.
Feel the power within it.
Open it.
When you open the book,
you find a door.
Pass through the door.
You discover a pathway.
Follow the path.
At the end of the path,
a teacher awaits you.
The teacher has a gift for you.
Receive the gift.
This gift connects you
to all space, all time, and all beings.
Offer thanks to the teacher.
Return along the path,
through the door,
and out of the book.
Close the book.
As you do so,
feel the power within it.
Feel the blessing
of the gift you have received
that connects you to all things.

Breathe out and open your eyes.

Practice: Engraving the Paths

Close your eyes and breathe out.

Before you is a stone.
Notice all the details of the stone:
size, shape, color, texture.
Reach out to the stone.
As you touch it,
a hollow channel appears in the stone.
Look up from the stone.
See what the channel carved in the stone
has created in the world.

Breathe out and open your eyes.

Chapter 1:2 · The Road Map

עשר ספירות בלימה
ועשרים ושתים אותיות יסוד
שלוש אמות
שבע כפולת
ושתים עשרה פשוטות

Ten inscriptions of the void
and twenty-two foundation-letters,
three mothers,
seven doubles,
and twelve simples.

This passage offers us *Sefer Yetzirah*'s imaginal library: ten *sefirot* (here translated "inscriptions"), three mother letters, seven doubles, and twelve simples. The ten *sefirot* of *Sefer Yetzirah* are cosmic structures that provide a frame for reality. Together they form the frame within which creation takes place. The twenty-two letters are the multiple forces that fill reality. They fall into three categories. First are the mothers or *imot*, the three primary elemental forces. Second are the double letters or *kefulot*, which take two different letter-forms. Third are the simple letters or *peshutot*, which take one letter-form. These are the tools the Creator—and the human creator—has to work with.

According to Hayman, this passage "is not securely anchored in the textual tradition of *Sefer Yetzirah*."[26] That is, it likely was not part of the earliest version. He suggests this paragraph was later included to bring together the ten *sefirot* or dimensions with the twenty-two letters, thus providing an integrated account of the thirty-two wondrous paths.[27] It is included here in order to introduce readers to the basic categories of *Sefer Yetzirah*.

Ten Inscriptions   עשר ספירות

The word *sefirot* shares a root with the word *sefer* or book—*samech-peh-reish*, which means "to tell." This implies that the ten *sefirot* are connected to the three books, which we will learn is in fact the case. *Sefirot* (singular *sefirah*) is a term usually understood to mean "aspects" or "dimensions."[28] Gershon Scholem derives the word *sefirah* from *lispor*, to count, and identifies the *sefirot* as the "ten primordial numbers": thus, the thirty-two paths include letters and numbers.[29] Similarly, Yehuda Liebes understands the *sefirot* as "things that are counted," and believes they represent "the fructive and creative possibility of the infinite numbers."[30] Yet the *sefirot* as they are listed are not only numbers, nor are they really "counted things" in the sense of a list where each thing relates specifically to its numerical position. Rather, the *sefirot* are sets of cosmic orientation points.[31]

How, then, should we translate *sefirot* in the context of *Sefer Yetzirah*? Kabbalah scholar Giulio Busi notes a Talmudic use of the word *sefirah* that means "writing." This is a rare use of the word, but it is the only one that relates directly to the word *sefer* or book. Applying this meaning to *Sefer Yetzirah*, Busi suggests that the *sefirot* are acts of divine writing—in other words, they are inscriptions. Busi notes that the verbs used as the Divine interacts with the ten *sefirot* are *chakak* (engraved), *chatzav* (hewed), and *chatam* (sealed)—all of which make perfect sense in a context where the *sefirot* are acts of cosmic engraving or writing. Busi therefore translates *eser sefirot belimah* to mean "ten immaterial writings"—writings that define the boundaries of the universe.[32]

We can see that the ten ethereal inscriptions correspond in their number to the Ten Commandments. Saadya Gaon notes this correspondence as well.[33] This supports Busi's theory that *sefirah* should be translated "inscriptions." The tablets are inscribed by God's finger on the stone tablets, and the *sefirot* too are inscribed by God's hand onto the world as it exists. Pirkei Avot, a section of the second-century text known as the Mishnah, notes:

> Ten things were created on the Sabbath eve at twilight...
> The writing, the inscription, and the tablets...[34]

Among the ten mysterious things created at twilight is the special writing used for the Tablets. Similarly, *Sefer Yetzirah*'s ten cosmic dimensions are primordial "divine writing," marking creation with its realities and tensions.

This is why this commentary translates *sefirot* as "inscriptions." The translation evokes the book's beginning images: a divine scribe engraving the *sefirot* and the letters upon the surface of reality. This world-writing is consistent with the first verses of Genesis in which God's utterances give rise to creation. It is also consonant with Jewish myths in which the Torah exists prior to creation and is used as a blueprint for the universe.³⁵

The Void   בלימה

The word *blimah* contains the words *bli* (without) and *mah* (what), and conveys "without substance." We first see the word in the Book of Job: "God stretched out Mount Zaphon over the void (*tohu*), suspended the earth over emptiness (*blimah*)."³⁶ *Tohu* is the void that exists before creation: "The earth was void and chaos, and darkness was on the face of the deep..." In choosing the word *blimah* to describe the *sefirot*, *Sefer Yetzirah* hints at primordial mysteries.

Giulio Busi suggests "immaterial" as a translation for *blimah*. He defines *blimah* as "without anything" as in "writing without anything." This immaterial writing is God's cosmic inscription, God's Logos as it is inscribed upon the world. Aryeh Kaplan offers "insubstantial," explaining that the *sefirot* are ideal, ineffable, abstract, rather than material, entities.³⁷

However, *blimah* in the Bible is not an adjective but a noun, referring to the substance in which the world is suspended.³⁸ I have translated *blimah* as "void" because biblically, it parallels *tohu*, the word for void or formlessness. In *Sefer Yetzirah*, it appears that beyond the limits God sets for the physical world, the divine inscriptions or *sefirot* extend beyond the realm of the earthly elements—into the void, so to speak.

There are other possible readings of the word. Gershom Scholem understands *blimah* to come from the root *bet-lamed-mem*, to stop up or close, and understands *blimah* to mean "secret" or "closed within itself."³⁹ That is, the *sefirot* constitute a closed system. *Sefer Yetzirah* indeed uses the word "blum" to mean "stop up" or "stay silent." However, in Job the word *blimah* clearly means "void," and *Sefer Yetzirah* is very sensitive to the nuances of biblical language. We might perhaps say that within the word *blimah*, the word "restrain or stop up," and the meaning of "void" poetically resonate with one another. *Sefer Yetzirah* understands the *sefirot* to be both immaterial and an ungraspable mystery that cannot be fully expressed.

Hayman has an entirely different approach, suggesting that "*eser sefirot blimah*" means "the ten *sefirot* are the basis." He takes this route because this phrase occurs paired with the phrase "*esrim veshtayim otiyot yesod*," which he translates as "twenty-two letters are the foundation."

Hayman thus understands *blimah*, in the context of *Sefer Yetzirah*, to mean something similar to foundation. Hayman seems to understand the verse in Job—"who suspends the earth on the *blimah*"—to mean "who suspends the earth on its basis." However, there is not much linguistic justification for translating *blimah* as "basis."

The *sefirot* that we must contemplate are *blimah*: they cannot be experienced in the way we experience most things. We have to engage with them differently—not shallowly, but at depth. They must be grappled with rather than seen clearly. The next sections of the book will help us to do the necessary grappling.

Foundation-letters   אותיות יסוד

Sefer Yetzirah refers to the letters as *otiyot yesod*, foundation-letters. The word *yesod*, in the Bible, means a foundation, as in the foundation of a city or house. Usage in the talmudic period is similar, with *yesodot* used to mean the foundations of the Temple.[40] So these letters are house-builders: they are the foundation of the Temple that is creation. The letters are written but they give rise to what is built. *Sefer Yetzirah* ingeniously sketches for us a cosmos that is both book and temple.

The letter-foundations, which compose both words and world, come in three categories:

1) Three mothers (explored in Chapter 3)
2) Seven doubles (explored in Chapter 4)
3) Twelve simples (explored in Chapter 5)

Sefer Yetzirah is structured so that each of the four subsets of the thirty-two paths (*sefirot*, mother letters, simples, and doubles) has its own chapter, identified by its own tagline. The sections of Chapter 1 (with a few exceptions) begin with the phrase *eser sefirot blimah*—ten inscriptions of the void. This tagline indicates the topic: God's ten inscriptions, and how they shape the universe.

Practice: The Void

Close your eyes and breathe out.

You are facing a cosmic void.
As you observe the void,
you see that a world begins to arise:
first large structures,
then smaller ones.
Observe all of the aspects of this world.
See that behind the world,
the void is still present:
a foundation for everything.

Breathe out and open your eyes.

Practice: Foundations

Close your eyes and breathe out.

Become aware of your body.
Now, feel that a web of pathways extends
from your body
into the earth beneath.
These pathways are like roots,
drawing up energy from the ground.

Feel the nourishing energy
that comes through the roots
into your body.
Send energy
from your body
back into the earth.
Feel what this is like.
Now, feel that pathways extend
from your body
into the sky above.
Feel the enlivening energy
that comes through the pathways
into your body.
Send energy
from your body
back into the sky.
Feel what this is like.
How does your body
feel different now?

Breathe out and open your eyes.

Chapter 1:3 · The Covenant

עשר ספירות בלימה
מספר עשר אצבעות
חמש כנגד חמש
וברית יחיד מכוונת באמצע
במילה ולשון ופה

Ten inscriptions of the void:
the number of ten fingers,
five opposite five
and a single covenant set in the center:

in word	in the genitals
and language	and tongue
and speech	and mouth.

This passage invites us to see in our mind's eye the Creator's hands reaching out to create: "the number of ten fingers, five opposite five." So too, we are invited to hold out our hands, see our fingers, and become aware of our own creative power. These are the hands that inscribe the void, that make the world.

Yet the passage also invokes the voice: language, speech, the tongue. This too is a sacred power of inscription. God and humans share this power to create via words. Without ever saying that people are "made in the image of God," the text here implies a parallel between humans and the divine.

The sets of five fingers on each hand echo the ten *sefirot*. The opposition of the fingers on one hand to the fingers on the other hand parallel the five tensions that the *sefirot* form when they are paired. The *sefirot*, which form the dimensional frame of the cosmos, come in ten "half-dimensions" that function as five whole dimensions. As we will see, these five dimensions are space (three dimensions), time (one dimension), and person (one dimension). Like the fingers on the two hands, the *sefirot* exist in dynamic, constructive tension. The structure of the world is built from these tensions.

At the center of the ten *sefirot* is the covenant: the inscription of the divine presence in the world. This single covenant is "centered" or "oriented" (*mekavven*) in the middle of the body, so that the body's appendages are on either side. We are going to see this word *mekavven* (oriented/centered) again, referring to the Divine Presence at the center of the world. That is, the body echoes the divine presence: just as the Divine Presence is located at the center of multiple opposing forces, so too the vocal apparatus is located at the center of opposing fingers and limbs. The human mouth, centered in the face and between the two hands, is parallel to the divine speech that pours out at the center of the world. When we speak, we approach divine creative power.

A Single Covenant ברית יחיד

For *Sefer Yetzirah*, the covenant (*brit*) does not primarily have to do with the revelation at Sinai. The Divine makes a covenant with anyone who masters the Hebrew letters and the *sefirot*, which are the universe-patterns. We might even say that the Divine makes a covenant with those who discover the secret of an expanded consciousness. All we need in order to access the covenant is the body and our own faculty of speech.

It is not observance of the Torah but awareness of the dimensions of the cosmos that typifies a "member of the covenant." The passage suggests that Jews, who have the Hebrew language as a heritage, can attain this covenant.[41] Yet the book also promises something much wider: the covenant is available to anyone who inscribes their own consciousness with the pattern of the cosmos.

The covenant as understood by *Sefer Yetzirah* has radically different implications from a covenant that is communal and tribal in nature. We ourselves are one of the "paths" between heaven and earth; when we become aware of this, we attain creative power. Our participation in covenant is not a membership in a religion but rather a shift in consciousness. Connected to the root of *mekavven*, "centered," is the word *kavvanah*, intention. This suggests that becoming centered means having intention, shaping one's own mind.

Creative consciousness involves holding opposites in tension rather than embracing one side of a polarity. The book returns again and again to the reconciling of opposites via balancing or centering. North opposes south, beginning opposes end, good opposes evil—but the Holy Place is precisely in the middle. To the centered mind, all phenomena are equally real and equally shifting. It is the divine center that offers stability in an ever-changing reality.

In word *(in the genitals)* ומילה
and language *(and tongue)* ולשון
and speech *(and mouth)* ופה

The word *etzbaot* means "fingers," but it can also mean "toes," and this is crucial to understand in examining this passage. Just as the fingers and toes parallel one another, the two "centers" of these ten extremities—e.g., the tongue, centered in between the fingers, and the genitals, centered in between the toes—are linked. The text says that the covenant is made in word and tongue and speech, but in Hebrew, "word," "tongue," and "speech" also have sexual/reproductive connotations. So too, the covenant with Abraham and his progeny is made via speech and also via the generativity of the reproductive organs.

Note the delicious double entendre in this passage: "Word" (Hebrew *milah*) also means "circumcision," as in the covenantal marking of the penis.[42] So *milah* is also a reference to the phallus—it holds both meanings (word and phallus) at the same time. *Lashon* can mean "language" and can refer to the physical organ of the tongue. It also has an intimation of the genitals.[43] In rabbinic Hebrew, the word "mouth" (Hebrew *peh*), can also refer to the *peh shel mata*, the "lower mouth," i.e., the vulva.[44] The shadow of the reproductive organs looms large in this passage. This reading is made even stronger by the use here of the word *k'neged*—opposite—as Genesis calls Eve the *ezer k'negdo* (helper-opposite, or helpmate) of Adam.

The implication is quite clear: the word and the reproductive organs are parallel vehicles for the covenant with the Divine. Why? Because both are creative. The word creates worlds, and the reproductive organs create life. In fact, an alternate text of this passage reads "a single covenant in the circumcision of the tongue and the circumcision of the genitalia"—referring directly to this duality of speech and reproductive capacity.

The text implicitly suggests that speech, writing, and reproduction are all a kind of inscription: an engraving of reality. The human voice, the hands, and the body all have the power to shape and form these inscriptions of reality. The implication is that we, like God, can create worlds. Here we have a new angle on the "word and world" duality that is central to the book. Just as a human can create life via the sex organs, humans can create life through their speech and through writing. This passage offers the promise that one who learns to inscribe the mysteries of this book will attain life-giving power.

Practice: A Single Covenant

Close your eyes and breathe out.

See before you the Creator
however you understand the Creator.

The Creator's mouth
is speaking Creation.
See what comes forth
from the mouth of the Creator.

The Creator's hands
are shaping creation.
See what comes forth
from the hands of the Creator.

The Creator's genitals
are birthing creation.
See what comes forth
from the genitals of the Creator.

See that these three creations are one.

Breathe out and open your eyes.

Practice: Five Opposite Five

Close your eyes and breathe out.

Your palms face one another.

The five fingers of one hand
touch the five fingers of the other hand.
See that each hand
is full of a primordial power.

See that these two powers are opposite.

See that each hand
is equally strong.

The ten fingers,
the two forces,
push against one another.

As these two irresistible forces,
these two immovable objects,
meet,
find the balance between them.

Feel the balance reverberate
throughout your body.

Breathe out and open your eyes.

Chapter 1:4 · The First Instruction: Understand in Wisdom

עשר ספירות בלימה
עשר ולא תשע עשר ולא אחת עשרה
הבן בחכמה וחכם בבינה
בחון בהם וחקור מהם
העמד דבר על בוריו
והשב יוצר על מכונו

Ten inscriptions of the void:
ten and not nine, ten and not eleven
understand in Wisdom
be wise in Understanding
examine them, delve into them
stand each thing on its clarity
on its absence
and return the Creator
to Their Dwelling Place.

Four passages into our journey, we haven't yet been told what the *sefirot* actually are. It appears that the journey begins with preparing our minds. Only then we can begin to interact with the powers of creation. This passage and the two that follow it tell us how to direct our minds toward the spiritual practice *Sefer Yetzirah* offers. That is why this commentary names them "The Three Instructions." This series of three preparatory passages is like an unfolding ceremony that involves the reader as a participant in the text.

The first instruction is to direct the mind to understand that the Creator dwells at the center of creation. As we direct the mind in this way, we discover that the Creator is also at the center of each human being. In order to understand this, we must develop a hollow clarity, a presence that is absence.

Ten and Not Nine, Ten and Not Eleven

עשר ולא תשע
עשר ולא אחת עשרה

Of course ten is not nine! Why does the text bother to tell us this? This somewhat odd phrase emphasizes that the ten *sefirot* are, as Liebes says, "things that can be counted."[45] They are genuine aspects of reality. That is to say, the ten *sefirot* are not metaphors. They are not the invention of a human mind. They are truly facets of what is.

The phrase "ten and not nine" may also allude to other thought-systems that posit ten fundamental dimensions of reality. Saadya Gaon, the ninth-century Jewish sage and commentator on *Sefer Yetzirah*, notes that Aristotle recognized ten categories of reality (substance, quantity, quality, relation, space, time, possession, position, action, and passivity). Saadya Gaon connects the *sefirot* and the Aristotelian categories to the Ten Commandments, making three sets of ten.[46]

The Gnostics of the first and second centuries CE believed in ten Aeons—ten spheres or personalities that emanate from the Godhead. Scholars Joseph Dan and Gershom Scholem have suggested that there may have been considerable Gnostic influence on the writer(s) of *Sefer Yetzirah*.[47] Gnosticism was a belief system (considered heretical by Christians and Jews)[48] that various sects embraced between the second and thirteenth centuries. Dan writes:

> The Gnostics in their various sects believed in the existence of a system of supreme divine forces, known in Greek as *pleroma*, within which there were different levels of divine figures, some good and others evil, some male and others female, and with the entire system perpetually in a state of dynamic ferment and with struggles between the different factors within it."[49]

A related term for these divine figures is "aeons." There are said to be ten aeons. In *Sefer Yetzirah* we also have ten emanated entities existing in polarized tension, two of which are identified as "good" and "evil." We can see the possibility that Gnosticism could potentially have been an influence on our passage.

This passage can also be read in another way: as an invitation to find out the truth. Are there really ten *sefirot*? Might there be nine or eleven? This is another case in which the text draws the reader into active engagement. "Check our conclusions," the words seem to be saying. "You'll see that we are right in our perceptions of the Real."

Understand with Wisdom, Be Wise With Understanding

הבן בחכמה
וחכם בבינה

In 1:1, *Sefer Yetzirah* calls the *sefirot* and the letters "paths of Wisdom." In 1:4, we meet Wisdom again. This time, She has two names: Wisdom and Understanding. She has these two names in the book of Proverbs itself: "I, Wisdom, dwell with Prudence... I am Understanding; courage is mine."[50] Like the two hands, or the ten *sefirot*, Wisdom has a dual aspect. The reader must learn the duality of Wisdom's ways in order to understand Creation.

Philo, the ancient Jewish philosopher, believed that Wisdom provided the means for knowing God—Wisdom was both the way to God and the guide on the way.[51] Wisdom was the divine word working in the world such that Scripture and Greek philosophy could both be influenced by it.[52] Interpreting Scripture allegorically, Philo sees Wisdom in the story of Rebecca drawing water for Abraham's servant:

> Rebecca therefore must be praised, who, in obedience to the injunctions of her father, having taken down the vessel of wisdom on her arm from a higher place, proffered her pitcher to the disciple...[53]

Philo's Rebecca is a vehicle for the flow of wisdom from a "higher place." She is similar in function to the Wisdom of *Sefer Yetzirah*, a force that channels a flow of divine meaning into the world.

The phrase "understand with Wisdom, be wise with Understanding" actively enjoins the reader to engage Wisdom. The phrase alternates between verb and noun—between the cosmic being (Wisdom) and the act that embodies her (to understand or be wise). Just as in the first section of *Sefer Yetzirah*, Wisdom is a process rather than a defined entity; so too in this passage Wisdom is noun but also verb. The reader must activate the paths of Wisdom by seeking to become wise.

It is important to separate *Sefer Yetzirah*'s mention of Wisdom and Understanding (*Chochmah* and *Binah*) from the later kabbalah's understanding of those terms. In the Zohar and other texts of classical kabbalah, *Chochmah* and *Binah* are separate masculine and feminine *sefirot* (divine personalities or realms) that join together to create the world.

In our passage, *Chochmah* and *Binah* almost certainly refer to the same entity: the mysterious "Wisdom" of our opening passage, the multifaceted vehicle by which the Divine creates paths within reality.

The text now instructs the reader to examine the *sefirot*. *Bechon bahem* means "examine them." *Chakor mehem*—"search or cross-examine them"—can also have the meaning "dig into them,"[54] which is why the phrase is translated here as "delve into them." This language hints at the hollowing/channeling action at the heart of *Sefer Yetzirah*. To attain Wisdom is to understand its hollow nature. We will soon be told that the *sefirot* are rays stretching from the divine center into the many directions of the universe without end. The text invites us, à la Robert Frost, to look down each one as far as we can.[55]

Stand Each Thing on its Clarity   העמד דבר על בוריו

The Hebrew words read *ha'amed davar al boryo*. This phrase appears in the Talmud, and there it means "clarify the matter"[56] or more literally, "stand each thing on its clarity." Hayman translates the phrase *"ha'amed davar al boryo"* as "get the thing clearly worked out." Kaplan translates the phrase as "make each thing stand on its essence."[57]

We should note that there are variant texts of this passage. The agreed-on part of the sentence is *"ha'amed davar al"*—"stand each thing on." The final word is variously rendered by manuscripts as *boryo* or *beryo* (its clarity), or as *bor'o* (its Creator).[58] The reading *"ha'amed davar al bor'o"*—"stand each thing on its Creator" is powerful, as it suggests tracing each *sefirah* back to its origin in the Godhead.[59]

And, as we have come to expect, there is a double entendre here. The word *boryo* (its clarity) is connected to *bar*, clear, but we might observe that *bor* can also mean "pit" or "emptiness." Indeed, in Talmudic Hebrew, the word *"bar"* can mean either "clear" or "empty." The image of the empty pit fits with the repeating image of hollowness: channeling, engraving, carving.

This passage invites the reader to contemplate the *sefirot* which are "depths" without end. We are to establish each thing on its hollowness, knowing that each of these dimensions is an empty channel for divine creative force. It is possible, then, to see all of the aspects of reality as the movements of divine energy through a world that is engraved, carved, hollow.

If we stand each thing on its "pit," we can see in the space below each solid thing the empty channel out of which it arose. If we were to make a parallel with a Buddhist text, we might turn to a Zen koan that says: "The true nature of phenomena is emptiness."[60] Or consider the *Kurna Purana*, a medieval Hindu work which describes the practice of abhava-yoga as "one's self is meditated upon as a void and without qualities."[61]

Bible scholar Avivah Zornberg speaks about this void that stands below creation in her book *The Murmuring Deep*. She writes: "The infrastructure of creation, the *tohu vavohu* (formlessness), is the void that leaves one aghast...the murmuring void is the ground and deep of human life..."[62] The void beneath us both terrifies us and inspires us to create, to make meaning.

This phrase in *Sefer Yetzirah*, in its plain meaning, invites us to see the *sefirot* clearly as they exist. But its subtext invites us to understand that they do not exist as separate entities—they are merely movements of the divine. The text poetically suggests that both things are true: void and substance, the many and the underlying oneness. This is the mystery we are to contemplate—the dual awareness that is Wisdom. This is perhaps why we are to "understand in Wisdom and be wise in Understanding." There is a back-and-forth quality to all that is, as we move between one and many.

Return the Creator to Their Dwelling Place
והשב יוצר על מכונו

Sefer Yetzirah's surprising finish to this passage is a direction to the reader to return God to God's proper place. We hadn't known that God was displaced, so the direction to return the Divine to the right place is surprising.[63] Or maybe it isn't surprising. Only when we are centered can God be centered in us. By perceiving and experiencing the divine energy behind all phenomena, we can restore God to the proper place at our core.

Meditation teacher Jay Michaelson says it like this:

> It is a very simple matter to know intellectually that all of spacetime is one field of matter/energy; that the individual self does not have any existence independent of the One; and that all creatures, matter, and energy are but fleeting manifestations of Being...

> However, to truly know it—that is, to experience this truth (to Be Here Now)—is to know one's real nature, to end the selfish desires which cause one's own and others' suffering, and to experience a peaceful yet indescribably, achingly, beautiful sense of spaciousness in the One that Is, here, now, everywhere and always.[64]

Yet there is something else in the phrase "return the Creator" in addition to the instruction to be present. There is an aspect of theurgy here: what humans do can affect the Divine. We are capable of returning the deity to a proper state. This theurgic impulse will be adopted by the later kabbalah, which will assert that human sacred practice can aid the Godhead in coming to complete unity.[65]

The Hebrew for God's (His, here translated in the gender-neutral singular Their) holy place is *mechono*. *Mechon* can mean a dwelling, fixed place, or foundation, and can be used to indicate the Temple. Its root (*kaf-vav-nun*) is the same root as in the word *mekavven*, which *Sefer Yetzirah* uses to mean "center" or "orient." The place of the Divine is at the center: the center of the world, the center of the mind, the center of the cosmic shrine. To come to center, to focus our contemplative attention, is to return the Divine to the proper place. This of course can only be true if the Divine is inside us, waiting to be brought to center.

This means that the Creator (*yotzer*) mentioned in the text is also us. We too can be creators of worlds—or, as Yehuda Liebes says, we can be creators of the self.[66] *Sefer Yetzirah* tells us that when we open our consciousness to the cosmos, when we develop the right state of mind, we come to our right place, and dwell at the center of the universe.

Practice: Stand Each Thing On Its Absence

Close your eyes and breathe out.

You are standing on a clear surface,
like a frozen lake, or a sheet of glass.

Beneath you,
you perceive
an upside-down reflection of you.

Look down into your reflection.

See that within it is
a void, a nothingness.

Feel into this hollowness beneath you.

Feel into the place where you are no-thing.

How does this feel?
Now, as you look down into your reflection,
feel into your hereness,
your body's substance
casting this reflection.

How does this feel?
See if you can hold both feelings—
substance and void—
at the same time.
See what happens now.

Breathe out and open your eyes.

Practice: Returning the Creator to the Place

Close your eyes and breathe out.

Focus on a central place in your body:
mind, heart or belly.

See that a creative power
dwells in this place.

Feel this creative power
radiating outward
through all the limbs of your body.

As creative power fills you,
observe what happens
in your body, heart, mind, and spirit.

What will you do with this creative power?

Breathe out and open your eyes.

Chapter 1:5 · The Second Instruction: Return to the Place

עשר ספירות בלימה
בלום פיך מלדבר
בלום לבך מלהרהר
ואם רץ לבך
שוב למקום
שכך נאמר
רצוא ושוב
ועל דבר זה נכרת ברית

Ten inscriptions of the void:

Stop your mouth from speaking,
stop your heart from murmuring,
and if your heart runs
return to the Place
for scripture says:
"running and returning."

Regarding this matter.
a covenant was made.

Over my many years of studying *Sefer Yetzirah*, I quote this passage the most. It is hard to think of a more eloquent description of the practice of meditation and contemplation than these words. In order to concentrate on divine reality, one must calm the internal narrative. We are all familiar with the experience of the mind rambling on uncontrollably, even when we try to silence it. Here the reader is invited, perhaps even at the moment of reading, to turn from the chatter at the surface and go deeper.

All meditation requires a focus (the breath, an image, a text, etc.). When one becomes distracted, one returns to the focus as a way of once again stilling the mind. For *Sefer Yetzirah*, the focus to which we must return is the *makom*. *Makom* has a wonderful double meaning. First, it is the "place"—the current place and time, the moment, the real. Second, *Makom* is a rabbinic term for God.[67] By returning to conscious presence, one is returning to the divine.

Stop your Mouth from Speaking and Your Heart from Murmuring   בלום פיך מלדבר
בלום לבך מלהרהר

We have all along been told that letters and words created the world, and yet now, ironically, we are told to stop speaking. Why this paradox? Because the inscriptions God uses to create are more than a language: they are the world itself. To truly know the *sefirot*, we too must go beyond verbal language and sit with the Real.

The verb *blum* (to stop up, to restrain) is critical to this passage. The root *bet-lamed-mem* recalls the word *blimah* (insubstantiality, void, ethereality). Biblically speaking, the word *lev* (heart) refers to the mind as well as what people today call the heart. "Stop your heart from murmuring" refers to the consciousness, as when Ecclesiastes says: "*natati et libi*/I set my mind (literally, *gave my heart*) to find out and probe with wisdom all that happens under the sun."[68] When we stop the inner dialogue rooted in personality and experience, we encounter *blimah*, non-substance. We meet the unspeakable—that which cannot be said.[69]

The word *hirhur* means anxious rumination, as in the kind of worried insomniac thinking one does late at night. In Jewish legend, Abraham, having committed to leave his father's home and land for an unknown place, has *hirhurim*—he wonders obsessively if the community will criticize him for abandoning his father.[70] To make one's heart stop ruminating (or murmuring, to use a word that sounds a bit like the Hebrew *hirhur*) is to refrain from the anxiety that haunts many of our inner lives, in order to attune to a different reality. In all meditation and spiritual practice, the practitioner has *hirhurim*, murmuring thoughts. The key then is to return to the focus, which is the Place.

If Your Heart Runs, Return to the Place

ועם רץ לבך
שוב למקום

Although Tzahi Weiss has argued that *Sefer Yetzirah* was written by non-rabbinic Jews with little awareness of rabbinic texts,[71] this passage would seem to undermine that claim somewhat. Rabbinic Jews used the epithet *haMakom* (the Place) to indicate God. The authors of *Sefer Yetzirah* embraced it, perhaps, because it fit with their notion of God as intimately interconnected with time and space.

Makom implies God in a very particular form: God as cosmic architecture. A place is bounded by space, time, and body/soul. For *Sefer Yetzirah*, these dimensions are all emanated by the divine. Therefore our place—our personal particularity—is one manifestation of the Place that is God.

"Returning to the place" can also refer to an ethical return, since the Hebrew word *shuv*/return can mean to repent. The practitioner is called to return to God via his/her actions as well. The spiritual practice of *Sefer Yetzirah* should affect ethics as well as metaphysical perceptions.

Yehudah Liebes notes that the word *makom*, in biblical Hebrew, is sometimes used to refer to the Temple.[72] Liebes contends that God has the rabbinic name *haMakom*, the Place, because God is the one who dwells in the "Place"—that is, in the Temple. To "return to the Place" means to return to the sacred center that is the cosmic Temple. *HaMakom*, the place, could also mean the body, for the body is our place as well. Or, the place could mean the meditative focus: the breath, the sacred phrase, or whatever we are concentrating on. The place could also mean the real: whatever is happening at that place and time. All of these could be regarded as the Temple of the moment.

Running and Returning

רצוא ושוב

Our passage now quotes the book of Ezekiel, in which the prophet describes a vision of angel-like creatures (*chayot*) running and returning.

> The appearance of the creatures was like coals of fire burning. Something like the appearance of torches was going among the creatures, the fire had a brightness, and from the fire came lightning. The creatures were running to and fro like the flash of lightning.[73]

The quoting of this verse is what is known in rabbinic literature as a "prooftext"—a biblical support for what the writer is saying. Yet the passage in *Sefer Yetzirah* uses the verse not to refer to angels, but rather to the human mind.

When we attempt to quiet the mind, it resists. It tries to go back to its ordinary thought patterns. Meditation is a process of becoming distracted and drawing the attention back to the meditative focus. Aryeh Kaplan writes: "As soon as a person attempts to clear his mind of thought, he immediately begins to think, 'Now I am not thinking of anything.'"[74] Few people can stay in a purely focused state for long. Most of us must oscillate back and forth. The text here borrows the biblical phrase *ratzo vashov* (running and returning) to name this process.

And, as we noted, *ratzo vashov* also means running and returning between the One (God) and the Many (the creations), in a constant process that links divinity with physical substance. Reality runs along the thirty-two paths of wisdom, back and forth, between the Creator and the world. When we enter a deeper consciousness, we begin to see this dual nature of the real. There is a placental quality to this running and returning. The network allows for the two entities, God and the world, unity and multiplicity, to be separate and connected at the same time.

A Covenant Was Made   נכרת ברית

The phrase *nichrat brit* ("a covenant was made") utilizes a passive verb. This means that the parties to the covenant (presumably God and the reader) are unclear. The reader must explore what this mysterious covenant, related to the "running and returning" of the mind, must be.

Covenant implies a structured relationship between parties. The word "covenant" seems to describe the relationship between God and the practitioner. In saying: "Regarding this matter, a covenant was made," this passage makes a promise that the practice will work reliably: the wisdom *Sefer Yetzirah* offers will permit an ongoing and trustworthy relationship with God.

Practice: Stop Your Heart from Murmuring

Before beginning, set a timer for 10 minutes. Choose a focus. It can be an image (like a circle or Hebrew letter) or a repetitive sound (like a word, phrase, or song that you repeat) or the sensation of your breath. It could even be the sound of the ocean.

Close your eyes and breathe out.

Bring your attention to the focus.

Try to keep your attention there.

When you find that you have other thoughts,
gently return to the focus.

You don't need to chase the thoughts away:
just try not to pay attention to them.

If feelings come up, allow the feelings.

Return to the focus.

When the timer goes off,
breathe out and open your eyes.

Practice: Return to the Place

Close your eyes and breathe out.

You are on a journey
toward a place that is sacred for you:
a mountain, cave, river, garden,
a place of prayer, a shrine,
or anywhere you imagine.

Move closer and closer
to your destination.

When you arrive at the place,
someone comes out to greet you—
someone known or unknown to you.

They say to you:
Welcome back. How wonderful
that you have returned.

Notice what you feel
as you receive this welcome.
Know that you were always meant
to come back to this place.

Look down at yourself
and notice how you are transformed
by your return to this sacred place.

Breathe out and open your eyes.

Chapter 1:6 · The Third Instruction: Before One, What Are You Counting?

עשר ספירות בלימה
נעוץ סופן בתחילן ותחילתן בסופן
כשלהבת בגחלת
שהיוצר אחד
ואין לו שני
ולפני אחד מה אתה סופר

Ten inscriptions in the void:
Their end is imbedded in their beginning
and their beginning in their end
like a flame in a fiery coal
for the Creator is one
and has no second
and before one,
what are you counting?

This passage alerts us to a paradox inherent in contemplating the *sefirot*: they are both One (divine) and many (earthly). They cannot be viewed as entirely one or the other. The reader needs a warning about this paradox because otherwise, in attempting to visualize the *sefirot*, we may become mesmerized or confused by the question of whether they are divine or not. The answer this passage offers is that they are both.

We now must recall Wisdom in the Book of Proverbs, who is "the beginning of God's path."[75] Wisdom is a created being, yet she is also God's counselor and witness to creation. According to the Bible, she is born even before the primordial deep that pre-exists the world.[76] This suggests a unique closeness to divine mystery. Just as Wisdom's nature partakes of the created world and also of the primordial divine, so too the *sefirot* have this dual nature.

Their End is Imbedded in Their Beginning, and Their Beginning in Their End

נעוץ סופן בתחילן ותחילתן בסופן

The *sefirot*, the engraved pathways of divine creative power, are the "end" of the creative process, yet they are interwoven with the beginning, which is God. So too, God is interwoven into the *sefirot*. The end and the beginning cannot be meaningfully divided from one another. Via the *sefirot*, divine energy interpenetrates creation.

The burning coal cannot be separated from its flame: if there is no coal, there is no flame, and if there is no flame, the coal ceases to burn. The *sefirot*, the divine inscriptions, arise constantly from their divine Inscriber. They are separate from the Creator, yet also conjoined: "engraved" into reality, they are eternally filled and refilled with divine creative power.

Like a Flame in a Fiery Coal

כשלהבת בגחלת

Sefer Yetzirah uses the image of fire to explain the link between God and the *sefirot*. Fire, in biblical tradition, indicates divine presence. Consider the fire of the burning bush in the Moses story, the lightning on Mount Sinai, and the burning torch that appears to Abraham.[77] There is also a biblical text in which an angel uses a burning coal to cleanse Isaiah's lips so he can speak prophecy:

> I said: "Woe is me, I am lost, for I am a man of unclean lips, and I dwell amid a people of unclean lips, yet my eyes have seen the King, the God of Hosts."
>
> Then one of the seraphim flew over to me with a burning coal which he had taken from the altar with tongs. He touched it to my mouth and said: "Behold, this has touched your lips, and your iniquity has gone away, and your sin is pardoned."[78]

While the word for "coal" here is *ritzpah*, not *gachelet* as in our *Sefer Yetzirah* text, it is notable that the coal in Isaiah is used to cleanse the lips so that the prophet may speak.[79] Just as Isaiah's coal purifies his speech, the *sefirot*, like flames arising from a coal, should purify ours. Speaking of these matters must be approached with careful intention.

For the Creator is One and Has No Second

שהיוצר אחד
ואין לו שני

The Shema, one of the central prayers in Jewish worship, states that God is One. Yet what does this mean? For some commentators, the Shema simply states that God is one entity and not many. Yet for the kabbalists of the thirteenth century, the Shema states that God is one and incorporates many divisions into that unity. Some kabbalistic texts assert that all of the world's diversity is divinely emanated; in other words, there is nothing but God.[80]

The analogy of the coal and the flame suggests that *Sefer Yetzirah* affirms this second reading of the Shema. The Divine Master is singular and has no second—this doesn't only mean there is no second God, but that there is no second *anything*. The *sefirot* (and by extension, the creation they frame) are extensions of God's existence rather than separate entities. This means that the world's multiplicity is ultimately not entirely real. There is one divine power acting through a multiplicity of channels.

And Before One, What Are You Counting?

ולפני אחד
מה אתה סופר

When I teach *Sefer Yetzirah*, I often note that this phrase sounds like a Zen koan to me. I have heard students in my classes spontaneously make the same observation. Like a Zen koan, this phrase seeks to interrupt the thinker, to catch us in the middle of thinking.

Prior to creation, there is no "one" as opposed to "two." There is no duality and therefore unity cannot be named or counted—God's unity is prior to "one," prior to the notion that anything can be separated and counted. In defining the *sefirot*, we must know them as ten things, and yet this text suggests to us that there is not even truly "one," never mind "ten." Multiplicity, this cryptic statement suggests, is an illusion.

Yet the phrase, which addresses the reader ("What are **you** counting?") implicitly acknowledges that in the world we live in, there are separate identities, separate beings.[81] We live in the world of counting. Yet when we contemplate the "flame in a fiery coal," we also have access to the world where there is no counting. In that world we are "before the One"—in the place of the One, another meaning of *lifnei echad*.

In saying *mah ata sofer* ("what are you counting?") the passage cleverly incorporates the verb *samech peh reish*, to **count**, also related to the words for **tell** and **write**: the same verb as the root of *sefirah*. Hidden in "what are you counting?" is also "what are you trying to tell me?" The phrase suggests that a mystery is being communicated. We could also hear in this phrase "what are the *sefirot* really?" For at the same time as we "count" and try to know the ten *sefirot*, we also cannot count them or know them, because they are One at the same time that they are ten. At the same time that we try to write/speak/count the *sefirot* in their separate forms, we cannot separate them into individual forms. They too are "before One."

Practice: A Flame in a Fiery Coal

Close your eyes and breathe out.

See that a burning coal is before you.
A flame rises out of the coal.
See its brightness and feel its heat.

Perceive that the flame and the coal
are inseparable.

See within this fiery coal
the mystery of oneness.

If you feel able, reach out to take the coal.
Feel its heat, without being burned.
Bring it to your mouth.

Hear the truth
that comes out of your mouth
when the coal touches it.

Breathe out and open your eyes.

Chapter 1:6 · The Third Instruction: Before One, What Are You Counting?

Practice: Before One

Close your eyes and breathe out.

Count backward slowly
from ten to one.

As you do so,
perceive the world shifting
from multiplicity
to unity.

When you get to one,
count backward one last time,
to whatever is before one.

What do you see, hear, or feel
when you encounter
what is before one?

Breathe out and open your eyes.

Chapter 1:7 · The Depths of the *Sefirot*

עשר ספירות בלימה
ומדתן עשר שאין להם סוף
עומק ראשית ועומק אחרית
עומק טוב ועומק רע
עומק רום ועומק תחת
עומק מזרח ועומק מערב
עומק צפון ועומק דרום
ואדון יחיד
אל מלך נאמן
מושל בכולם ממעון קדשו
ועד עדי עד

Ten inscriptions of the void:
their measure is ten, yet they are infinite:

A depth of beginning and a depth of end
A depth of good and a depth of evil
A depth of above and a depth of below
A depth of east and a depth of west
A depth of north and a depth of south

and a singular Master—
a faithful Divine ruler—
rules over them all
from God's holy dwelling
and out to eternity.

Chapter 1:7 · The Depths of the Sefirot

Now that we have been prepared for an encounter with the *sefirot*, we finally meet them, and it is a dizzying moment. The ten *sefirot* are a frame for the whole cosmos. They inscribe the void with order and meaning. This passage finally explains the mystery of the *sefirot*: they are ten partial dimensions that, when combined into pairs, provide five whole dimensions. The whole dimensions are the basis for space, time, and subjective experience (the body/soul).

The ten partial dimensions are, essentially, rays: lines that begin at a point and extend infinitely in one direction. Each ray combines with another to form a line that extends infinitely in both directions. (Since the rays are called "depths," we might also choose to think of them as broader than a line: more like a field, maybe—but we'll first imagine them as lines.)

Two rays, called beginning and end, join together to create the dimension of time (*shanah*). One direction of the "time" dimension is "beginning," and the other direction is "end," but the dimension of time is infinite: it has no end in either direction. It is an infinite line along which every point between "beginning" and "end" can be plotted.

Similarly, two rays, good and evil, join together to create the spectrum of human experience (body-soul or *nefesh*). One direction is "good," and the other direction is "evil," but the dimension of subjective experience is an infinite line along which every point between "good" and "evil" can be plotted.

It takes six rays—up, down, north, south, east, west—to create the dimension of space (*olam*). Each pair of attributes (up/down, north/south, east/west) creates an infinite line. All together they create a three-dimensional space, a kind of infinite cube.

Together, these ten rays delineate the three realms of space, time, and body/soul, and build a five-dimensional universe. All phenomena occur within these three realms: the three "books" (to refer back to what we read in 1:1). We are now invited to open the three books of the cosmos and plumb their depths.

The language of this passage is poetic and elegant in its simplicity. The poem also reads like a spell, as if we are summoning the outline of creation out of the void, just as God once did. Yehuda Liebes notes that the structure of the language here is similar to the structure of ancient Hebrew poetry.[82] The poetics of the passage convey its message: the profoundly beautiful and graceful balance of opposites within the created world.

A Depth   עומק

Each of the *sefirot* is described as an *omek*. *Omek* means a "depth" as in a profundity or a mystery, but also a literal depth, as in a valley.[83] One can enter into the depth of study, as in the Talmud's tractate Megillah where Joshua spends the night "in the depths of the law." One can also enter a feature of the landscape that is a depth.[84]

The choice of the word *omek*/depth continues *Sefer Yetzirah*'s consistent fascination with empty space.[85] The ten "depths" are not solid entities; "depth" is by its nature empty. The divine creative power can come "through" a depth, can fill a depth the way water fills a valley.

It also may be significant that the Aramaic word *umkah* is used for the foundation of a building.[86] If each depth is a "foundation," then the whole cosmic structure is a house. This house is "founded" on its five-dimensional hollow frame.[87] Its center is the Divine's dwelling-place. In other words, our passage describes the cosmos as a universe-sized Temple. Ronit Meroz writes: "The very structure of the world... indicates its holiness!"[88]

The emptiness of "depth" has a uterine fecundity to it, as if the ten *sefirot* form a womb space. Feminist scholar Kathryn Silverstein defines depth as "an expansive interiority, a space of possibility."[89] She applies this definition to our passage by noting: "the word 'engrave'... highlights the paths as avenues of potentiality, rather than substance. One can perhaps envision the figuration of depth here as the emptiness of possibility... In linking these *sefirot* together, the *Sefer Yetzirah* subverts any clear divide between divinity, temporality, and corporeality."[90] The positioning of these ten "depths" in relationship to one another, with God at the center, gives the Divine, and also the human being, a web-like network of channels of creative possibility, each one intersecting the next. By extension, God intersects with the created world.

Christian feminist theologian Catherine Keller offers a definition of depth that signifies "a layered complexity, a multidimensionality of becoming, in which differences are neither kept separate (as in a clearly bounded dyad of Creator/creature) nor fused (as in a pantheistic substance) but held in contrast."[91] If we apply this understanding to our passage, we can posit that this passage within *Sefer Yetzirah* supports a multidimensional view of existence, in which human experience and divine experience are not entirely separate or joined but rather overlap via a shared network of dimensional "depths."

Seeing the passage as a prompt for meditation, Aryeh Kaplan offers this visualization:

> Attempt to picture an infinity of time in the past. Let the mind travel back to a moment ago, an hour ago, a day ago, a year ago, continuing until you reach a level where you are trying to imagine an infinity ago. Then do the same with regard to the future.... In this matter, one gradually trains the mind to depict the infinite.[92]

Peter Hayman describes the goal of this passage as "thinking God's thoughts after Him." Looking at 1:13, Hayman identifies the desire of the text as "to experience imaginatively what it is like to be God."[93] So too, in this passage, the reader positions him or herself at the center of the universe and looks down all the infinities, taking God's perspective.

This passage is perhaps where the meditative and the magical meet. Magical practice tends to envision spiritual power in the hands of the practitioner. By allowing the reader to imagine God's creative power, the text invites the reader to envision spiritual power in their own hands.

From God's Holy Dwelling ממעון קדשו

There appears to be a central point where all the infinite "depths" meet, and *Sefer Yetzirah* calls this central point *ma'on kodsho*, God's holy dwelling. *Ma'on kodsho*, "God's holy habitation," typically means the Temple. Section 1:7 imagines the Divine in a house at the center of the universe, ruling over all dimensions from a central point. Ronit Meroz writes of this text: "The Holy Tabernacle serves as the axis mundi."[94]

As Yehuda Liebes writes, "The God of *Sefer Yetzirah* is found in being."[95] God is in the midst of the world, and the practitioner seeks God within creation.

This house where God lives rests on the hollow depths of the *sefirot*. This image of a solid entity resting on hollow depths echoes 1:4, in which we hear "stand each thing on its clarity/absence." Moreover, the image reminds us of a Talmudic legend that hollow tunnels ran beneath the Temple: tunnels known as the *shittim* or foundations. According to this legend, the tunnels went down to the *tehom*, the primordial depths.[96] Similarly, the author(s) of this passage imagine God's cosmic Temple as permeated by hollow depths. As Liebes writes, "The foundations of the world and the foundations of the Temple are one."[97]

And Out to Eternity   ועד עדי עד

From the center, one can look down any one of the rays of the *sefirot* into infinity. This perch at the cosmic center is meant to transform us, to change our way of perceiving and knowing. Joseph Campbell wrote: "The center of the world is the axis mundi, the central point around which all revolves. The central point of the world is the point where stillness and movement are together. Movement is time, but stillness is eternity. Realizing how this moment of your life is actually a moment of eternity... this is the mythological experience."[98] In offering us God's perspective, the text welcomes us into a mythic experience in which we understand ourselves as part of a larger cosmos.

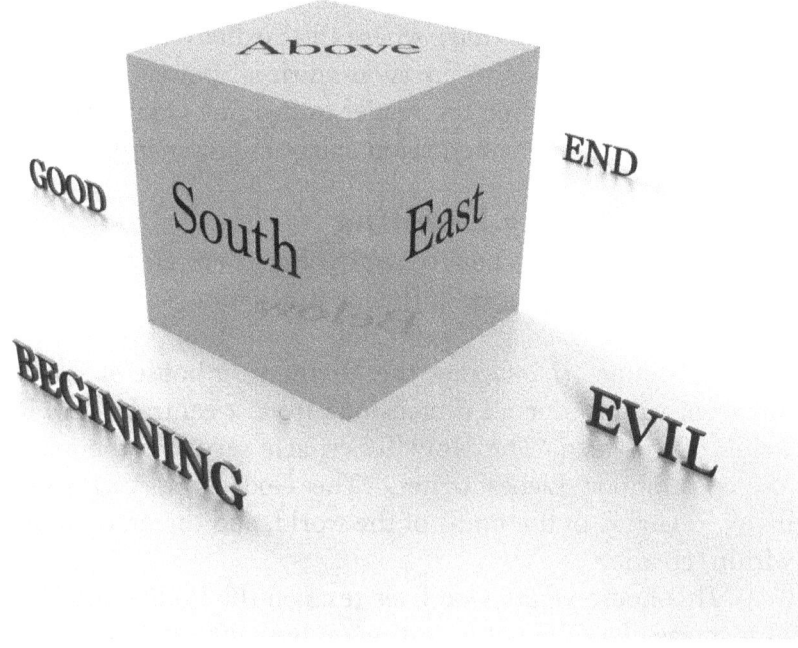

Figure 1. The five cosmic dimensions of the *sefirot*: space (the six directions), time (beginning-end), and body-soul (good-evil).

Practice: The Depths

Close your eyes and breathe out.

You are looking down into a well.
This well contains all space and time
and all beings that have ever been.

Look into the well
and see the past that shaped you.
Look into the well and see the future you are shaping.

Look into the well and see what is above you.
Look into the well and see what is below you.

Look into the well and see the good in your life.
Look into the well and see what is harmful in your life.
Look into the well and see your life as an integrated whole.

Look into the well and see the sacred center.
Look into the well and see yourself at the center.

What do you feel and know
at the center of all things?

Breathe out and open your eyes.

Practice: Until Eternity

Close your eyes and breathe out.

You are in a tunnel.
The tunnel is infinite
and goes on forever in both directions.

Look down the tunnel in one direction.
What do you see or feel?

Now, look down the tunnel in the opposite direction.
What do you see or feel?

Now, bring your attention to the center of the tunnel, the midpoint.
What do you find here
at the center of the tunnel?

Breathe out and open your eyes.

Chapter 1:8 · The Flash of Lightning

עשר ספירות בלימה
צפיתן כמראה הבזק
ותכליתן אין להם קץ
ודברו בהן כרצוא ושוב
ולמאמרו כסופה ירדופו
ולפני כסאו הם משתחוים

Ten inscriptions of the void:
Their appearance has the look of lightning
and their end—they have no end.

God's word in them
is like "running and returning."

They chase after God's utterance like a whirlwind
and bow before God's throne.

This passage seems to be one of the "instructions" that helps us to understand how to contemplate the *sefirot*. As Ronit Meroz notes, this passage suddenly upends what we thought we knew, and suggests a completely new way of looking at the *sefirot*.

In the book of Ezekiel, we hear of the *chayot hakodesh*, the angelic creatures bearing the Divine chariot: *vehachayot ratzo vashov kemareh habazak*—"the creatures were running and returning like the appearance of lightning."[99] *Sefer Yetzirah* borrows this image to describe the *sefirot*. The *sefirot* are not simply stationary features in the architecture of space and time. They are not only the walls of the world. They also move, and God's word moves in them. The *sefirot* channel the oscillation of the Divine word, as it travels from the one to the many and back again.

The Look of Lightning   כמראה הבזק

In the previous passage, we heard that the divine dwelling place is at the center of the *sefirot*, so that the *sefirot* reach out in endless rays from the divine. The hollow *sefirot* and the engraved letters seem meant to conduct divine energy, power, or intention throughout the cosmos. Our current passage tells us that these ten rays are in fact infinite, and that they have the "appearance of lightning." It seems that they are flashes of energy, or that flashes of energy appear in them, moving back and forth. God's word, like lightning, flashes from the sacred center, moves through the depths of the *sefirot* and out into their endless reaches, and returns to the sacred center. *Sefer Yetzirah* calls this movement "running and returning."

The use of lightning to describe the *sefirot* is evocative. Physicist Kared Barad writes: "Lightning is a reaching toward, an arcing dis/juncture, a striking response to charged yearnings."[100] Lightning arises from "electrical potential buildup and flows of charged particles."[101] While the physics of lightning may not have been available to the author(s) of this text, the flash of lightning certainly was. The lightning that moves within the *sefirot* is very much like a flow of charged particles, an electrified reaching toward divine presence.

Ronit Meroz understands this section to be describing the *sefirot* as a group of angels, similar to the "holy beasts" in Ezekiel who bear the divine throne. Meroz argues that beings that can "bow" before God must be "personified" supernatural beings—angels, in the form Jewish tradition usually understands angels, rather than anything "abstract." Meroz writes: "It is the angels who always set out on God's mission, and of whom one may therefore say that 'his word is in them.'" Meroz asserts that the *sefirotic* angels have "humility and reverence" for God—they are entities capable of having a personal attitude toward the Divine.[102]

Yet are the *sefirot* truly personified? God's word in these beings does not "command," but rather "runs and returns"—the *sefirot* are conduits, not servants. Perhaps we might call them angels, but they are also hollow endless entities, and the divine word runs and returns in them like an electric current through a charged wire. They may be conscious, but they hardly seem like Michael or Gabriel. It may be that the *sefirot* bow not (or not only) because they are reverent in a personal way but because they are channels sensitive to the movement of divine creative power. The bowing of the *sefirot* is a theotropism of the whole universe.

The *sefirot* act as a collective—they are a multiplicity with a single purpose. They move together after God's word, and they bow together before God's throne. These multiple forces are channels for one "singular master." Yehuda Liebes indicates that many of the sections of Chapter 1 start with multiplicity and end with oneness, as if to show the reader how all is drawn toward the One.[103]

Running and Returning כרצוא ושוב

When we think of God's word "running and returning," one can almost imagine God's utterances as a tide that moves in and out within the architecture of the *sefirot*. The *sefirot* themselves are not rigid and immobile, but rather are animate, organic receptacles for a fluid divine will. Alive to God's desires, the *sefirot* move to follow God's word.

Sefer Yetzirah is trying to explain how space and time respond to the divine will. The *sefirot* attempt to emulate God's word, yet the perfection of God's intention can never be fully realized. The physical universe, as embodied in the ten *sefirot*, cannot fully manifest divine will but can only "chase after it."

This exactly mirrors God's relationship with the human mind. In 1:5, we were told: "If your heart runs, return to the Place, for the sacred text says 'running and returning.'" God's movement within the world is like the movement of thoughts within the mind: periphery to sacred center, sacred center to periphery. The meditating consciousness chases after God yet bounces back to the periphery of awareness. The movement of the *sefirot* and the movement of the consciousness are one. The distractibility of the mind, and its potential for refocus, echoes the fleeting way God's presence appears in the world.

Yet the process of distancing and returning, which introduces imperfection, also allows for movement. It is the running and returning that fills life with infinite variety and possibility rather than leaving it to stagnate or simply dissolve back into oneness. This movement from oneness to fragmentation and back again is the basis for creativity, both divine and human.

Meroz imagines that this passage expresses the desire of its author "to join the dance of the angels... he seeks the fragile, tempting and fascinating experience of that which is not and which is, the *belimah* on which the world is suspended."[104] The reader, encountering this longing, also longs to run and return between the finite and the infinite, to be a channel for the lightning of God's presence.

Like a Whirlwind   כסופה

The *sefirot* "chase after God's word like a whirlwind (*sufah*)." This image depicts the ferocious oscillation of the *sefirot* and continues to evoke the image of a lightning storm. The *sefirot* do not only move back and forth in a line: they whirl, flash, branch like lightning.

The word *sufah* is a biblical word. Isaiah and Jeremiah both use this word to describe the wheels of the divine chariot.[105] That the text chooses this precise word cannot be an accident. The *sefirot* are the wheels of the divine chariot, moving in response to God's direction. The architecture of the universe is God's ever-moving vehicle. A whirlwind implies a round movement. This contrasts with the "cube" of the *sefirot* and shows us that the universe's dimensions are not stationary and angular but organic and alive.

The term *sufah* is also a play on words. It hints at *sof* (end). The creatures follow God's word as if there is an end to reach, though both the *sefirot* and God are infinite. Thus there is a tension between finite (*sof*) and infinite (*ein sof*). The word *sof* is also a play on *suf*, reed, The *sefirot* are like hollow reeds, channeling God's will and bending in the storm of God's wind.

Practice: The Flash of Lightning

Close your eyes and breathe out.

Lightning flashes before you.
As you observe, the lightning becomes ten creatures:
the *sefirot*.

The lightning creatures
move in a circle.
They bow toward its center.

As the lightning flashes again, it reveals
what is at the center of the circle.

Breathe out and open your eyes.

Practice: A Reed in a Whirlwind

Close your eyes and breathe out.

You are a hollow reed
among other reeds.
A strong wind blows.
You bend in the wind.

Feel the power of the wind
as it moves you
and all the other reeds.

Let yourself surrender
as you bow in the wind.

What do you feel
as you let the wind bend you?

When the wind stops,
return to your place
among the other reeds.

See what the wind has left
in the hollow within you.

Breathe out and open your eyes.

Chapter 1:9 · The First *Sefirah:* Divine Breath

עשר ספירות בלימה
אחת רוח אלוהים חיים
זו היא רוח הקדש

Ten ethereal inscriptions.

One:
Breath of the Living God—
She is the Holy Spirit.

Chapter 1 now embarks on a creation story in which the first four *sefirot* unfold from one another, thus making the world. God becomes the artist (or maybe the lover, depending on how you read the language) of the elements, engraving elemental diversity into the fabric of existence. The breath of the Divine becomes the four winds and the mortal breath of all life. The Divine then shapes wind into water, molds water into fire. God then seals this elegant creation by means of the six final *sefirot*: the six directions.

In 1:7, we were told that the ten *sefirot* are beginning, end, good, evil, north, south, east, west, up, and down. We have called this the dimensional version. In this new rendition, the first four *sefirot* are divine breath, breath/wind, water, fire, north, south, east, west, up, and down. While the dimensional version of the *sefirot* shows us ten coequal *sefirot* in an architectural structure, the elemental version shows us one *sefirah* arising from the next. The first is about structure, the second about process.

One, Breath of the Living God   אחת רוח אלוהים חיים

The first of the *sefirot* is the breath/wind/spirit of God, or *ruach Elohim chayyim*. (*Ruach*, in Hebrew, has all of these meanings, and is translated throughout the book as one of the three, depending on context.) This divine breath is reminiscent of the "wind of God hovering on the face of the water" (*ruach Elohim merachefet al pnei hamayim*) in Genesis 1:2. It also reminds us of the breath that God blows into Adam to bring the first human to life:

> YHWH God formed the earth-being (the *adam*) from the dust of the earth, and blew into his nostrils the breath of life (*nishmat chayyim*), and the earth-being became a living being (*nefesh chayah*).[106]

In a sense, *Sefer Yetzirah* is reinterpreting Genesis. Where Genesis specifies that it is the human that comes to life via God's breath, 1:9 invites us to envision that God's breath breathes the entire cosmos. (The sixteenth century kabbalist Isaac Luria's image of the divine glassblower exhaling a breath to expand glass vessels of creation comes to mind.)[107] This reinterpretation of Genesis widens the intimate relationship between God and humanity to include all creation. All things, says the *Book of Creation*, begin with God's breath.

The transcendent breath that begins the chain of *sefirot* is a reformulation of the idea that God spoke to create the world. Here, God's speech is not just the expression of an abstract intention, but a tangible breath. Notice how here, *Sefer Yetzirah* elides the distinction between creation and the Creator. The breath of the living God is different from God (since it has been "breathed out") but it is also part of God's substance. The first *sefirah* is clearly an intermediate entity, much as Ronit Meroz suggests that Wisdom is an intermediate entity between divine and mortal.[108] It is "holy spirit"—emanated from God and partaking of God's nature.

She Is The Holy Spirit   זו היא רוח הקדש

Kodesh means holiness. *Ruach hakodesh* can therefore mean "holy spirit" as in divine inspiration. The Talmud uses *ruach hakodesh* to describe the way God inspires prophets to speak—and sometimes it uses the term to mean God.[109] Yet the phrase can also mean "holy wind," as in the *ruach Elohim*, the divine wind that hovered on the face of the water in Genesis 1:2, or "holy breath," as in God's breath breathing out creation. The text takes full advantage of the polysemy of this phrase to imply all three.

There is another resonance in the term "holy spirit." According to the Bible and then the Talmud, the holy spirit inspires Betzalel, the builder of the Tabernacle space, with divine knowledge: "Betzalel knew how to combine the letters that created heaven and earth, as it says:

'And he filled him with the spirit of God *(ruach Elohim)*.'"[110] "Holy spirit" is needed for the creation of sacred space—and here, it is used in the creation of the cosmic temple.

The holy spirit, *Ruach haKodesh*, is, grammatically speaking, a She. *Ruach Elohim Hayyim*, breath of the living God, is also a feminine term. This female gendering of divine spirit/breath is consistent with the female gendering of Wisdom and of the element-letters *Aleph, Mem* and *Shin* (i.e., the mothers). The other elements in the chain of creation—air, water, fire—will also turn out to be feminine.

The male God and the female elements form a creative, organic partnership: in fact, given that the "holy spirit" is a term for God and also a female element (divine breath), there is no easy distinction between the male creator and the female elements. It could be said that they are parts of a divine creative system, rather than separate entities. Once again, we have multiplicity and oneness.

The kabbalah will later expand the notion of masculine and feminine aspects of the Divine to include the divine Bridegroom and Bride, Cosmic Father and Cosmic Mother, and a host of other personae. Here in the Book of Creation, the facets of creative power are less personalized. God and the holy wind are not bridegroom and bride, but something wilder and less human.

Hayman notes there are a variety of expanded versions of 1:9, many with more masculine-sounding language. For example, a number of versions add: "His Throne is established of old." Others add: "Blessed and twice blessed is His name."[111] Assuming that the briefest text is the original, perhaps later Jewish copyists or commentators were not so comfortable with the feminine ring of the language and tried to change it by adding more masculine phrases. Yet the image remains: God and the Holy Breath—creator and creatrix.

Practice: Holy Breath

Close your eyes and breathe out.

As you breathe out,
your breath becomes a being.

As you breathe again,
the being becomes clearer in form.
You can fully perceive him/her/them/it.

The being breathes in what you breathe out.
You breathe out what the being breathes in.

Feel the love and trust
that arises between you
as you share one another's breath.

If you wish,
you can ask this being a question
and receive an answer.

Or, you can simply breathe in silence,
feeling the connection between you.

Breathe out and open your eyes.

Practice: Holy Wind

Close your eyes and breathe out.

A wind begins all around you.
It starts as a gentle breeze
and builds to a strong gust.

Let the wind enter your body
and move through you.

Within you
and all around you,
the wind whispers.

Accept what the wind whispers
as a truth,
a gift of the holy wind.

Breathe out and open your eyes.

This practice can be undertaken
outside on a windy day.

Chapter 1:10 · The Second *Sefirah:* Breath

שתיים רוח מרוח
חקק וחצב בה ארבע רוחות השמים

Two:
Breath from Breath.

He engraved and carved within Her
the four winds of heaven.

The second *sefirah* in the elemental version is *ruach meruach*: "breath from breath," "wind from wind" or "spirit from spirit." The divine breath gives rise to (we might even say gives birth to) wind, air, breath, or spirit. As "divine breath" becomes simply "breath," the elements move farther away from their divine source and out into the world. Yet the two words are identical: breath (the divine version) and breath (the worldly version) are both *ruach*. Even in the individuation of breath from the divine breath, the two remain of the same substance.

God then separates the newly created "breath" into the four winds. One (God) becomes two (God and Holy Spirit) becomes four (the four winds). Diversity arises out of oneness. The four winds move out to the four directions, and the world becomes a wider place.

Creation thus far seems almost without container. God's wind gives rise to the world's winds without any solid earth to provide a place to stand. In *Sefer Yetzirah* breath comes first; the world of substance comes later.

Engraved and Carved   חקק וחצב

Just as in our previous passage, the word for wind or breath, *ruach*, is feminine: God carves within "her" the four winds. There is a fecund quality to this "hollowing" that the *ruach* undergoes, as if God is making the wind pregnant with four offspring. The feminizing of the elements yields subtle yet unmistakable erotic imagery: as the chapter unfolds, God "engraves" wind, water, and fire and thus engenders a whole world. The hollow engravings of the Hebrew letters now relates to the hollows in a uterine body. When seeded with the right material, these hollows contain and nurture substance and life.[112]

There are multiple feminine entities present in this passage. The divine breath, the earthly air, and the four winds are all feminine, and their successive generational expansions—as if they are mother, daughter, granddaughters—show how the Artist gives rise to ever-multiplying creations. The feminine forces of breath, though they have an element of passivity in that the god-artist "carves" them, are active partners in that they make possible the drawing out of one entity from the next. Without breath there are no words and no letters, and without the letters, the Creator cannot create.

Sefer Yetzirah, in showing us this image, says something profound: Eros does not only apply to romance, but also to the creative process. *Sefer Yetzirah* here intimates that God's creation is not devoid of emotion or desire: it is an intimate act of love and pleasure. So too, the human who creates may find delight and yearning.

The Four Winds of Heaven   ארבע רוחות השמים

Peoples around the world, from the Lakota to the Mongols, invoke the four directions as a structure of creation, a way of including all places in a unity. The "four winds of heaven" or "the four winds of the sky" also appear in the Bible, in the book of Zechariah.[113] In Zechariah, the winds present themselves before the divine throne, embodied in four chariots. They are God's messengers to the far reaches of the world. The four winds are also reminiscent of the four rivers that flow out of Eden to water the regions of the world.[114] Later, the Babylonian Talmud speaks of God being crowned[115] "above and below and in the four winds of heaven"—in other words, everywhere.

The four winds are a language for the sum total of the diversity of creation. The breath that is One divides into the breath of Many. It is this flow from One to Many and back again that 1:10 is training us to observe, when it invites us to follow in our mind's eye the journey from divine breath to the four winds.[116]

Practice: Breath from Breath

Close your eyes and breathe out.

See, hear, and feel before you
the *ruach hakodesh*,
the divine wind, the holy breath.

This divine wind
divides
and becomes four winds.

Each of the four winds
has a face.
Let each face
greet you
and make itself known to you.
What do you meet
in the faces of the four winds?

Now, the four winds
become one divine wind again.

The divine wind now also has a face.
Encounter this face
that unifies the four winds.
The face breathes into yours,
filling you with its unity.

Feel what happens
as you breathe the divine breath
that holds the four winds of the world.

Breathe out and open your eyes.

Practice: The Four Winds

Close your eyes and breathe out.

See that the four winds
carry your breath
to all living beings on earth.

Mammals, insects, birds, fish, trees
all breathe your breath.
The four winds bring their breath back to you.

You are breathing the breath
of all life on earth.
When they breathe out,
you breathe in.
When you breathe out,
they breathe in.

Breathe out.
Breathe in.
Feel how the four winds join you
to all living things.

Breathe out and open your eyes.

Chapter 1:11 · The Third *Sefirah*: Water

שלש מים מרוח
חקק וחצב בהם תוהו ובוהו
רפש וטיט
חקקן כמין ערוגה
הציבן כמין חומה
סיככן כמין מעזיבה

Three:
Water from Wind.

He engraved and carved in Them
chaos and void,
mud and clay—

engraved Them like a kind of garden,
carved Them like a kind of wall,
wove Them like a kind of ceiling.

In the third stage of creation, *ruach* (here translated wind) gives birth to Water. Water is the third of the *sefirot*.[117] Out of water, God forms earth. Out of earth, God carves and weaves a world that will hold all life. This house-like or basket-like earth-structure is enclosed, with walls and a ceiling. This womb-like container God creates is "like a kind of garden"—ready for life to enter it.

Water from Wind   מים מרוח

The wind, or the breath, now produces another elemental generation: the water. There is some question as to whether the "wind/breath" (*ruach*) that creates the water is divine wind/breath (that is, the first *sefirah*), or earthly wind/breath (that is, the second *sefirah*). If the *sefirot* derive from one another in a chain, one to the next, then it must be the earthly wind from which water derives.

In Them   בהם

The waters are the first of the elements to be plural rather than singular. However, they are not plural in every manuscript.

Hayman notes a variety of manuscripts that read "God engraved and carved *in her*" (*bah*). In other words, water, like breath/wind, is yet another feminine element. In the manuscripts where water is plural, sometimes "God engraved and carved *in them*" is feminine plural (*bahen*) and sometimes is masculine plural (*bahem*).

Hayman suggests that "in them" (masculine plural) is the earliest recoverable text—and in fact it is also the grammatically correct construction for water (*mayim*) which in Hebrew is masculine plural. That makes it even more fascinating that many texts use a feminine singular or feminine plural for water (*bah* or *bahen*), despite this not being grammatically correct. Those who copied or edited the manuscript could sense the intention of the text to describe the elements as female. In fact, the later verbs that have water as their object (*asa'an*/He made Them, etc.,) also to refer to water.

The plurality of water in many versions of the text emphasizes that God pairs with multiple elemental partners to create the world. God is an artist with many media. Or, God is a lover with many beloveds. The impression we receive is not of a deity with a single divine or mortal consort, but a succession of relationships built with many substances. God's eros with the world (which itself is a divine entity) multiplies exponentially as the creative process unfolds.

This creation story offers the human creator a model for erotic relationship with the world. We are not to cling to one form of creation, one vessel for deity. Rather, we are to find new potential in each encounter with the world. Annie Dillard writes of this erotic relationship with the present moment, saying: "Every day is a god, each day is a god, and holiness holds forth in time... I wake in a god. Someone is kissing me—already. I wake, I cry, 'Oh.' I rise from the pillow.... Today's god rises, his long legs flecked in clouds."[118]

Chaos and Void, Mud and Clay   תוהו ובוהו רפש וטיט

Tohu vavohu or chaos and void are the Hebrew words used to describe the formless state of creation in Genesis 1, before the Divine began to create the world: "The earth was without form and void, and wind of God hovered over the waters." *Sefer Yetzirah* offers a midrash or interpretation of this text: when Genesis says: "a wind of God was hovering on the face of the waters,"[119] it means that "wind" gave rise to "water" and carved into that water the primordial earth. In Isaiah 57:20, the sea precipitates "*refesh vetit*," mud and clay—a similar case of earth arising out of water. The mud and clay suggest a fluid earth that God can shape at will.

Itamar Gruenwald, a translator of the *Sefer Yetzirah*, believes that the words "chaos and void, mud and clay" and the phrases that follow, are a later addition to *Sefer Yetzirah*—he argues that these phrases are more elaborate and stilted than the usual language of *Sefer Yetzirah*.[120] The phrase *kemin* ("a kind of") has a rabbinic ring to it, as when a rabbinic text suggests that it is "as if" (*ke'ilu*) God has hands. This possibly added language is perhaps meant to include the element of earth within the element of water, to harmonize *Sefer Yetzirah*'s elemental system with a four-element system that includes earth.

Yet water is associated with earth elsewhere in the *Sefer Yetzirah*—notably in chapter three, where fire forms heaven and water forms earth. So it is perhaps not accurate to say that water was not originally associated with earth in the earliest sources or versions of *Sefer Yetzirah*. The association between water and earth seems to be an intrinsic quality of the book as it has been composed. Earth is not dust, but mud.

This implies that the earth is not as solid as it looks. The solidity of the world, we soon learn, comes from the seals God has set in place around it. Were it not for these seals, the world would perhaps leak away into the void. For *Sefer Yetzirah*, the elements are always in motion.

This image holds meditative insight. If the elements are always in motion, then the contemplative must always be ready to shift perspective. Just as the *sefirot* are running and returning, flashing like lightning, the one who meditates must be prepared for radical shifts in what he or she experiences.

Engraved Them Like a Kind of Garden   חקקן כמין ערוגה
Carved Them Like a Kind of Wall   הציבן כמין חומה
Wove Them Like a Kind of Ceiling   סיככן כמין מעזיבה

Out of the watery mud, God now engraves[121] a world—a "garden," as in the garden of Eden. As in many other passages of *Sefer Yetzirah*, the world is not an open space but a house-like space that God encloses. Water is the floor, walls and ceiling for the cosmos.[122] It is as if a terrarium has been placed inside a giant muddy raindrop.

The verbs here that describe the making of these watery borders are "made them" (*asa'an*), "carved them" (*chatzivan* or *chatzavan*, depending on the manuscript), and "wove them" (*sikhekhan*). The final verb means to interlace or entangle, and is related to the word *schach*, the entangled branches placed on top of the harvest booth at the festival of Sukkot.[123] In other words, God is basket-weaving: creating interlaced walls that will hold the newly made world. "Carving" and "making" are already words we expect in *Sefer Yetzirah*, but "weaving" is new.

The image of God basket-weaving is surprising: it evokes weaving a wicker basket. We could even compare this image to Moses' mother Yocheved weaving a basket so her infant can float on the Nile in Exodus 2. God floats the human world on a great flood of waters just as Yocheved floats her baby on the vast river. The language of "engraved" is softened and complicated by the inclusion of "wove." "Wove" suggests interlacing, overlapping, entanglement.

There is something relevant and contemporary about the notion of "entanglement" as a mode of creation. John Preskill, a theoretical physicist, writes: "Everything points... to space being emergent from deep underlying physics that has to do with entanglement."[124] Entanglement, in physics terms, means that particles are found to have correlated attributes such that they act not as individual particles but as an inseparable whole. *Sefer Yetzirah* provides us with a spiritual language to talk about the entanglement of entities and relations that is inherent to our world.

The word *maazivah*, translated here as ceiling, means a concrete pavement that serves as a ceiling and also may serve as a floor for the story above.[125] This word feels very specific. The ceiling of the created world has another story above it, and below it as well. The world humans live in is only one layer of the house. Outside the walls God has made, a larger, chaotic, cosmos looms. This is why God must seal the newly made world within its woven borders.

Practice: Like a Kind of Garden

Close your eyes and breathe out.

Before you, a drop of water
condenses and hangs in the air.
The inside
of this drop of water
is visible to you
in all of its minute detail.

Inside the drop of water,
a world appears.
Earth spreads out. Plants grow.
Creatures emerge.
All forms of life appear.

Each time you breathe on the drop,
the image clarifies.
The world is contained
within this drop of water.

Reach out and take this drop,
this infinite blessing,
in your hand.

What do you feel and understand
as you hold this garden of life
in your hand?

Breathe out and open your eyes.

Practice: Water from Breath

Close your eyes and breathe out.

Your breath becomes a mist.
The mist surrounds you.

The mist becomes a stream of water.
The stream flows around you,
cleansing and renewing,
washing away any detritus
or impediment that clings to you.

When all has been cleansed,
the stream becomes a mist again.
The mist dissolves.

You feel clear and new
after your immersion in these waters.

Breathe out and open your eyes.

Chapter 1:12 · The Fourth *Sefirah:* Fire

ארבע אש ממים
חקק וחצב בה כסא הכבוד
וכל צבא מרום
שכך כתוב
עשה מלכיו רוחות
משרתיו אש לוהט

Four:
Fire from Water.

He engraved and carved in Her
the Throne of Glory
and all the heavenly hosts,

for so it is written:
He makes the winds His messengers,
flaming fire His ministers.

Having shaped the earth via water, the Creator now draws forth fire from water, in order to shape the heavens: the divine throne and all the angels. The passage quotes Psalms 104:4—"He makes the winds His messengers, flaming fire His ministers"—as a proof of its claim. Presumably *Sefer Yetzirah* understands the prooftext to affirm the elemental chain of being from wind to fire, as well as the idea that angels are made of flame.

We should note two things: first, the heavens are part of the creation story—they are not treated as some other world but as part of this one. Second, in *Sefer Yetzirah*, creation moves from earth to heaven and not vice versa. Here and in Chapter 3, the element of earth (water) is mentioned before the element of heaven (fire). For *Sefer Yetzirah*, the earth comes first. God's primary place as creator is not in the heavens; God only takes a seat there late in the process. The Creator is most deeply invested, not in heavenly realms, but in the physical universe.

Engraved and Carved in Her All the Heavenly Hosts חקק וחצב בה וכל צבא מרום

Like the divine spirit and the wind, the fire is feminine, and God engraves "in her" the attributes of the celestial realm. The carving and engraving of the fire gives us a view of God as a blacksmith as well as a lover. We could see the fire as a forge where God shapes the heavenly throne. Or, we could imagine that fire conceives from the Creator and gives birth to the stars and all the heavenly hosts.

The water gives birth to the fire that is its opposite. The sky's light: sun, moon, stars, angelic hosts—contrasts with the earth's darkness: water, soil. The tension of opposing elements, as well as their partnership, exists from the world's beginning,[126] yet the tension is defused in favor of a dynamic cooperation. With the Creator's help, great-grandmother (divine breath), grandmother (air), mother (water), and daughter (fire) go on proliferating from one another. The first four *sefirot* provide a dance floor for the many creations yet to come.

Winds His Messengers מלכיו רוחות

It is no accident that *Sefer Yetzirah* quotes a biblical text in which the elements seem alive. We might say that "He makes the winds His messengers, flaming fire His ministers" is a poetic phrase and does not literally mean that the wind is a conscious worker on behalf of the Divine—but we might also say that the biblical text suggests a universe in which all things are animate and in service to holiness, even the wind.

Sefer Yetzirah, in quoting this text in reference to angels, is suggesting that the elements themselves are angelic—that wind and fire are messengers of divine creativity. This is entirely consistent with the book's depiction in 1:8 of the *sefirot* as "chasing after God's utterance." In its description of the creation of fire, the passage asserts that the elements that we experience all around us are God's messengers to us. The world is animate and charged with purpose.

Fire from Water אש ממים

If we consider the book's genre as ritual rather than narrative, we may come to imagine that the progression of the four elements, as it is written down in these passages, is meant to be enacted rather than merely read. That is, a practitioner could re-enact the creation of the world by invoking the four elements of divine breath, wind, water, and fire. The beginning of the ritual would in some way evoke God's holy spirit, and then human breath and/or the four winds, water (perhaps with earth added), and fire would be progressively introduced (either via pronouncing their names or by encountering the actual substances). The text of these four sections could be used as a liturgy for this ritual.

If we read the progression of the elements as a liturgy, it is significant that we end up with the divine throne. This could be a reason why fire is last rather than first. The unfolding of creation brings us face to face with the divine presence on the throne and with the elements that are God's angels. That encounter leads us directly to the next passage of the book and the next part of the ritual, in which God will stand at the center of the universe to seal the world and protect it.

Practice: Divine Throne

Close your eyes and breathe out.

Before you is a fire.
Out of the fire
a throne arises.
Heavenly hosts surround it.

The Creator arrives to sit upon the throne.
The Creator invites you
to sit on the heavenly throne.
What do you see from this vantage point?
What do you learn
from the perspective of the divine throne?

Step down off the throne.
Breathe out and open your eyes.

Practice: Firelight

Close your eyes and breathe out.

Find in your body
a place where your life-force is strong.

See and feel within this place
a bright and powerful flame.
Feel the warmth of this flame
as it spreads through your body.

What feeling arises
as you sense the flame within?
What action or intention
does the flame invite in you?

Breathe out and open your eyes.

Practice: Fire from Water

Close your eyes and breathe out.

You are plunging your hands into a pool.
From the pool, you draw out a handful of water.
In your cupped hands, the water becomes a jewel.
The jewel bursts into flame.

The flame does not burn you.

You hold it up
and it lights up everything around you.

This flame reignites
all the light in the world
that has gone out.

See and feel the hope
that has been reignited
by this fire drawn from water.

Breathe out and open your eyes.

Chapter 1:13 · The Fifth through Tenth *Sefirot*: The Six Directions

Five: God sealed Above
and faced upward
and sealed it with *Yud Heh Vav*.

חמש חתם רום
פנה למעלה
וחתמו ביהו

Six: God sealed Below
and faced downward
and sealed it with *Yud Vav Heh*.

שש חתם תחת
פנה למטה
וחתמו ביוה

Seven: God sealed East
and faced front
and sealed it with *Heh Vav Yud*.

שבע חתם מזרח
פנה לפניו
וחתמו בהוי

Eight: God sealed West
and faced behind
and sealed it with *Heh Yud Vav*.

שמנה חתם מערב
פנה לאחריו
וחתמו בהיו

Nine: God sealed South
And faced to the right
and sealed it with *Vav Yud Heh*.

תשע חתם דרום
פנה לימינו
וחתמו בויה

Ten: God sealed North
and faced to the left
and sealed it with *Vav Heh Yud*.

עשר חתם צפון
פנה לשמאלו
וחתמו בוהי

Chapter 1:13 · The Fifth through Tenth Sefirot: The Six Directions

Having created and ordered the elements into a world, the Creator now stands at the center of the universe and performs a sealing ritual to make the world a safe place for life. "Sealing" is a magical practice of firming up a created reality or rendering a space free from negative influence. Both may be occurring here. The Creator moves around the cosmic stage, using six combinations of the letters of the divine name to seal the six directions. These six directions are the final six *sefirot*—the final elements in the frame of the cosmos.

Peter Hayman writes: "There are two principal images of God in *Sefer Yetzirah*: the Great Artist and the Great Magician... We have God standing in the middle of what was to become the universe and sealing its boundaries with the six possible combinations of the three constituent letters of the Divine name YHWH."[127] This sealing approximates the work of a magician or sorceress conducting a spell. Yehuda Liebes concurs: "God appears like a magician who confines the *sefirot* [to their assigned boundaries] with the help of a seal composed of holy names."[128]

The space sealed by the six directions is not called a temple, yet one cannot help feeling that it corresponds to the "holy dwelling place" at the center of the created world in Chapter 1:5, and to the "holy Temple set in the center" that will be described in Chapter 4:4. Hayman refers to this cosmic temple-space as God's "power-house,"[129] and expresses that this "cosmic Temple" image appears in Philo and Josephus. Rabbinic texts allude to this concept in their image of the *beit hamikdash shel maalah* or the heavenly Temple. Since God seals from the center, God is within this cosmic temple along with all creation.

In a variety of sources, the directions play a significant role in both earthly and cosmic Temples. I Chronicles describes the keepers of the four gates of the Temple: "The gatekeepers were on the four sides: east, west, north, south."[130] Hayman notes that the Temple Scroll found at Qumran depicts a Temple with four inner gates—north, south, east, and west—and twelve outer gates (similar to the twelve diagonal boundaries mentioned in *Sefer Yetzirah* 5:2). The Book of Enoch describes the heavenly temple as having the "twelve openings of the four heavenly directions." Josephus describes the Temple as having four directional gates: north, south, east, and west.[131]

There is a rabbinic parallel with God's sealing ritual in 1:13:

> How did the Holy One of Blessing create the world? Rabbi Chanina said: The Eternal took two balls, one of fire and one of water, and worked them into each other, and from these the world was created. Rabbi Chanina said: Four balls, for the four corners of the universe. Rabbi Hama said: "Six, for the four corners and one for above and one for below.... Stretch out your hand to east, west, north, and south. Even so was the work of creation before the Holy One."[132]

In this fifth-century Midrash, God creates the world by mingling the substance of fire and water, or mingling the substance of the four directions, or mingling the substance of the six directions. The similarity between the elemental and directional image evoked by the Midrash and our *Sefer Yetzirah* passage is notable. If a fifth to seventh century date is correct, the two are roughly contemporaneous, which suggests that the view of God as a magician who created using the elements and directions was more widespread than just one text or community.

What lies outside the sealed boundaries of the elemental/directional cube? The text carefully does not say. Yet we have been told in 1:11 that *tohu vavohu*, formlessness and void, arise out of the water along with the earth. It may be that this primordial void is what God places outside of the sealed cube. Liebes specifies: "The intention of the sealing of the directions is not to separate between the world and God, but to defend the created world... from the formlessness which is not divinity but chaos and primordial void."[133] Biblical scholar Jon Levenson writes "The confinement of chaos rather than its elimination is the essence of creation, and the survival of ordered reality hangs only upon God's vigilance in ensuring that those cosmic dikes do not fail."[134]

We know that in the first, dimensional set of *sefirot*, the depths of time and space go on forever. It appears that, in setting limits for each of the six directions, God makes a distinction between the entire cosmos and the habitable, ordered part of it. Just as an ancient Babylonian Jewish sorceress would seal a house from demonic powers, God is designating and protecting a particular "house," the house that holds all human life, via this sealing ritual. "What people do to protect their homes from evil forces, God must have done to protect his universe from the threat of chaos."¹³⁵ In fact, one incantation bowl seals angels into the four corners of a house—a similar procedure to sealing the six directions.¹³⁶

We perhaps now see why the dimensional version of the *sefirot* in 1:7, and the elemental version in 1:9-12, agree that the final six *sefirot* are the six directions. Those six directions are essential to shaping a cosmos people can live in. Taken together, the six directions indicate the whole world—just as the letters, taken together, indicate a whole cosmos.

If the text is a ritual, this stage of the ritual calls us to stand in the center of a sacred circle and seal the six directions. In doing so, we not only protect our own space but strengthen the cosmic Temple. As readers gifted with the secret of God's protective spell, we help hold the shape of the universe.

The One, here, also refers to God's holding of the unity of the universe in contrast to its multiplicity, embodied in the six directions. Through the act of sealing, the One and the many interface. The One writes the name of oneness on the walls that represent multiplicity: a powerful embodiment of the inextricable threads of unity and diversity.

Sealed   חתם

We can understand the practice of sealing of the universe better when we compare it to the Jewish Mesopotamian practice of making incantation bowls to seal a home (a practice contemporaneous with the writing of *Sefer Yetzirah*).¹³⁷ The bowls, written in Aramaic or Syriac, were often buried at the corners of houses, and were meant to seal the house and send demons back to the netherworld. The bowls received their power via the inscription of powerful words: another similarity to *Sefer Yetzirah*. The makers of the bowls included women as well as men, and some have speculated they were mostly women.¹³⁸

The bowl inscriptions use the language of sealing demons out of the home. For example:

> Sealed and countersealed are the house, dwelling, possessions, sons, daughters, cattle, and soul of Ahai son of Ispandarmid and Ispandarmid daughter of Qiomta his wife, and all the members of their household. They are sealed and countersealed from a demon, from a persecutor, from a male and female idol, from a Lilith... and from anything evil.
>
> They are sealed and countersealed by the name Yah YHWH Tzevaot. Amen amen selah, haleluyah haleluyah.[139]

The incantation on the bowl is meant to protect the house itself and everyone in it. Similarly, God's inscribed incantation is meant to protect the created world and everything in it. The divine name mentioned, YHWH Tzevaot, is one of the divine names invoked at the beginning of *Sefer Yetzirah*.

The language of sealing is ubiquitous. A bowl from the collection of the British Museum, reads: "Written, bound, and sealed, and doubly sealed be the house and threshold of Aban Gusnas son of Anosafrit from evil spirits and from evil sorceries and from all hateful magic practices..."[140] Another reads: "Sealed and countersealed and fortified are Ahat, the daughter of Imma... and Shilta the daughter of Immi—they and their houses and their children and their property are sealed with the seal-ring of El Shaddai, blessed be He."[141] One bowl invokes "the seal of the Holy God"[142] and another "the seal of YHWH of Hosts."[143] Incantation bowls are unusual in Jewish literature in their frequent invocation of sealing: Scholar Erica Hunter notes that "amulets [of other kinds] rarely invoke the sealing motif."[144]

An incantation bowl meant to expel demons has particular relevance to our text:

> They are bound and sealed, bound by the bond of heaven and sealed by the seal of earth (*isirin b'isra d'shemaya vechatimin bechatma d'ara*), bound by the seven bonds that are not loosened and sealed by the seven seals that are not broken... sealed by their foundations (*oosheyhon*), by the great seal (*chatma raba*) that is not loosened.[145]

The "bond of heaven and seal of earth" is an image parallel to 1:13's image of God sealing heaven and earth. There is reference to a "great seal" which may be the divine name, the seal upon the entire world. Yet another bowl mentions: "the great seal by which are sealed heaven and earth"[146] and another asserts: "I am binding you with the bond with which heaven and earth have been bound."[147] These phrases all allude to a divine seal of creation: the exact image being offered by our text.

Some Mesopotamian incantation bowls also mention the directions. For example, Hunter notes a bowl that protects from "sorceries of the west and east, sorceries of the north and south," while Moriggi describes a bowl that reads "north wind and west wind, south wind and east."[148]

However, there is a major distinction between the incantation bowls and the text of *Sefer Yetzirah*: incantation bowls always mention the demonic explicitly, and *Sefer Yetzirah* never does. The effect of this is that what lies outside the boundaries is mysterious, while what lies inside is strongly in focus. The book's passages focus not on what is being kept out, but the order and beauty of what is being held in.

For the contemporary practitioner, the idea of "sealing" lends itself to an individual practice of consciously making a bounded space—in other words, engaging in ritual or meditation that gives us rest, safety, and structure. Using a "sealing" practice, we can summon a space around ourselves within which we find serenity.

The Divine Sealed Below   חתם תחת

Sealing the direction of "below" is particularly important. In searching for rabbinic parallels to the "sealing" narrative, Hayman and others quote the Talmud story in which King David, while laying the foundations of the Temple, finds the primordial deep rising toward him:

> When David dug the drainpipes [in the foundation of the Temple], the depths rose and sought to inundate the world. David said: Is there anyone who knows whether it is permitted to write the Divine name on a pottery shard, so that we may throw it into the depths and they will subside?... He wrote the name on a pottery shard and cast it into the depths, and the waters in the depths subsided...[149]

Apparently, the Divine has sealed the world, and kept the primordial waters out, by imbedding a shard with the Divine name beneath the spot that will one day be the Temple. While David is digging the Temple's foundations, he dislodges this primordial seal and thus frees the waters. (In other versions of the legend, it is the foundation stone, the *even hashetiyah*, navel of the world, that holds back the deep and that David dislodges.)[150] David acts to replace the divine name that stops up the deep, and the waters recede. Note the use of a pottery shard: similar to the ceramic incantation bowls.

Earlier in Tractate Sukkah, we hear a related legend:

> The drainage pipes [built under the Temple altar] were created during the first six days of creation... They are hollow and descend to the primordial depths (*tehom*). They are the handiwork of the Holy One of Blessing. It was taught in the school of Rabbi Ishmael: Don't read *bereisheit* (in the beginning) but rather *bara sheit* (God created the drainage pipes).[151]

Here, God, not David, is the digger of the pits under the Temple. In both of these legends, the word for drainage pipes is *shittim* which means "foundations." God digs the world's foundations beneath the Temple, and they go down to the primordial deep. The text goes out of its way to point out that the pipes are hollow—very much like the engraved hollow channels of the letters, or the "depths" of the *sefirot*. The *otiot yesod* or

Figure 2. The six combinations of the letters of God's name that God uses to seal the six directions of the world.

letter-foundations, which are engraved and hollow, should remind us of the hollow foundation of the Temple.

The sealing of the *shittim* and the sealing of the six directions have a similar function: to keep out the primordial depths. The philosopher Paul Tillich calls these depths: "the form-destroying eruption of the creative abyss of things."[152] The primordial waters in the David legend and the unnamed depths outside the six walls created by God's name both have these qualities: they are "form-destroying" and thus must be kept out of God's world of forms, and yet they are also "the creative abyss of things"—it is out of these depths that God carves and defines all of reality.

With *Yud Heh Vav* ביהו

Scholar Tzahi Weiss notes that *Sefer Yetzirah* affirms all twenty-two letters of the Hebrew *aleph-bet* as the primary powers of creation.[153] Weiss believes this twenty-two-letter philosophy, though Jewish, arises from a Syriac Christian milieu in which twenty-two letters were the basis for divine creation.[154] The emphasis on the three mothers (the beginning, middle, and end of the *aleph-bet*) seems to be in sync with this twenty-two letter philosophy.

Weiss notes a separate philosophy, espoused by many rabbinic midrashim, in which the letters of the divine name (*Yud*, *Heh*, and *Vav*) are the powers that make creation. This passage, by using combinations of the letters of the divine name as cosmic seals, seems to support that philosophy. In fact, many, though not all, manuscripts of *Sefer Yetzirah* contain the below paragraph at the beginning of our section. In this paragraph, the text explains that the letters *Yud*, *Heh*, and *Vav* were chosen "from among the simple letters" to be fixed in God's name (i.e., in the name YHWH) and to seal the six directions.

> The Divine chose three letters
> from among the simple letters,
> in the secret of the three mothers
> Aleph Mem and Shin
> and fixed them in God's Great Name
> and sealed with them the six directions.

Weiss believes that this added passage was edited into *Sefer Yetzirah* early in its development to harmonize the twenty-two-letter philosophy with the letters-of-the-divine-name philosophy.[155] This addition claims that Yud, Heh, and Vav though they are the letters of the Name, are not a separate class of letters but rather from the category of "simple letters" (*peshutot*). Their specialness lies in that they are chosen "in the secret of the three mothers." In other words, it is the *Aleph, Mem,* and *Shin* (the three mother letters) that are special, and the letters of the divine name are echoes of them. Elsewhere in the book, these three simple letters are called fathers, and are said to derive from the mothers. The passage seems to intend that when we see the divine name YHWH in a prayer or sacred text, we should understand that the mothers (*Aleph, Mem, Shin*) are the secret behind the divine name.

In the sealing spell, the three letters *Yud Heh Vav* are recombined to form six different three-letter combinations, and each combination is assigned to a direction. *Sefer Yetzirah* does not explain why certain combinations of the letters of the divine name are assigned to particular directions, and in fact the different manuscripts have different combinations assigned to each direction—except that a number of texts do report the first combination as YHV.[156] (The list in this translation is from a Baghdad manuscript of 1262.[157]) It might be that *Sefer Yetzirah* doesn't intend for us to ascribe meaning to the particular combinations of the letters: it is the fact of combining the letters that matters.

The passage also doesn't explain how God or the reader is to speak each of the combinations. Tzahi Weiss suggests that, unlike certain Greek traditions, which understand the vowels as especially holy and elevated, *Sefer Yetzirah* diminishes the importance of vowels, and doesn't even mention them.[158] (The letters of God's name may represent vowels, as Scholem and Weiss both point out, but that still doesn't tell us how to pronounce them.)[159]

It might be that the intention was for a student to learn of the mysteries of the book with a teacher in order to learn how the six combinations of the letters of the divine name are to be spoken. If this is so, then the book is meant to be studied with a teacher who leads the student through the text as a ritual. It is not to be accessible to anyone who happens to pick it up. A random reader might understand the concepts, but would not know how to conduct the ritual.

It is also possible that the book is being quite plain here, and that the letters are not to be pronounced at all but rather to be written. In that case, one would not need vowels, and the three-letter combinations would be written as shapes on the "walls" of the cosmos—or of the mind.

Yet the primary force of the book is that the letters *Yud*, *Heh*, and *Vav* are not the only powerful letters. *Sefer Yetzirah* claims in Chapter 2:5 that "all that is created and all that is spoken comes from a single Name"—and the twenty-two letters are a name for God. *Sefer Yetzirah* does not reject the idea of the power of God's name, but claims that in reality, all of speech is the divine name. And if all of speech is the divine name, then to speak the holy language is to stand in the presence of God.

Practice: Sealing the Directions

Before you engage this meditation, you will need to learn the six combinations of letters for the six directions in 1:13 or, alternatively, decide on a single letter or symbol you will use to seal each of the directions.

Close your eyes and breathe out.

There is a cube around you.
It may be visible or invisible.
It has walls, a ceiling, and a floor.
Reach out to the walls, ceiling, and floor of the cube.
What do they look and/or feel like?

A writing implement appears in your hand.
Reach up to the ceiling.
Feel the vastness of what is above.
Inscribe the seal of the Above.

Reach down to the floor.
Feel the depths of what is below.
Inscribe the seal for the Below.

Reach ahead of you to the eastern wall.
Feel the brightness of the east.
Inscribe the seal for the East.

Reach behind you to the western wall.
Feel the glow of the west.
Inscribe the seal for the West.

Reach left to the northern wall.
Feel the power of the north.
Inscribe the seal for the North.

Reach right to the southern wall.
Feel the power of the south.
Inscribe the seal for the South.

Return to the center.
Look around at the cube.
Look down at yourself.

What is different?
How have the walls, floor, and ceiling of the cube changed?
How have you changed?

Breathe out and open your eyes.

Practice: God Sealed Above, God Sealed Below

Close your eyes and breathe out.

You are a channel
between heaven and earth.

If you reach upward,
you touch the Above
and feel its vibration.

If you reach downward
you touch the Below
and feel its vibration.

Let the two vibrations
mingle inside you
and become one.

What happens within
as the two vibrations merge?

What happens in the world around you
as the two vibrations merge?

Breathe out and open your eyes.

Chapter 1:14 · Completing the Ritual of the Ten *Sefirot*

אלו עשר ספירות בלימה
רוח אלהים חיים
ורוח מים אש
מעלה מטה
מזרח מערב
צפון ודרום

These are the ten
inscriptions in the void:
breath of the living God
wind, water, fire,
above and below,
east, west,
north and south.

Our first chapter ends with a kind of benediction: a recapitulation of the four elements of divine breath, wind, water, and fire, and the six directions. These elements and directions form a closing poem: a spell, an architecture, a coalescing of being out of the void. The substance of the Divine, breathed out into the created world, has now congealed as the elements and directions.

The concluding section is not merely a recounting, it is a summoning of a cosmic network of paths of wisdom. It is a kind of alternate ten commandments: an elemental ten commandments, a ten commandments that is a diversity of being. Having named and invoked these ten entities, we have now formed a ritual space for the twenty-two letters to work their magic. The twenty-two letters that fill the space formed by the *sefirot* will be the focus of Chapter 2.

Wind, Water, Fire   ורוח מים אש

We are once again, as if in hindsight, standing beside the Creator as the Creator reaches out to the directions and to water, fire, and air. The reader—the adept who learns this creative magic—repeats these ten inscriptions and learns to invoke their power. Hearing the elements named, we can easily imagine a Temple being summoned out of the void.

The temple of divine elements is a vast and majestic edifice, a cosmic temple, far beyond the power and understanding of mortals, yet *Sefer Yetzirah* makes the bold offer that we can stand at its center and name it for what it is.

Practice: Temple of Elements

Close your eyes and breathe out.

See that you are surrounded by four walls:
one of wind, one of water,
one of fire, and one of holy divine breath.

Turn to each wall.
See that inscribed on each wall
is an image, word, or phrase:
a message for you.

Receive the messages that the elements offer.

Now, inspired by these messages,
call wind, water, and holy breath
to fill the space within the walls.
Wind, water, breath and fire
meet one another
and begin to create.

What do the elements create
as they join with one another?
Observe how this creation
enriches you and the world.

Breathe out and open your eyes.

Chapter 2:1 · The Twenty-Two Letters

עשרים ושתיים אותיות יסוד
שלשׁ אמות
שבע כפולות
ושתים עשרה פשוטות

Twenty-two foundation-letters:
three mothers,
seven doubles,
and twelve simples.

As Chapter 1 ended by naming the ten *sefirot*, Chapter 2 begins by naming the twenty-two Hebrew letters.[1] The opening passage divides the twenty-two into three categories of letters: mother letters (*imot*), double letters (*kefulot*), and simple letters (*peshutot*). Just as the *sefirot* are multiple yet join together to form a frame for God's world, the letters are multiple yet join to form the diversity within that world. All of these multiple entities lead back to the One.

This chapter will not explicate the categories but rather will introduce a spiritual practice: that of combining, or exchanging, letters. This practice has power because the letters constitute the substance of the cosmos, and also because the twenty-two letters together constitute God's name. A Syriac Christian text, "The Cause of The Foundation of the Schools," asserts that God teaches humans the twenty-two letters, "arranged with the great name of the construction of the firmament" in order that they may understand the power of the Creator.[2] God thus "handed over to [humans] the visible creation, that like letters they might write them in their continuous variation..."[3] Weiss concludes from this and similar texts that *Sefer Yetzirah*, though it privileges Hebrew rather than Syriac, is communicating a similar tradition: the twenty-two letters comprise the divine Name. The *aleph-bet* is the Name that gives a person access to the mysteries of creation.

Twenty-Two Foundation-Letters עשרים ושתיים אותיות יסוד

As we enter a new chapter, we begin with a new tagline: *esrim veshtayim otiyot yesod*, or "twenty-two foundation-letters."[4] (Remember that a "tagline" is a phrase that begins each passage of a chapter, to indicate which chapter one is reading.) There is a variant of the new tagline: *esrim veshtayim otiyot*—"twenty-two letters." One of these two lines will appear at the beginning of each section of Chapter 2 (with the exception of 2:5).

The phrase *otiyot yesod* (foundation letters) is somewhat complex. Hayman believes the phrase should be translated: "the letters are the foundation of... the three mothers, etc."[5] This reading does not work perfectly throughout the chapter, as the phrase does not always have an object. Weiss points out that *otiyot yesod* can mean "element-letters," and thus is a perfect translation of the Greek *stoicheion*, which means both elements and letters.[6] We will follow a reading in which "foundation letters" is a phrase that suggests the letters are both word and matter: both letters and foundational elements. This understanding of the letters hints at the core practice of *Sefer Yetzirah*, which is the entwining of word with matter.

Practice: Scribing Letters

Close your eyes and breathe out.

Before you is a page.
You write a letter on it.
It becomes a creation
and flies off the page to its proper place.

You write another letter.
It becomes a creation
and flies to its proper place.

Perceive with wonder
the beauty and uniqueness
of each creation
that arises out of the letters you form.

When you are finished forming letters,
look up and see the world that you have made.

Breathe out and open your eyes.

Practice: Tapestry

Close your eyes and breathe out.

Before you is a tapestry.
As you observe its colors and textures,
you become aware that this tapestry
is a vast network of many forces.

Reach out to one of the threads
and let it vibrate between your fingers.
What is the power of this thread?
Let its power enter you.

Reach out to another thread.
Let it vibrate between your fingers.
What is the power of this thread?
Let its power enter you.

Reach out to another thread.
Let it vibrate between your fingers.
What is the power of this thread?
Let its power enter you.

Now feel within.
What is different?
What have the three threads woven in you?

Breathe out and open your eyes.

Chapter 2:2 · Engraving the Letters

עשרים ושתים אותיות
חקוקות בקול
חצובות ברוח
קבועות בפה
בחמש מקומות

א ח ה ע בגרון
ב ו מ פ בשפתים
ג י כ ק בחיך
ד ט ל נ ת בלשון
ז ס ש ר צ בשינים

Twenty-two letters
engraved in the voice
hewn in the breath
fixed in the mouth
in five places:

Aleph Chet Heh Ayin	in the throat
Bet Vav Mem Peh	in the lips
Gimel Yud Kaf Kuf	in the palate
Dalet Tet Lamed Nun Taf	in the tongue
Zayin Samech Shin Reish Tzadi	in the teeth

Letters can be carved not only in stone but in the body: "engraved in the voice, hewn in the breath, fixed in the mouth." This engraving of sound happens via the shaping of a hollow space: the human vocal apparatus. In other words, speech is a vehicle for creation. The implication is that God specially designed human speech as a vehicle for creative expression. Human biology is made to accommodate the sounds—and the magical powers—of the Hebrew *aleph-bet*.

We now know that the power of the letters does not only exist by their written form but also in their spoken form. This appears to be true for both human beings and God—as Genesis says, God spoke to create the world. The mention of voice (*kol*), breath (*ruach*), and mouth (*peh*) is ambiguous as to whether it refers to God or humans, since the creation story in Genesis, describes God as having a voice, and breath (which God breathes into the first human). Later in the Bible, God speaks to Moses *peh el peh*, mouth to mouth.[7]

The "engraving" of speech using the mouth parallels God's "engraving" of written letters to create the world. The difference between speech and writing vanishes—both ways of making meaning inscribe realities on the world. Speech, therefore, is as fructive as writing: speech lasts, because speech creates.

Based on its presence in many manuscripts, Hayman includes this passage in brackets in his earliest recoverable version. Yet he wonders whether this passage may not have been part of the original form of *Sefer Yetzirah* at all.[8] Scholars Gruenwald and Scholem both believe this passage was not part of the original text; Gruenwald indicates that "this division [of the letters] is nowhere repeated in the book, and it has no bearing on its doctrines."[9] Scholem writes that "it may not have been included in the first version of the book."[10] Hayman points out that a fivefold division of letters does not have much to do with anything else in *Sefer Yetzirah*.[11] However the reference to speech as engraving is profoundly relevant to the themes of the book as a whole.

If we try to visualize the passage, we might imagine a prophet preparing to speak divine words: shaping power with tongue, lips, and throat. *Sefer Yetzirah* invites us to see, even become, the one who holds the letters in potential, then sends them into the world by the power of mouth, voice, and breath.

In Five Places   בחמש מקומות

The passage divides the Hebrew letters into five categories.

The italicized phrases here (which are not in Hayman's earliest recoverable version but are included in some versions of the Long Recension) suggest that each of the five letter categories is formed by a different part of the human vocal apparatus.[12] Each speech organ has letters "engraved" in it, to enable that organ to shape and utter the letters.

It is as if the humans and the letters are a single organism that has evolved together for the expression of these sounds and their meanings.

This fivefold division may help us see the influence of other cultures on this passage. A number of scholars have pointed out the similarities between Arab linguistics of this time period and the linguistic theory expressed in this passage. Hayman writes that "The closest parallel to the theory of phonetics expressed here...is found in an Arabic treatise Kit'ab Al-Ayin produced by the Muslim scientist and linguist Al-Halil (c. 710-775/91).[13] Liebes has suggested that the books' linguistic theory is reminiscent of Indian ideas about language,[14] and there are a few other indications that the authors of the book were aware of ideas from India.[15]

For example, the notion of the voice/speech as a kind of fluid creative entity resonates with ancient Hindu texts: for example, "wherever there is a word, there is Brahman, wherever there is Brahman, there is a word"[16] or "The hymn is truly to be considered as the earth, for from it all that exists arises."[17] The Hindu goddess Vak or Vach (literally *Speech*) personifies the gift of speech: divine speech, human speech, and even the sounds of animals.[18]

Brahma creates Vak first of all things and she partners with Brahma in creating the world, using speech to create substance. As Brahma's first creation and confidante, Vak has much in common with Wisdom as She is portrayed in the Bible and *Sefer Yetzirah*. In the ancient Hindu text known as the Rig Veda, the Devisukta (Hymn to the Goddess) proclaims: "The gods diffuse me in every direction, my presence abiding in many places and revealed in manifold ways.... Having created all the worlds and beings, I move freely like the wind."[19] Given the great age of the Rig Veda, it is possible these notions of divine breath made their way to Mesopotamia over time and influenced Jewish thought about the ways that speech, word, sound and sacred text embody divine essence.

Practice: Engraved in the Voice

Close your eyes and breathe out.

You are at the mouth of a cave.
You hear a voice within the cave:
a song, or hum, or words,
or simply breath.

Descend into the cave.
The voice calls you deeper and deeper
into the cave.

You come to the innermost chamber.
Here, the voice surrounds you,
penetrates your being.
You respond to the voice
with your own voice.

You find
that the source of the voice
is within you.

Still singing or sounding,
you climb out of the cave
into the light.

Breathe out and open your eyes.

Practice: Hewn in the Breath

Close your eyes and breathe out.

A hollow ball spins before you,
engraved with shapes and designs.

The ball makes a sound.
This single sound emerges from
all the openings
and the engravings.

Allow the sound to fill you,
awaken you,
and heal you.

As you heal and awaken,
the meaning of the shapes and designs
becomes clear.

Know in this moment
what the ball's design
communicates to you.

Breathe out and open your eyes.

Chapter 2:3 · The Wheel of Letters

עשרים ושתים אותיות
קבועות בגלגל
פנים ואחור
סימן לדבר
אין לטובה למעלה מענג
ואין ברעה
למטה מנגע

Twenty-two letters
fixed in a wheel
that cycles forward and back.

A sign of the matter:
No good
higher than thrill.
No evil
lower than ill.

In Chapter 1:7, God and the reader were at the center of the *sefirot*, from which position they could reach out to east, west, north, south, etc. Now, 2:3 places the reader (and presumably God) at the center of a wheel of letters that rotates forward and backward. This wheel is a bit like a round walled garden—with a wall that moves. The wheel is a tool for combining letters. We will soon learn that this round wheel-wall has "two hundred thirty-one gates." That is, the number of possible combinations of the twenty-two letters in groups of two is two hundred thirty-one.[20]

How should we imagine this backward-and-forward-moving wheel? Jews across time have drawn different images of it.[21] One possible image of the wheel is that it is doubled—there are two rings of letters, one within the other. These two rings of letters can be rotated separately so that any two letters of the *aleph-bet* can line up with one another. Whenever two letters combine, a gate appears in the wheel that allows the divine creative force associated with that letter to flow through into its particular form. The human reciter acts as a kind of safecracker, listening carefully for the combined sound that will unlock a particular creative energy. (A manuscript of Moshe Cordovero's commentary on *Sefer Yetzirah*, written in 1584, presents this same image of a double wheel of letters.)[22]

This combining, or permuting, activity is a visual as well as aural process. When the physical letters line up, along with their sounds, the gate opens. This image of hollow gates is consistent with the fundamental image of engraving: two letters can merge with one another and create a channel together.

A Sign of the Matter: סימן לדבר
No Good Higher than Thrill אין לטובה למעלה מענג

The end of the passage offers a *siman ledavar*, a "sign of the matter." In the Talmud, this phrase could indicate a demonstration of something (such as the appearance of stars to indicate the time for evening prayer)[23] or a biblical prooftext.[24] Here, the "sign" is neither. It appears to be a cryptic saying: "no good higher than delight (*oneg*), no evil lower than plague (*nega*)."[25]

Here the phrase has been translated "No good higher than thrill; no evil lower than ill" to capture something about the Hebrew: the words *oneg* (delight) and *nega* (plague or suffering) both contain the letters *ayin*, *nun*, and *gimel*. The meanings are opposite only because the letters are ordered differently. The "sign" suggests that the order of the letters matters deeply, because even if the letters are the same, their order can produce two different meanings. This is key, because all things are composed of the twenty-two letters in different combinations.

The text "No good (*tov*) higher (*lemaalah*) than thrill, no evil (*ra*) lower (*lematah*) than ill" links back to the *sefirot*. The list of the *sefirot* in 1:7 includes good (*tov*) and evil (*ra*) as two fundamental qualities in the cosmos. Further, *maalah* and *mata*, high and low, are *sefirot* in 1:13. These connections to the *sefirot* seem to allow those ethereal inscriptions to hover in the background here, reminding us that the ten *sefirot* provide a sacred frame for the combining of the letters.

The invocation of good and evil also suggests that the permutation of letters can yield phenomena as diverse as perfect good and perfect evil. Good and evil, delight and suffering, are each composed of the same letters: they are merely rearranged. All of this is an instruction and a warning to the reader, the one who is performing the incantation of the text. The combination of the letters can yield any outcome, from perfection to horror. One must therefore turn the wheel of the letters with tremendous care. The human creative power, like God's, has consequences.

Yet the similarity of *oneg* and *nega*, delight and suffering, also offers a contemplative truth. Even things so diverse as pleasure and pain are still made up of the same building blocks, the same human consciousness and experience, the same divine creative force. The wheel of letters contains all phenomena. All happenings are ultimately one, even when they appear radically different. When we understand this, we can come to a state of equanimity within the cosmos.

Practice: Cycling the Wheel

Close your eyes and breathe out slowly.

You are standing at the center
of a ring of standing stones.
There is a letter carved into each stone.

The ring of stones
lifts, and whirls around you.
When the ring stops whirling,
two of the stones
have formed a gateway.

Look through the gateway.
See the world's greatest good,
and the world's greatest injury.

See that the good
reaches out to heal the harm.

See your own greatest good,
your own greatest injury.
See that the good
reaches out to heal the harm.

Breathe out and open your eyes.

Practice: Higher than Delight, Deeper than Sorrow

Close your eyes and breathe out.

Three glowing globes hang in the air,
just within reach.
The globes radiate joy, vitality, and serenity.

Now the globes rearrange themselves.
In this configuration,
the globes radiate sorrow, fear, and anger.

Reach out and rearrange the globes
into a third configuration
that holds all of these feelings together.

Breathe out and open your eyes.

Chapter 2:4 · Combining the Letters

עשרים ושתים אתיות
חקקן חצבן
צרפן שקלן והימירן

כיצד שקלן והימירן
אלף עם כולם
וכולם עם אלף
בית עם כולם
וכולם עם בית
וכלן חוזרות חלילה
נמצאו יוצאות במאתים ושלושים ואחד שערים

נמצא כל היצור וכל הדיבור
יוצא בשם אחד

Twenty-two letters
engraved, carved,
permuted, weighed and exchanged.

How did God weigh and exchange them?
Aleph with them all
and all of them with Aleph
Bet with them all
and all of them with Bet
and they all repeat in a cycle.
Thus they emerge from 231 gates.

And so it is that all creation and all speech
emerges from one name.

Again we enter God's workshop. God is busily at work, forming each letter with its unique traits, engraving and carving it as a channel for creation. God smelts the letters as a silversmith or blacksmith might—the root of the word *tzerafan*, he permuted them, also means to smelt. God is working with the letters in combination, "weighing" them against one another and "exchanging" them one for another. "Exchange" (*heimir*) seems to mean "permute," as in arrange the letters in various combinations. Like a jeweler, God is stringing the letters in different orders to make different creations.

The verbs that describe God's actions—*chakakan, chatzavan, tzarfan, shakalan, heimiran*—have a beautiful sound when one says them together. These words have a mantra-like quality: one could repeat the words and shift one's consciousness. This entire passage seems to point toward the experience of trance.

The passage now instructs the reader in a practice of combining all the letters, in groups of two, from *Aleph* to *Taf*. This process spells out a massive and complex divine name, composed of all twenty-two letters in combination with one another (231 combinations). This complex divine name is a way of naming a vast array of diverse creations. Using larger and larger combinations of letters, we can name, or even create, an infinity of distinct sounds, distinct entities.[26]

It might be that the combination process, an intense mantra-like process that occupies the mind deeply, is a trance-inducing ritual that allows the reader to re-enact God's creative process. It also may be that the combining practice is magical, and allows the reader to create reality using the letter combinations, just as God did. In the *Book of Creation*, the power to change one's consciousness and the power to create worlds are inextricably linked.

Weighed and Exchanged שקלן והימירן

In the Bible, the word *heimir* means "to exchange."[27] In the Torah, the word means "to exchange one sacrificial animal for another" (in which case both animals become holy). The word choice suggests that each letter is like an offering in the cosmic Temple. As they are exchanged and permuted, they all become holy.

The word *shakal*, "weigh," has a different implication. To weigh something suggests selling it in a market. Biblically speaking, one is enjoined to have honest weights when one buys and sells things.[28] The root *shakal* also is related to *shekel*, a coin.[29]

The market has holiness to it also. Novelist Lian Hearn writes: "There is a sort of magic going on at markets. Goods are bartered; one thing transformed into another."³⁰ Nam Lin Hur, analyzing the marketplace in early modern Japan, concurs: "Street markets were not purely places for trade.... the first form of trade had a religious component: prospective traders first ritually offered their commodities to deities and then proceeded to deal with commoners."³¹ So too, the biblical marketplace and its associated weights and currencies (*shekalim*), apply both to humans and to God: the half-shekel census tax is dedicated to the sanctuary and therefore given into God's possession, and individuals may donate *shekalim* in place of their fields or their own bodies:³² "All your valuations shall be according to the *shekel* of the sanctuary."³³ In combination, the words *Heimir* and *shakal* imply a sacred market, a temple market, where things are exchanged and transformed.

The letters are therefore a means of changing from one state to another. We might imagine that the recitation of the letters is a means of entering a sacred mindset, a way of being "exchanged" and given into a holy realm. Once we enter this realm, we become empowered to also "weigh and exchange," to shape and transfer divine energies.

Aleph with Them All³⁴   אלף עם כולם

The passage now offers a practice for the combination of letters, in which the first letter, *aleph*, is combined with all the other letters in succession (i.e., *aleph-bet*, *aleph-gimel*, *aleph-dalet*, etc.) and then *bet* with all the remaining letters in succession (*bet-gimel*, *bet-dalet*, etc.) It appears that this is done both visually (by imagining the letters) and orally (by speaking each pair of letters). So the practice might sound like "ab," "ag," etc., and look like a series of two-letter combinations. According to the text, the letters "repeat in a cycle," meaning one moves through them in a pattern from *aleph* to *taf*, and presumably can begin again with *aleph*.

Later Jews understood the practice of letter combination to be magical, capable of enlivening a *golem*, a human-like being created by humans. The permutation of letters was a technique that could make life.³⁵ Aryeh Kaplan notes that it was said that doing the process in reverse could "unmake" a golem.³⁶ This is consistent with the idea that the *aleph-bet*, when permuted, comprises a name of God, since the name of God can create and destroy, according to Jewish tradition.

231 Gates   במאתים ושלושים ואחד שערים

There are 231 combinations of two Hebrew letters, assuming that *aleph-bet* is the same as *bet-aleph*; that is, combinations of two letters are not to be repeated even if they come in a different order. This number does seem to contradict the text's saying "*aleph* with all of them, and all of them with *aleph*, as if *aleph-bet* would be different than *bet-aleph*. (There is a variant text in which the number of gates is 462, which would include both *aleph-bet* and *bet-aleph*.[37]) However, the text as we have it seems to assert 231 gates. (Hayman notes most manuscripts say 221, but he concludes this is a scribal error that occurred, most likely, because a scribe left the long top off the letter *lamed* [equaling 30], forming a *kaf* [equaling 20] instead.[38]) In Appendix III, the reader will find instructions for the practice of 231 letter combinations.

The language of "gates" and of "emerging" or "going out" seems to mean that the combinations of letters form not solid forms, but gateways. The combinations of letters seem to be visualized as some sort of doorway created by the alchemy of those two particular letters. This doorway, perhaps, admits a particular kind of creative energy into the world, in order to form a particular creation.

This language of gateways is related to Wisdom itself, to the web of channels through which God emanates creation. In the Book of Proverbs, Wisdom cries out "at the gates, by the city's entrance, at the coming-in of the doors."[39] Wisdom, God's partner in making the world, is specifically associated with gateways and doorways, with the negotiation of the boundaries between the physical world and what lies beyond it. Her *netivot*, her pathways, apparently have doors that need to be opened in order for divine creative force to flow.

The "gates" must admit something, but what exactly? Once again, the divine energy, or solidified will, that flows through the channels into the world is implied rather than stated. It is as if *Sefer Yetzirah* has an awe about this divine substance that is disseminated by the web of Wisdom's channels, such that, like the divine name, it cannot be explicitly pronounced. The gates remain empty of anything visible: what pours through them cannot be grasped.

All Creation and All Speech Emerges from One Name

כל היצור וכל הדיבור
יוצא בשם אחד

The phrase *kol hayetzur vechol hadibur yotzei b'shem echad*—"all creation and all speech emerges from One Name"—illustrates that word is matter and matter is word. God is the author of words and things—channeling both into being by means of the letters which are the Name. The human practitioner who undertakes the combination ritual also enters into a mythic reality where intentional speech becomes real.

Each and every being arises from a combination of letters that is part of the Name. We might say that the world is the Divine Name, and all of its myriad phenomena are syllables of that Name. Nature is a manifestation of God, albeit in a complex and multiple form. One sacred Reality combines and recombines itself to form all things. Once we know this, our relationship to the world is transformed. This image is surely meant to induce peace and equanimity in the one who contemplates it.

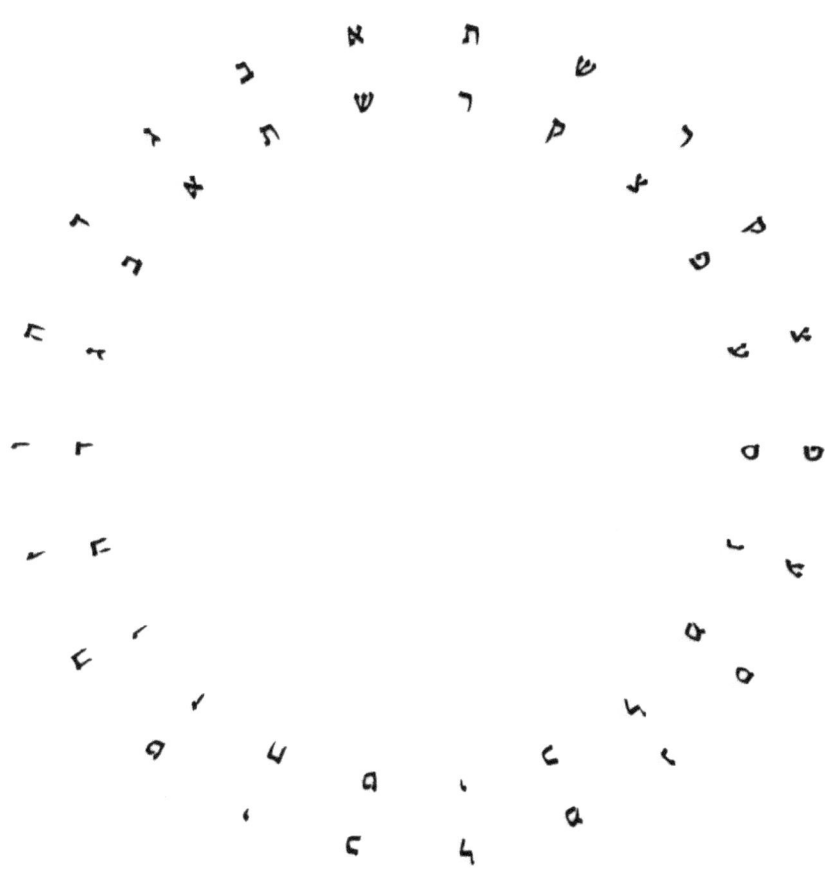

Practice: All Creation and All Speech Emerges from One Name

Close your eyes and breathe out.

You are transported to a realm
where angels are singing.

You hear the angels
pronounce the Divine Name.

However you hear this Name
is the right way.

As the angels sing or speak or dance the Name,
a universe comes into being.

You are a witness to this new universe,
this moment of beginning.

See your own life beginning anew
as you hear the Divine Name.

Breathe out and open your eyes.

Practice: The Wheel of Letters

Close your eyes and breathe out.

You are at the center of a double circle of stones
carved with Hebrew letters.
One by one, the letters are shining and sounding their sounds.

Two stones begin to shine,
sounding their letters together.
As they do so,
a ray of light enters the circle.

Now two other letters glow and sound,
then two others.
Each time a pair of letters glows and sounds,
a ray of light appears within the circle
until there are many, many rays of light.

What do you hear, see, or feel
as the lights interweave with one another?

The lights dim
and the circle of stones falls silent.
In the silence, know
that you have heard and seen
a name of God.

Breathe out and open your eyes.

Chapter 2:5 · Pillars Made of Air

יצר מתהו ממש
ועשאו באש וישנו
וחצב עמודים גדולים
מאויר שאינו נתפס

The Divine formed
substance out of void
and worked it in fire,
and it became,
and carved great pillars
out of air that cannot be grasped.

Chapter 1 ended with what we might call a "summary ritual," a creation spell summoning the elements and directions—all ten *sefirot*. Chapter 2 also ends with a "summary ritual" that immerses us in the magic of the twenty-two letters. Though some versions of *Sefer Yetzirah* include other passages in this chapter, Hayman's version ends here, with God forming substance out of void.

In the Divine Artist's workshop, the creation of the world is in progress. Using fire as a catalyst, God works the void into substance—yet the "great pillars" that constitute the world's substance arise from intangible air. What is this "air that cannot be grasped"? Presumably, this refers to spoken letters and words that cannot be held in the hand. It is word that creates world.

Tzahi Weiss mentions a fifth-century Syriac Christian source, a verse-homily by the Christian poet and theologian Narsai, in which letters are hewn out of spirit yet become solid as stones:

I saw the five letters that he set down at the beginning of the verse [Genesis]... With the iron toll of the spirit he hewed the signs like stones/and built upon them a house, vast from top to bottom.[40]

Here, as in 2:5, God hews the letters out of spirit, yet the letters take on substance: they are like stones and can build the cosmic temple. 4:4, in fact, contains this exact image of letter-stones that build a house. And here, the air that becomes solid pillars suggests a similar image: Weiss suggests that Narsai's words and the words of the *Sefer Yetzirah* stem from a common Syriac cultural trope featuring letters hewn out of air that become building blocks for the world.[41]

Substance Out Of Void יצר מתהו ממש

The word *tohu* means primordial chaos or primordial void. This passage clearly refers to Genesis 1, in which the universe begins in "chaos and void"—*tohu vavohu*. In 2:4, God makes *tohu* into *mamash* ("something" or "substance"). *Mamash* implies something tangible, sensual—something one can touch. In modern Hebrew or Yiddish, *mamash* has come to mean "real" or "really," as in "It's *mamash* raining."

Scholar Yehudah Liebes believes that the word *mamash* is a midrash on the word *bohu*, which follows the word *tohu* in the Genesis text and which seems also to mean "void." When *bohu* is divided into two words, it yields the phrase *bo hu*—"something is in it."[42] Matter is already concealed in the void, and waits for God to shape it using the letters.

God makes the world—here called *yeshno* or existence—out of this primordial nothingness. In evoking the language of *tohu*, the book here evokes the Genesis model, in which God creates using speech, and then introduces a different model in which God works the world in fire, creating as an artist does, using physical tools and materials.

Worked in Fire ועשאו באש וישנו

The image of God as a blacksmith appears earlier in the chapter in verbs like *tzaraf* which refer to letter permutation but can also mean "smelt." God works the world as a smith works metal—or maybe as a glassblower blows glass. If the image is in fact related to glassblowing, then we have returned to the image of God as creator of "engraved" or hollow channels. The channels, forged in air and fire, are the letters themselves.

The passage says that God worked the void in fire and it "became" or "existed" (*yeshno*). Hayman notes that some versions of *Sefer Yetzirah* contain the phrase *ve'asa et eino yeshno*—"God made something out of nothing."[43] This phrase resembles later Jewish theology in which God creates out of nothing. Yet the versions which Hayman relies on imagines creation occurring, not out of nothing, but out of a lump of matter in a blacksmith's fire.[44] The creation *ex nihilo* image may be a later imposition by Jewish writers who felt more philosophically comfortable with "something out of nothing" than with God working a primordial mass.

Hayman notes that the "fire" here may allude to a rabbinic legend in which the heavens are made of "fire and water."[45]

The pillars of air worked in fire also connect to an image from the Hebrew Bible: the pillars of cloud and fire that accompany the Israelites through the wilderness.[46] So too, the text suggests, these pillars of air, these holy letters, are guides and protectors for mortal beings.

Great Pillars out of Air   וחצב עמודים גדולים מאויר

We should notice two more things about the image of pillars. First, the Bible speaks of the pillars of the Temple. In 1 Kings, Solomon sets up two pillars at the entrance to the Temple and names them Yachin and Boaz.[47] The mention of pillars here suggests the building of the cosmic Temple.

Second, in Proverbs, we have a verse in which Wisdom hews pillars: "Wisdom has built her house, she has hewn her seven pillars."[48] The word for "to hew" (*chatzav*) is the same in the biblical passage and in our passage. The hewing of pillars in this passage strongly suggests the presence of Wisdom, God's energetic matrix for the process of creation. The house that Wisdom builds is the world, and its pillars are the breath.

The columns of air are a way of talking about our own shaping of words. Spoken sounds are "pillars out of air that cannot be grasped," as they are made from the shaping of breath within the throat. Yet these sounds produce meaning: poetry, sacred text, things that last. In a similar vein, the ancient poet Sappho writes: "Although they are/only breath, words/which I command/are immortal."[49]

It seems we are meant to recite this passage as a re-invoking of creation. The very words of this passage hold the intent to create worlds. The breath we use to speak the words is an embodiment of the vast pillars made of air.

That Cannot be Grasped   מאויר שאינו נתפס

The Hebrew root *tafas* (to grasp) has multiple meanings. It can mean to grasp or seize a physical object, but also to intellectually grasp an idea. The Talmud famously says: *tafasta meruba lo tafasta*—one who tries to grasp too much, grasps nothing.[50] In other words, don't intellectually bite off more than you can chew.

God is able to create out of an intangible and invisible substance; so, the passage seems to imply, is the reader. Yet that which we create out of our breath cannot be held. Chapter 2 concludes with an insight meant for the practitioner: the cosmic structures can be imagined, yet they also escape the imagination. They are "great pillars" that "cannot be grasped." The experience of touching divine creative power is profound, yet we cannot hold onto it. We must treat all the insights and revelations that come from our inner journeys as pillars that cannot be grasped.

Practice: Working in Fire

Close your eyes and breathe out slowly.

A fire is before you.
A fire-keeper is tending it.
This fire is your life-force.
See how carefully the fire-keeper tends it,
and breathes on it to keep the flame alive.

As the fire burns,
a pillar of smoke arises from within it.
Within this pillar
is a new creation.
What new thing
arises from the fire
that is your life?

Breathe out and open your eyes.

Practice: Pillars of Breath

Close your eyes and breathe out.

Each breath you take
is forming a pillar between sky and earth.
Soon you are surrounded
by many great pillars.

Reach out to one of these pillars.
Try to grasp it.
What happens
when you try to grasp the pillar of breath?

As you breathe, the pillars multiply.
Observe the structure they form.

This form, whatever it is,
is the holy temple.
Rest within the temple.
Notice how it feels to be here.

Know that you yourself are the Holy Temple,
connecting sky and earth.

Breathe out and open your eyes.

Chapter 3:1 · The Three Mothers

שלש אמות

א מ ש

יסודן

כף זכות וכף חובה

ולשון חוק

מכריע בינתיים

Three mothers:
Aleph, Mem, Shin.

Their foundation is
a palmful of merit
a palmful of guilt
and a tongue of engraved law
balances between them.

We have now considered both the *sefirot* (the frame for the universe) and the letters (which provide the content within the frame). Chapter 3 introduces us to the first subset of the letters: the three mothers, *Aleph, Mem,* and *Shin*. These are three Hebrew letters that channel the great powers of nature: air, water, fire. *Aleph, Mem,* and *Shin* stand for *avir* (air), *mayim* (water), and *eish* (fire).[1] They are the first, middle, and second-to-last letters of the *aleph-bet*, which would suggest they are beginning, middle, and end—the totality of reality. The term "mothers" implies sources, origins, matrices, birthgivers. The mothers are the forms of sky, earth, and everything in between. As we have noted, these elemental letters overlap with the elemental *sefirot* of air, water, and fire. This overlap gives us the sense that the three mothers are more than letters—they are nature in her most massive and timeless shapes and forms. They are sky, sea, and everything in between.

Like Wisdom, the mothers are forces rather than persons, though it's not hard to imagine them as watery, fiery, windy presences gathered in some field somewhere to conjure the world into being. The trio reminds one of the ancient view of the world in which humans exist between sky above and underworld below. This cosmology has its roots in ancient Mesopotamian myth.[2]

Ronit Meroz believes that *Sefer Yetzirah* intended, or once contained, a tradition in which the three mothers give rise to the three realms of space, time, and soul.[3] If for a moment we imagine this to be the case, the power of the three mothers increases exponentially. They become co-creators with the Divine in forming every dimension of the universe.

Aleph, Mem, Shin   ש מ א

Indologist David Shulman suggests that the *Aleph*, with its role as unifier and harmonizer of opposing forces, plays a similar role to the "a" in Sanskrit thought, which is understood to be the primal sound, and in some traditions embodies deity.[4] *Mem*, which has a humming sound and whose original Hebrew pictogram indicated "water," also has an elemental quality. Avivah Zornberg points out that the primordial deep, *tehom*, has associations with a humming "m" sound.[5]

Yet why not choose *Tav*, the final letter of the Hebrew alphabet, as a mother letter instead of *Shin*? The answer seems to be simple: the letter Tav takes two sound-forms, depending on its placement in a word. Thus it belongs in the category of double letters rather than mother letters. This leaves the *Shin*, the second-to-the-last letter, to be the third mother letter.

Yet this inclusion of *Shin* instead of *Tav* introduces a kind of imperfection into the mother letters: *Aleph* is beginning, *Mem* is the middle, but *Shin* isn't really the end. There's something unsatisfying about this. Some even believe *Tav* is the third mother letter, rather than *Shin*, but that the *Sefer Yetzirah* text is deceiving us in order to conceal the mystery of the three mothers from non-initiated readers. One support for this belief is that, in Aramaic, the *Shin* and the *Tav* often switch (one becomes the other). This grammatical oddity could be a hint that the practitioner should switch *Shin* and *Tav*.[6]

And, one can see a long-standing Jewish belief in *Aleph*, *Mem*, and *Tav* as the letters of power. These three letters spell *Emet*, or truth. There is a later Jewish legend that the golem had the letters *Aleph*, *Mem*, and *Tav* inscribed on its forehead.[7] When the *Aleph* was erased, the word on the golem's forehead became *Met*, or "dead," and the golem's life-force disappeared.

But *Tav is* a double letter (i.e., it fits without controversy into the category of letters that take two sound-forms) and therefore cannot be a mother letter. It is listed with the double letters and acts like one of them. And, the shape and hissing sound of *Shin* goes easily with *eish*/fire, in ways that *Tav* would not. (The letter *Sin*, which looks like *Shin* but is pronounced with an "s" sound, is not a "double" of *Shin* but rather a separate letter, so it does not make *Shin* a double letter.) We may provisionally conclude that *Shin* is an authentic mother letter.

However, *Tav* does in some way remain in the background of the mother letters. It is the end, after all. In some way, the "shadow" of *Tav* among the mother letters is like a fourth element—a secret earth element, a hidden messianic future, a final outcome that remains a mystery.

A Palmful of Merit, A Palmful of Guilt   כף זכות וכף חובה

Aleph, Mem, and *Shin* don't exist only as triangle. The *Mem* and *Shin* are opposites—"merit" and "guilt"—and must be resolved by a third entity, which is the "tongue of law." For *Sefer Yetzirah*, all dualities can be resolved into multiplicity-within-unity. In Chapter 1, the polarities of good-evil, beginning-end, north-south, etc. fit together into a unified architecture. In Chapter 2, the multiplicity of the letters can be combined into a single divine name. In Chapter 3, the polarity of water and fire can be resolved via the energies of air, which bring these forces together and harmonize them.

In this passage, the three mothers arrange themselves like a scale, with two equally balanced powerful forces, one on each side, and a balancing force at the center. The image is of a courtroom, in which a decision about merit or guilt must be made. The word *kaf* or palm also can mean a "pan" as in the pan of a scale. The image here is like a person holding out two hands (or a scale with two pans), one containing a verdict of innocent, and one containing a verdict of guilty. The tongue of the person (*lashon chok*, the language or tongue of law), or the balancing element of the scale, must speak the judgment. Aryeh Kaplan calls this image of opposing forces, with an integrating/balancing force in the middle, "thesis/antithesis/synthesis"—a thing, its opposite, and what reconciles the two.[8] Yehuda Liebes suggests that in the language of merit and guilt there may be a connection here with the *sefirot* of *tov* and *ra*, good and evil.[9] If so, then the *Aleph, Mem,* and *Shin* also represent moral/experiential dualities and their resolution.

But how do the elements relate to moral good and evil? Up until this point, *Sefer Yetzirah* has largely deal with cosmic forces—physics, more or less. How does the moral realm integrate into this view of reality? Word order would indicate that *Mem* goes with merit and *Shin* with guilt, yet later in the chapter, *Mem* is associated with earth and *Shin* with heaven. If we were to read this exactly as it appears, the watery realm (earth) would be associated with merit, and the fiery realm (heaven) would be associated with guilt. Given that usually it's earth that is labeled sinful and heaven that is labeled pure, it's a bit hard to make sense of what *Sefer Yetzirah* is telling us. We might perhaps say that it is fire/heaven that condemns, and water/earth that forgives. If so, *Sefer Yetzirah* is once again privileging earth, and physical reality, as foundational for human life.

Or, we might understand "merit" and "guilt" a little differently. In rabbinic Hebrew, *chovah* can mean a debt as well as a judgment of guilt, and *zechut*, acquittal or merit, can also mean "to have authority or possession."[10] In this reading, the polarities are "to have" and "to owe." On earth, we have a certain freedom to act and experience. And we "owe" heaven a great deal. In this sense, we are both free and not free. *Sefer Yetzirah* may be alluding to a fundamental human mystery: we have a sense of acting alone, and yet we are constrained by the larger whole that is the universe. We are also often faced with a shifting sense of our goodness and our moral liability.[11] In its first description of the mother letters, *Sefer Yetzirah* invites us to see our own dual nature—free and bound, innocent and guilty—and integrate those two understandings into a third kind of awareness, in which many truths exist simultaneously.[12] Similarly, later kabbalists understood *Mem*, *Shin*, and *Aleph* to relate to the divine attributes of *chesed* (love), *gevurah* (limitation), and *tiferet* (balance)—opposite qualities that resolve into a third integrating attribute.[13]

A Tongue of Engraved Law Balances Between Them

ולשון חוק
מכריע בינתיים

The phrase *lashon chok* is a triumph of double meaning. *Lashon* can mean tongue or language, and *chok*, law, comes from the word "to engrave." So, the phrase can mean "the tongue of decree" (i.e., the one who speaks the decree) or the "language of law" (as in the rule of law itself). But the word law, *chok*, comes from the same root as "*chakak*, to engrave." The tongue/language must engrave the judgment, just as God engraves the letters into the world. The translation here reads "a tongue of engraved law" to try to capture the double meaning.

In a sense, the *Aleph* that balances and integrates the duality of *Mem* and *Shin* is doing so by engraving a path between them.

The verb *machria*, here translated as "balances," generally means "to decide." Many translate the phrase *lashon chok machria beintayim* as "the tongue of decree decides between them." But there is no permanent "decision" between water and fire, as both are required for the world to exist. In rabbinic Hebrew, the word *machria* can also mean to balance, harmonize, or compromise between two opinions.[14] (Hayman translates *chok machria beintayim* as "the balancing item.")[15] This fits more closely with the action of the *Aleph*, which stands between sky and earth and tempers the effects of cold and heat. The two perspectives must be reconciled, not opposed to one another.

It is notable that it is *Aleph*, the air, the intangible breath, that offers integration and reconciliation. This passage contains wisdom for practitioners: what helps us keep the balance between our conviction of righteousness and our feeling of guilt, our sense of constraint and our awareness of freedom, is the breath. The breath allows us to become present to what is, to gain perspective and integrate different ways of knowing. When we come to presence, we are able to hold multiple truths without straining. Recent scientific research shows that deep breaths allow synchrony between brain areas and thus makes for greater calm, focus, and emotional control.[16] This ancient book is correct that the breath helps us reconcile what appears to be contradictory.

Practice: A Palmful of Merit, a Palmful of Guilt

Close your eyes and breathe out.

You are holding all of your merits in one hand.
Look at them and feel their weight.
Notice their size, texture, color.

You are holding all of your guilts in the other hand.
Look at them and feel their weight.
Notice their size, texture, color.

Breathe.

Bring your hands together.

Allow merit and guilt
to integrate and come into balance.

Open your cupped hands.

What do you see
in your cupped-open hands?

What has become
of your guilt and innocence?

Breathe out and open your eyes.

This is a version of a meditation created by Dr. Catherine Shainberg, used by permission.

Practice: Balancing Between

Close your eyes and breathe out.

You see two of yourself.

One of you is completely constrained:
by others, by your situation, by the universe.

One of you is completely free,
and completely unconstrained by anyone or anything.
See these two versions of you clearly.

As you observe,
the two of you
step together and become one.

What is the nature of this self/that is both free and unfree?
Know this as your true nature.

Let this self
step into you
and become you.

Breathe out and open your eyes.

Chapter 3:2 · The Six Rings

שלש אמות א מ ש
סוד גדול מכוסה ומופלא
וחתום בשש טבעות
וממנו יוצאין אש מים רוח
ומחותל בזכר ונקבה

Three mothers: Aleph, Mem, Shin.
A great secret veiled and mysterious,
sealed by six seal-rings.
From them come fire, water, and air
enveloped in male and female.

The language that describes the three mothers and their seal-rings is magical language. The three mothers are a "great secret, veiled and mysterious." Nothing else in *Sefer Yetzirah* is described as a secret. We have not seen the word "mysterious" (*mufla* or *pele*) since 1:1 when we first heard of the thirty-two mysterious paths. It is striking that these terms are used here. The three mothers, the elements of the world, are a cosmic mystery.

To decode this passage, we will need to return to the incantation bowls of sixth- to eighth-century CE Mesopotamia and Syria, and to Jewish practitioners of ancient magic. The language of seals and seal-rings is also used in incantation bowls to protect Jewish homes. The seals that the Creator places around the three mothers protect them and make them a safe "home" for life.

Veiled and Mysterious   מכוסה ומופלא

The Hebrew *mekhuseh* means "covered" and/or "wondrous." The "veiled" mothers are similar to the Holy of Holies at the center of the Temple, which is hidden behind a curtain and cannot ever be visited except by the High Priest on Yom Kippur. Their status as "covered" implies that these three entities form the center of the cosmic temple.

Their being covered or hidden suggests that an adept will need to work hard to see them. This seems counterintuitive: fire, water, and air are not particularly difficult to notice. Yet plumbing their mysteries may take a special perception—a parting of the veil of ordinary reality.

As feminine entities, the "veiled" three mothers have an alluring quality. One wants to approach them, find out more about them. Similarly, the Zohar of thirteenth-century Spain will later describe the quest of the mystic to encounter the Divine Presence in her secret hiding place:

> From her palace, she reveals her face to him, and gives him a hint of love, and then retreats to her hiding place. No one sees or knows, only he alone, and he is drawn to her with his whole heart and soul and with all of his being. And when he arrives, she begins speaking with him, at first from behind the veil she has hung before the words... until she stands revealed, face to face with him.[17]

While the romance in our text is not nearly so explicit, there is a call to the initiate to draw closer to the secret. The mention of male and female suggests an erotic secret, a joining of some kind. What deep mysteries and intimacies we might encounter, the text whispers, if we were to peer beneath the veil of the three mothers and know them for what they are: the root and foundation of all forms in our world.

Six Seal-Rings   בשש טבעות

Sealing is a ritual practice used to keep out demonic forces or keep in blessings. In Chapter 1:13, we discussed the uses of sealing in Jewish magic. In many incantation bowls, the process of sealing requires multiple "rings." For example:

> You may not come near the house and threshold of 'Adaq son of Mahlapta that is sealed with three rings and countersealed with seven seals (...) from this day and forever, *amen, amen, selah.*[18]

> I have sealed with the signet ring of El Shaddai and with the signet ring of Joshua son of Perachia the savior (*vechatmit be'iyokna d'el shaddai...*)[19]

The bowl-writers include sets of seal-rings as extra magical security against demons. So too, the rings mentioned here in our passage are almost certainly seal-rings, with letters engraved into them. Since there are six rings, the seals that would be inscribed into these rings are likely the six permutations of *Aleph, Mem,* and *Shin*. We might imagine that these three letters are a hidden name of God—"a great secret veiled and mysterious"—and hence the permutations of them are powerful.

While the *sefirot* exist in the void, the mother letters are not void but world, and they require a sealed space in order to exist. The seal-rings keep out the *blimah*—the void—and protect the structures of creation. Like the atmosphere that envelops the earth, the seal-rings provide a barrier between a livable space and an alien infinity. They are not edged like the walls of the cosmic temple, but round like rings, suggesting a move toward the organic. The seal-rings of the mothers offer a kind of womb, a shelter where life can thrive.

This image suggests a ritual practice: the successive combination of the mother letters in six permutations in order to create six seals (just as the *Yud, Heh,* and *Vav* were combined to make six seals). One could imagine practitioners chanting the six combinations as a protective prayer or spell. In fact, later versions of *Sefer Yetzirah* explicitly list six combinations of the mother letters, making two seals for each of the three letters.[20] The passage here itself may be meant as the text of a sealing ritual.

Enveloped in Male and Female   ומחותל בזכר ונקבה

The great secret, within its six seals, is enveloped in male and female. The word that appears in the text is *mechutal*, a rare word that means "wrapped" or "bundled." The translation would thus be "fire, water, and air, wrapped in male and female." Suddenly, a gender binary is introduced into our perception of the three mothers. In what way are the elements "wrapped in male and female"?

These words may suggest that the "wrapping" of the mothers is the body itself. As we will later learn, air, fire, and water manifest as chest, head, and belly. These are relatively non-gendered parts of the body. Perhaps the text means to suggest that the gendered parts of the body, the genital and secondary characteristics that society uses to designate us as "male" or "female," are mere wrappings around the most important human organs (head, chest, belly). "Male" and "female" are a secondary part of our identity—the core thing about us is our connection to the elements, the three mothers.

Another reading is also possible: the text might indicate that every being formed of the elements has male and female aspects that "envelop" it. Maybe these wrappings are different for different entities, or maybe we might have access to multiple genders at different moments. If we follow this reading, we could have a text in which multiple genders exist within a single person, and maybe even within God—since in Chapter 1 God is an intrinsic part of the chain of elements. (Perhaps this phrase "wrapped in male and female" also hints at the gendered nature of the Hebrew language, in which words are "wrapped" in male or female forms.)[21] The later kabbalah, which imagines God as a multi-gendered being, is consistent with such a reading.[22]

As is well known, it is common in the ancient world for men and women to be construed as two completely different kinds of being, with the male considered dominant and/or superior. Within this binary model, men and women often are regarded as complementary beings with opposite qualities. *Sefer Yetzirah* does not use these hierarchical gender models. The text suggests that the male and the female are equally related to the three mothers/three elements. There is no suggestion that women are deficient in any element. There is no suggestion, for example, that women contain more water and men more fire, or vice versa. There is simply an acknowledgement of different forms and/or energies. We might understand this text to say that the sex of one's body does not define one's essence. Again, the text seems to be speaking equally to multiple types of practitioners, including women.

Enveloped ומחותל

Let's take a moment to focus on the word *mechutal*, which in its biblical meaning means to enwrap, swathe, or swaddle.[23] The root of the word (*chet-taf-lamed*) is a somewhat unusual root, though it does appear in Job and Ezekiel. The idea of the elemental mothers being "swaddled" in male and female is fascinating.

And, there is possibly an alternative for the wording of this passage. The Aramaic *machtam*, "countersealed" or "double-sealed," is a word consistently used in incantation bowls and always paired with the word *chatim* or *chatum*, "sealed."[24] Here in our text, we have the word *chatum*, and then a few words later, *mechutal*. Perhaps the unusual word *mechutal* (enveloped) somehow hints at the Hebrew word *mechutam*, the Hebrew of *machtam*.[25] If the word *mechutam* is hinted at somehow, the reader might be meant to hear the phrase "sealed and countersealed"—sealed by six rings and countersealed in male and female. The genitalia might then be imagined as seals on the body, impressed into the flesh like a seal ring.

It is even possible that the word here was once *mechutam*. The phrase "sealed and countersealed" appears in magical literature rather than rabbinic literature. One could perhaps imagine that, early in the history of the book, a scribe or editor might have been surprised by the word *mechutam*, "countersealed" in this context, and might have substituted another plausible word (i.e. *mechutal*) which differed from *mechutam* only in one letter).[26] There is no proof to suggest this alternate text existed— but the words *mechutal* and *mechutam* do resonate in an interesting way, and even a hinting at the word *mechutam* would tie *Sefer Yetzirah* further to the incantation bowls and to Jewish magical literature, and would suggest that bodies of all genders "seal" the three mothers within them.

Practice: Six Rings

Close your eyes and breathe out.

You are holding a many-petaled rose
of any color you imagine.

A petal falls off, then another,
until six layers of the rose fall away.

At the center of the rose
is the secret
of the three mothers:
air, water, and fire.

Perceive and know the secret
as it manifests to you
within the rose
at this moment.

Breathe out and open your eyes.

Practice: Enveloped in Male and Female

Close your eyes and breathe out.

Woven in a cloak of light around you
are the energies of male and female.

Feel the power
of the two energies
as they manifest to you right now.

Feel how they are similar
and different.

Feel their profound and equal power.

The energies
of female and male
now gift you their power
in the form most appropriate to you.

Breathe out and open your eyes.

Chapter 3:3 · The Three Worlds

שלש אמות
אש למעלה
מים למטה
ורוח בנתיים

Three mothers:
Fire above,
water below,
and wind in the middle.

The three mothers give rise to three horizontal world-zones: fire above, water below, and wind/air in the middle. They provide the axis (heaven, earth, underworld) for the known world. This is essentially the same world-map as the Bible has: heaven/sky/divine above, humans in the middle, and underworld/deep waters below. We can see this worldview in Isaiah's words to King Ahaz: "Ask for a sign from YHWH your God, anywhere from the depths of She'ol to up in the heights."[27] This three-layered map of the cosmos can also be seen in Norse, Navajo, Mayan, Celtic, Greek, Egyptian, Siberian and other indigenous cultures through the world.

The term "mothers" emphasizes the fecundity of the elements. The notion of elemental fecundity already exists in Jewish sources. In Genesis, each zone is a place teeming with entities: heaven has its angels and birds, the realm of air has humans, animals, and plants, and the realm of the sea/underworld has fish and its sea monsters—and maybe spirits and demons. Consider the biblical texts in which God says: "Let the earth bring forth vegetation"[28] and "Let the waters swarm with living creatures."[29] The elements are not inert; they bring forth life.

The elements are interwoven in partnership. In Chapter 1, the first four *sefirot* (Divine Breath, Wind, Water, Fire) give rise to one another in a particular order. In Chapter 3, none of the three mothers precedes the other. They come into being as a whole.

The elements are a landscape. We can walk around inside the three mothers. We can look up at their bright skies or down into their deep waters. Though the three mothers exist within the cosmic frames of the *sefirot*, the mothers too provide a frame for our experience. They nourish us with their rivers, rain, sun, and soil. We might say they are the three levels of the world-temple.[30]

Fire Above   אש למעלה

In understanding fire as the element of heaven, *Sefer Yetzirah* is drawing on biblical material. Rabbi David Cavill has written a definitive study of the ways that biblical fire "represents a manifestation of the divine."[31] For example, a "fiery ever-turning sword" guards the Garden of Eden.[32] Fire "from YHWH out of heaven" consumes Sodom,[33] and "YHWH comes down in fire" on Mount Sinai when God reveals the commandments.[34] The blazing fire of Moses' burning bush, and the pillar of fire that leads the Israelites out of Egypt, are also examples of the connection between fire and divine presence.[35] When an angel appears to Manoah and his wife, the proof of his heavenly status is that their offering is consumed in fire, and "the angel of YHWH ascended in the flames of the altar."[36] There is a strong case to be made, biblically speaking, that fire belongs to heaven rather than earth. Rabbinic texts also speak of fire as coming down from the heavens.[37] *Sefer Yetzirah* understands fire to be a heavenly substance forming God's throne and the angels.[38]

Yet in *Sefer Yetzirah*, the heavens do not appear to be "another world," nor do they appear more important than the other realms. The heavens are not an unthinkable transcendent "Other," but simply one element of the physical universe, balanced by other elements. Heaven is not the center of the cosmos, but one of its poles.

This is a fundamental part of the worldview of the *Book of Creation*. The center of the cosmos is the physical world, where human beings live in their bodies. Heaven, earth, and underworld are part of this physical world, part of the vast engraved network of divine creativity. Human beings can perceive and access sky, earth, and everything in between.

Water Below   מים למטה

From the darkness of the fish's belly, Jonah prays: "From the belly of She'ol I cried out, and you heard my voice. You cast me into the depths, into the heart of the sea."[39] She'ol is a word for the underworld, where the spirits of the ancestors dwell. In the Book of Job, God asks: "Have you come to the sources of the sea, or walked in the bosom of the deep? Have the gates of death been revealed to you, and have you seen the gates of deep darkness?"[40] In the Bible, the world below is associated with water.[41] We may imagine that it is this dark underworld ocean upon which the wind of God hovers at the beginning of Genesis. Indeed, biblical texts describe God drawing a "line on the deep" in order to form the world.[42]

In the model presented by this passage, the below matters just as much as the above. The *Mem* and the *Shin* balance one another; neither one dominates. *Sefer Yetzirah* asserts a dynamic unity rather than a hierarchical duality. This is part of why the book's philosophy is so radical—it invites us to embrace an earth characterized by complex but unified systems, in which all components of the system are equally necessary.

The view of water in Chapter 3 is a little different from the view of water in Chapter 1. In Chapter 1, water gives rise to earth and is the source of the land humans live on. In Chapter 3, water seems to extend a little below the earth, into a mythic realm directly opposite the divine throne. We can only speculate what might be in this realm of deep water: maybe the Leviathan and the sea monsters, or maybe the ancestors. Whatever dwells in the deep, it is a part of the whole.

Wind in the Middle ורוח בנתיים

We often think of our world as "earth." Yet we do not breathe earth but air. It is the layer of air around our planet that allows oxygen-breathing creatures to live and thrive. The Bible also sees air or wind as crucial to human life. The words for soul and spirit—*ruach, neshamah, nefesh*—all mean breath. So when *Sefer Yetzirah* understands the world of humans as a world of air, that is consistent with the biblical portrayal of breath/wind as the definitive quality of living beings.

There is another reason it makes sense that *Sefer Yetzirah* would define its middle world as made of air or wind. *Sefer Yetzirah* frequently focuses on what is empty, carved out, or hollow. The middle world in which humans live is a carved-out world, a world with empty space for us to move and create. God too moves within this world of air, manifesting as the *ruach Elohim* (divine wind) floating on the face of the water, or the *ruach hakodesh* or holy spirit that inspires prophets. Ecophilosopher David Abram makes the beautiful suggestion that the notion of an invisible God may have come from the Hebrew ancestors' experience of the invisible but tangible force of air.[43]

In some manuscripts, this final phrase *ruach beintayim* ("wind between them") reads *ruach chok machria beintayim*: "wind is the engraved law balancing between them." The two opposites are separated by an element that is a buffer between them. Air can absorb the heat of fire and the cool of water, mixing and integrating the two. So too, the human world mixes and integrates heaven and the underworld.

In the book's ritual unfolding, this section seems to invite adepts to take a journey to all three realms. One goes upward with the *Shin*, downward with the *Mem*, or inward with the *Aleph*. The three mothers are spirit guides, leading seekers to the various landscapes of God's world and then inviting them to return to the breath.

Practice: Fire Above, Water Below
Close your eyes and breathe out.

You are at a point
between heaven and earth:
maybe on a mountaintop
or an immense ladder.
You can see a long way in all directions.
You can feel the wind.
Take a breath of this good clean air
to draw strength for your journey.
Ascend from this place
(by climbing, flying, or in any other way)
and enter the realm of fire.
What does this realm look and feel like?
Whom or what do you find here?
What is the wisdom
of the realm of fire?
When you leave,
take some of the fire
in a form you can bring with you.
Return to the point where you started.
Now, descend and enter the realm of water.
What does this realm look and feel like?
Whom or what do you meet here?
What is the wisdom
of the realm of water?
When you leave,
take some of the water
in a form you can bring with you.
Return to the point where you started.
Take out the water and fire you have gathered.
Mix them together.
What happens when you do this?
Breathe this mixture into yourself.
Feel the transformation
as air, water, and fire mix within you.

Breathe out and open your eyes.

Practice: Three Mothers
Close your eyes and breathe out.

The *Shin*, *Mem*, and *Aleph*
arise before you
as three beings:
a fire-being,
a water-being,
a wind-being.
The fire-being
offers you a secret doorway
to the world of fire.
See what you find there,
what you see, hear, and feel.
This world
is your world.
Return to where you started.
The water-being
offers you a secret doorway
to the world of water.
See what you find there,
what you see, hear, and feel.
This world
is your world.
Return to where you started.
The wind-being
offers you a secret doorway
to the world of air.
See what you find there,
what you see, hear, and feel.
This world
is your world.
Return to where you started.
Thank the three beings.
Come to awareness
that each one of them
is part of you.

Breathe out and open your eyes.

Practice: Three Worlds

Close your eyes and breathe out.

It is night.

You are standing on a beach
with your feet in the ocean.

You breathe in the cool air.

Above you are the stars.
You hear and feel the waves.

You are standing in all three worlds at once,
touching the sky,
the earth,
the sea.

Breathe out and open your eyes.

Chapter 3:4 · The Three Soundings

שלש אמות א מ ש
מם דוממת
ש שורקת
אלף רוח
חוק מכריע בינתיים

Three mothers:
Aleph, Mem, Shin.

Mem hums,
Shin hisses,
Aleph is the breath,
the engraved law balancing between them.

This passage contrasts the sounds of the three mother letters. The word "hums" (*domemet*) contains the letter *Mem*. The word "hisses" (*shoreket*) contains *Shin*. And *Aleph*, which makes a sound only when it is voweled, is the sound of the breath. The mothers exist not only in space but in sound. They are still letters, even though they embody worlds. In the ritual of *Sefer Yetzirah*, this passages invites the sounding of the letters as a way of invoking the elemental powers.

The sounds offer a meditative practice: the alternation of the "mmm" and the "shhh" of the *Mem* and *Shin*, with the breath of *Aleph* as a transition between them.

When we hum, we feel it in the belly—the point in the body associated with *Mem*. When we hiss, we feel it in the lips, in the head, which is associated with *Shin*. And *Aleph*, which we might pronounce as "ahh," or as a breathing sound, can be felt in the chest, which is associated with *Aleph*.

Shefa Gold, a master chanter in the Jewish tradition, writes that "chant is the marriage of sound and silence…. When the chant ends, there is a door that must be opened in the silence."[44] The *Aleph*, as part of a sound practice, may introduce this element of silence.

In a similar vein, the *Mem* and *Shin* seem to indicate a kind of constant sound, a background noise to creation. Avivah Zornberg describes God's speech as an interruption of the "murmuring deep," the tehom at the dawn of creation.[45] Zornberg notes the potential dynamic between humming (the sound of the *Mem*) and silence. She quotes Frosh: "... silence itself breaks, interrupts, the continuous murmur of the Real, thus opening up a clearing in which words can be spoken." If we apply this notion to our passage, the shhh or mmm is the sound of being, which is then interrupted by the silence of the *Aleph*. This silence, or open space, makes meaningful sound possible. All words require silence in order to distinguish them from one another.

Yet the hum (or hiss) of being is also powerful and necessary: "The background hum of life—desolate, excessive, neither language nor silence—is what links us to one another."[46] Reading Zornberg's view of the murmuring deep into our encounter with *Sefer Yetzirah*, we might say that the *Mem* and *Shin* provide us with the background hum of life, and *Aleph* provides the silence that allows for speech. To sound the three elemental letters is to resonate with, and to add one's own creative intention to, a hissing, humming, teeming universe.

The Engraved Law   חוק
Balancing Between Them   מכריע בינתיים

As in other passages, the text describes the balancing act of the *Aleph* by saying *Aleph ruach chok machria beintayim*, "*Aleph* is the breath, the law balancing/deciding between them." Remember that the word *chok*, meaning law or rule, also means "engraving." The breath is "engraved" in the body—it moves through open channels. *Aleph* is the engraved hollow space that contains the hum of *Mem* and *Shin*—and perhaps all other sounds as well. So we might say: "*Mem* hums, *Shin* hisses, and *Aleph* is an engraved breath that moves between them."

Practice: *Mem* Hums, *Shin* Hisses

Close your eyes and breathe out.

Sound the *Mem*
מ
a deep mmm sound.
Feel the resonance of *Mem*
through your whole body.
Notice where *Mem* resonates most.

Sound the *Shin*
שׁ
a hissing shhh sound.
Feel the resonance of *Shin*
through your whole body.
Notice where *Shin* resonates most.

Sound the *Aleph*
א
a breathy ahh sound.
Feel the resonance of *Aleph*
through your whole body.
Notice where *Aleph* resonates most.

Now, come to silence.

What happens
in your heart, mind, and body
in the silence after the sound?

Breathe out and open your eyes.

Practice: Elemental Sounds

Close your eyes and breathe out.

As you sound the *Mem*,
a deep mmm sound in the belly
waters flow in you.
Let the waters cleanse you.

As you sound the *Shin*,
a soft shh sound in the head
fires stir in you.
Let the fire enliven you.

As you sound the *Aleph*,
an open ahh sound in the chest,
breath moves in you.
Let the breath heal you.

Breathe out and open your eyes.

Chapter 3:5 · The Father Letters

שלש אמות א מ ש
ומהן נולדו אבות
שמהם נבראו הכל

Three mothers: Aleph, Mem, Shin
And from them were born three fathers
from whom everything was created.

Peter Hayman, on whose critical edition this translation relies, does not believe this passage is original to *Sefer Yetzirah*, but rather is a later addition. Hayman notes that in the Saadyan Recension this passage is entirely missing.[47] However, the passage is included here to allow us to reflect on the "three fathers" and their impact on the image of the mothers.

As noted in the introduction, the three fathers may be an editorial product of discomfort with the book's focus on feminine entities as primary cosmic forces. In 6:2, the fathers substitute for the mothers as the primary elemental sources. In 1:13, we noted that the manuscript of *Sefer Yetzirah* used by Aryeh Kaplan adds the "three fathers" and describes them as entities/letters stemming from the three mothers.[48] There, the three fathers are synonymous with the letters *Yud*, *Heh*, and *Vav*—the three letters of the divine name. In one version of Chapter 5, the three fathers embody the elements of air, water, and fire (thus superseding the mothers).[49]

The three fathers hint at the "three fathers" of Genesis (Abraham, Isaac, and Jacob). In this sense, they seem like partners to the three mothers. Yet if the three mothers have anything like a partner, it is God, not the three fathers. It is notable that the fathers are not spouses of the mothers; they are *noldu* (born) from the mothers. The root (*yud-lamed-dalet*) implies the birth of one entity from another. Another way to read it is as a kind of alchemical statement: the fathers proceed from the mothers or can be titrated from them.

The image of fathers being born from mothers is reminiscent of Middle Eastern traditions in which goddesses and their sons form powerful pairings (Isis/Horus, Mary/Jesus, etc.). the mothers remain a prominent force. Still, this image of fathers changes the primary nature of the three mothers. In the earlier layers of the text, God and the three mothers form an intimate partnership. In the "three fathers" tradition, it seems that the mothers and the fathers are paired, with God as the distant source of all of them. This introduces more of a monogamous, heterosexual ethos into the text—even though the fathers are "born" from the mothers, it is hard not to think of the mothers and fathers as paired. Thus, the "couple" becomes the prominent image, rather than the threefold grouping of the mothers.

This coupling, though it may come from a later layer of the text, allows later kabbalists to square their masculine-feminine-balanced system with the *Sefer Yetzirah*.[50] The later kabbalah concerns itself a great deal with the balancing and pairing of masculine and feminine forces. Such pairings are sometimes framed as love relationships and include the relationship of *Chochmah* (Wisdom) and *Binah* (Understanding), also known as *Abba* (Father) and *Imma* (Mother)—and, the pairing of *Tiferet* (Beauty) and *Malkhut* (Sovereignty), also known as the Bridegroom and Bride, or the Holy One of Blessing and Shekhinah. The Zohar also describes mother-son and father-daughter pairings within the Godhead—*Binah* (mother) and *Tiferet* (son), *Binah* (mother) and *Malkhut/Shekhinah* (daughter), or *Keter* (father) and *Malkhut/Shekhinah* (daughter).[51] These richly imagined male-female partnerships reflect Jewish mystics' diverse imaginings of the role of gender pairings in the understanding and experience of the Godhead. The "mothers and fathers" can be reconciled with this complex gendered theological system far more easily than the mothers on their own.

Yet in the earliest layers of *Sefer Yetzirah*, the text is not concerned with pairing mothers and fathers. The relationship between God and the creative feminine forces is enough. No further duality is necessary.

Practice: Three Fathers

Close your eyes and breathe out.

Air, water, and fire,
the three mothers,
are before you.

Perceive them fully
in whatever way they appear to you.

As you observe,
each of the three mothers gives birth:
air, then water, then fire.

Take note of the three entities
born to the three mothers.

How do you envision them?

Observe as these three newly born entities
find their right place in the world.

Breathe out and open your eyes.

Return to the Place

Chapter 3:6-9 · Three Mothers in Three Worlds

These passages likely do not stem from the earliest recoverable version of *Sefer Yetzirah*.[52] They are omitted from the Saadyan Recension (one of the most important manuscripts), and, they duplicate too closely the passages that come after them. However, they have been included here because they clearly show how the three worlds of space, time, and person interact with the three mothers.

3:6 · Mothers in the World

שלש אמות א מ ש
בעולם
רוח ומים ואש
שמים נבראו מאש
וארץ נבראת ממים
ואויר נברא מרוח
מכריע בינתיים

Three mothers Aleph, Mem, Shin
in the world:
air, water, fire.
Sky was created from fire,
earth from water,
and air was created from breath
balancing between them.

3:7 · Mothers in the Year

שלש אמות א מ ש
בשנה
אש מים ורוח
חום נברא מאש
וקור נברא ממים
ורויה מרוח
מכריע בינתיים

Three mothers Aleph, Mem, Shin
in the year:
fire, water, air.
Heat was created from fire,
cold from water,
and the overflowing
from the air balancing between them.

3:8 · Mothers in the Body

שלש אמות א מ ש
בנפש
ראש נברא מאש
ובטן ממים
וגויה מרוח מכריע בינתיים

Three mothers Aleph, Mem, Shin
in the body-soul:
the head was created from fire,
the belly from water,
and the chest, from air,
balances between them.

3:9 · Three Mothers in Three Worlds

שלש אמות א מ ש
חקקן חצבן צרפן
וחתם בהם שלש אימות בעולם
ושלש אימות בשנה
ושלש אימות בנפש
זכר ונקבה

Three mothers—Aleph, Mem, Shin—God
engraved them, carved them, combined them,
and sealed with them
three mothers in the world
three mothers in the year
and three mothers in the body-soul,
male and female.

Each of the letters manifests in three forms, for each of the "books" of space, time, and soul.[53] The mother letters, double letters, and simple letters all have a spatial form, a temporal form, and a form in the human body. The forms of the three mothers correspond to the primary divisions of space, time, and body-soul.

In space (*olam*), the three mothers *Shin*, *Mem*, and *Aleph* are (respectively) sky, earth, and the space in between. The space in between is called *avir*: air or atmosphere. Within the frame of the six directions set by the spatial *sefirot* (north, south, east, west, up, down), the three mothers provide the three strata that constitute the world-space.

In time (*shanah*), the three mothers *Shin*, *Mem*, and *Aleph* manifest as heat, cold, and a third season called *revayah* or "overflowing." *Revayah* seems to equal a season between the cold winter and hot summer. Within the frame set by the temporal *sefirot* of "beginning and end," the three mothers provide a cyclical pattern of changing seasons.

In *nefesh* (body-soul), *Shin*, *Mem*, and *Aleph* are the head, belly, and chest, with the chest (air) as a midpoint between the head and the belly.

Gaviah, the Hebrew word translated here as "chest," actually means "body" or "torso."[54] The word is also connected to *gav*, the word for "back." So the *gaviah*, or body, is the middle torso, that which connects the head with the belly. Within the frame set by the ethical/experiential *sefirot* of "good" and "evil," the three mothers provide the primary zones of the human body.

The mind, heart, and belly are all seats of experience, where we tend to locate our feelings and thoughts. These three centers of consciousness give us access to good and bad, suffering and joy. These areas of the body—mind, heart, gut—let us know what is right and wrong, what hurts and what heals. That the zones of the body arise from the three mothers means that the body is always connected to heaven and earth. The structure of the human person reflects the world's structure, and our internal powers reflect the great elemental powers of sky and the sea and the land. This ecospiritual insight, arising from a text fifteen hundred years old, is profoundly relevant to our current understanding of life on this planet.

Air   אויר

The dimension of space more or less duplicates what we have already been told: the three mothers form the sky, the earth, and the atmosphere in between. Here, however, the middle space is called *avir* (air) rather than *ruach* (breath/wind). This separates the element of air somewhat from the primordial element of wind/spirit—as if, as the world develops, it moves farther away from its divine origins.

As we have noted, because of *Sefer Yetzirah*'s unusual "three-element" system, there is no mother letter for earth. Instead, *Mem*, the water, gives rise to *eretz*, land, just as the Psalmist writes: "You spread out the earth upon the waters."[55] In the psalm and in our current passage, *eretz* implies the "land" rather than the "soil," which would be *afar* or *adamah*.

Overflowing   ורויה

In the dimension of time, the seasons are "heat," "cold," and *revayah*. "Heat" is clearly summer, and "cold" is clearly winter. But what season is *revayah*? Clearly it is some kind of balance between summer and winter, just as the *Aleph* balances between *Mem* and *Shin*. In the Bible, *revayah* means "saturated" or "overflowing" with liquid, as in "my cup overflows."[56] We aren't told whether *revayah* refers to one season (thus dividing the year into three seasons for the three mothers) or two seasons, autumn and spring (the "moderate" seasons, in contrast to winter and summer).

In 3:9 Kaplan translates *revayah* as "temperate"[57] (i.e., spring and autumn, when warm air mixes with cool air and temperatures are just right). In this translation, *revayah* seems to mean "saturated with warmth," that is, a beneficent mixture of cold and heat. Hayman, however, translates *revayah* as "humidity," presumably referring to a season when there is moisture in the air: not the dryness of summer, but not the cold rains of winter.[58]

However, there is another possibility. If *Sefer Yetzirah* was written in Mesopotamia as Weiss has posited, we should note that for thousands of years, the spring in Mesopotamia has been characterized by the flooding of the Tigris and Euphrates rivers. This flooding then waters the fields and makes the land fertile (hence the name Fertile Crescent). It is possible that *revayah* or "overflowing season" refers to springtime and the overflowing of the rivers which makes the land fertile. If we read the text this way, the word means exactly what it appears to mean: "overflowing."

How would a flooding season be a balance of water and fire? Winter, with its rains, would be cold and wet, and summer would be hot and dry. Spring would be a mixture of cold (snow) and heat (which melts the snow and thus floods the rivers). Therefore, *revayah* could refer to flooding season. However we translate it, *revayah* is clearly the season that balances and integrates heat and cold, just as the *Aleph* balances and integrates *Mem* and *Shin*.

Sealed with Them וחתם בהם

As we have noted elsewhere, "sealing" is a magical concept that involves expelling negative forces from a place or entity. The sealing of space, time, and body-soul marks all of these entities as sacred spaces—temples, if you will—that the Divine protects with a magical spell. The three mother letters become the seals for the three mother elements as they manifest in the three "books" or realms of existence.[59]

The "three mothers" seal the "three mothers." Hayman reasons that this does not make sense: a set of letters shouldn't seal itself. Yet according to these passages, the mothers manifest both as letters and as forms in the physical universe. If that is the case, the words may mean that God used the *Aleph*, *Mem*, and *Shin* to seal the sky, earth, and air. There are parallels between this language of "sealing" earth and sky in other Jewish magical literature of the time: one incantation bowl speaks of a bond of heaven and a seal of earth,[60] and another speaks of "the great seal of heaven and earth."[61] *Aleph*, *Mem*, and *Shin* function as the seals of

Body-Soul   בנפש

heaven and earth, just as in 1:14 the *Yud*, *Heh*, and *Vav* function as the seals of the six directions.

Body-Soul   בנפש

As has been noted in Chapter 1, it is extremely difficult to translate the word *nefesh*. In many biblical and post-biblical texts, *nefesh* means "soul" or "spirit" as when the Psalmist says "bless the Lord, my soul" or when Rachel's soul/life-force leaves her in Genesis 35.[62] Yet in many other texts, *nefesh* means a body. In Genesis 1, a living animal creature is called a *nefesh chaya*, a living being. In Genesis 2, the new human being Adam is called a *nefesh chaya*, a living being. In Leviticus, a person is called a *nefesh*. And in Deuteronomy, *nefesh tachat nefesh* means "a life for a life" (Deut. 9:21).[63] In Numbers, a *nefesh met* means a dead body.[64] Later, in rabbinic literature, *nefesh* also means "soul," "life-force," or "person"—the word *nefesh* is used, for example, when Rabbi Akiva's soul leaves him[65] but it is also used to designate "a person."[66] Later kabbalah certainly understands *nefesh* as soul, though it sees the *nefesh* as the aspect of the soul most connected to the body.[67] *Sefer Yetzirah* seems to use a meaning of *nefesh* that spans the body and the soul and assumes the two are one entity.

Male and Female   זכר ונקבה

The phrase "male and female" qualifies the word *nefesh*, and seems to imply that the body-soul comes in two varieties: male and female. The two varieties of human being are listed as equal, without any hierarchy being established. This would seem to hearken back to Genesis 1, where God creates the human in God's image, male and female.[68] Again, *Sefer Yetzirah* is leaning toward a more egalitarian interpretation of human experience.

In some versions of *Sefer Yetzirah*, gender doesn't only apply to the human being. Seals also can be male or female. There are versions of *Sefer Yetzirah* that list two seals for each of the three mother letters—one male, one female.[69] The two seals of *Aleph* are *Aleph Mem Shin* (male) and *Aleph Shin Mem* (female); the two seals of *Mem* are *Mem Shin Aleph* (male) and *Mem Aleph Shin* (female); the two seals of *Shin* are *Shin Mem Aleph* (male) and *Shin Aleph Mem* (female).[70] These six seals of the three mother letters are comprised of the six different combinations of *Aleph*, *Mem*, and *Shin*. This later addition spells out the implication that the six "seal-rings" of 3:2 are the six combinations of the three mother letters. This listing of the six seals also implies that each element—air, water, and fire—has a dual, gendered aspect.

We might imagine that these seals would manifest as air, water or fire in a male or female form: differently gendered element-angels. (Similarly, in one Jewish legend, the cherubim were said to be male and female, and even to engage in intimate embrace.)[71] We also might imagine these gendered seals as codes for creation. The gendering of the elemental seals might be an explanation for how gender arises in human beings: different combinations of the letters might form chest, belly, and head differently for differently gendered people. We might even imagine that gender-elements can be mixed and matched to produce a whole host of genders.

Practice: Three Breaths

Close your eyes and breathe out.

Breathe into your chest.
This is the *Aleph* breath.
Imagine the branching shape of the *aleph*

א

in your chest,
or simply breathe "*Aah*."
Feel the air, the *aleph*,
moving in your chest
and through your body.
Now, breathe into your belly.
This is the *Mem* breath.
Imagine the rounded shape of the *mem*

מ

in your belly,
or simply breathe "*Mmm*."
Feel the water, the *mem*,
moving in your belly
and through your body.
Now, breathe into the crown of your head.
This is the *Shin* breath.
Imagine the flaming shape of the *Shin*

ש

at the crown of your head,
or simply breathe "*Shhh*."
Feel the fire, the *Shin*,
moving in your head
and through your body.
Cycle through these three breaths again:
chest: air, *Aleph*, *Aah*.
belly: water, *Mem*, *Mmm*.
head: fire, *Shin*, *Shhh*.
Cycle through them a third time.
As you breathe,
feel the three parts of the body,
the three elements come together into a whole.

Breathe out and open your eyes.

Practice: Two Beings

Close your eyes and breathe out.

Two wind-beings face you,
male and female or of non-binary gender.
How are they the same and different?
What are their gifts for you?

Two water-beings face you,
male and female or of non-binary gender.
How are they the same and different?
What are their gifts for you?

Two fire-beings face you,
male and female or of non-binary gender.
How are they the same and different?
What are their gifts for you?

Envision the six beings
in a circle around you,
offering you their blessing.

Notice which being
among these six
draws you,
and invite that being
to be your guide
throughout this day.

Breathe out and open your eyes.

Chapter 3:10 · *Aleph:* Wind

המליך אות אלף ברוח
וקשר לו כתר
וחתם בו
אויר בעולם
רויה בשנה
וגויה בנפש

God made the letter *Aleph*
rule over wind
and tied a crown to it
and sealed with it
air in the world
the overflowing in time
and the chest in the body-soul.

As Chapter 3 winds to its conclusion, the final three passages list (as if in a magical encyclopedia) the three mother letters, the elements they govern, and the entities that arise from them. The letter *Aleph* is first in this sequence. *Aleph* shapes and seals the entities in space, time, and body that connect to air: the breathing-zone of earthly beings, the "overflowing" season of spring, and the chest or torso—the lungs and heart, where air circulates through the body.

Aleph is the mediator/integrator/fulcrum of opposing forces. *Aleph* is the middle world, the middle of the body, the middle of the year. Its shape lends itself beautifully to this position, since the *Aleph* is formed by a single diagonal stroke with a balancing leg on either side. The shape of the *Aleph* (which arises from the pictogram of a horned ox) seems to embody its function as the holder of "middle" space. Stretching its arms to either side, *Aleph* becomes the letter of balance.

The passage introduces a new term—*himlich* (to make king, or to cause to rule over). In other words, God is delegating some of God's sovereignty over the universe to the *Aleph*. As part of this delegation of power, God ties a crown to *Aleph*. This is both metaphysical and calligraphic. Some of the letters of the Torah are written with crowns, which is a kind of calligraphic artistry. In one Talmudic legend, God embellishes the letters with crowns in order that future sages should find meaning in them.

> When Moses went up to the heights, he found the Holy One of Blessing sitting and tying crowns to the letters. He said to the Holy One: "Master of the Universe, who prevents you [from giving me the Torah without crowns]? God said: A person will exist many generations in the future—his name is Akiva ben Yosef—and he will interpret piles and piles of laws from every crown and embellishment.[72]

In other words, the crown of the *Aleph* is an indication of its many layers of meaning. In the Talmud, the Hebrew phrase for embellishing the letters with crowns is *kosher ketarim*—tying or connecting crowns to the letters. A version of the same phrase appears in our passage. Yet God does not tie crowns to the letters for the purpose of interpretive embellishment, but for the purpose of connecting the letters to their respective phenomena in the cosmos. The tying of the crown becomes not only a scribal flourish, but a metaphysical connection between word and world.

The *Aleph* does not only "rule;" it also "seals." As if wielding a signet ring, God engraves the *Aleph* into the world. This magical action serves to solidify, confirm, and protect phenomena, and make the world a contained and supportive space for created beings. As a letter, *Aleph* communicates sound, shape, and meaning, but as a seal, *Aleph* shapes the features of the world and gives them God's blessing and protection.

In the spell that is *Sefer Yetzirah*, this passage is the only one that focuses specifically on the *Aleph* as an independent entity. It seems meant to invoke and summon *Aleph* by naming its powers. We could imagine reciting it as part of the larger ritual of *Sefer Yetzirah*, or as a particular invocation of the *Aleph*'s balancing gifts.

Practice: *Aleph*

Close your eyes and breathe out.

See the *Aleph* before you:
א
Breathe in the gift of *Aleph:*
wind, breath, spirit.
Feel *Aleph* spreading in your chest.

As you breathe,
let the shape of *Aleph*
extend through your body.

Sound the sound of *Aleph:*
Aah.
Let the sound vibrate and resonate through you,
cleansing and expanding.

Let this sound hold a blessing:
a blessing for movement, balance, unfurling.
Envision the impact of this blessing
inside your body.

Breathe out and open your eyes.

Practice: Rule over Wind

Close your eyes and breathe out.

You are sitting in a high windy place,
wearing the *Aleph* as a ring.
This ring appears exactly as you imagine it.

The ring allows you to summon the power of wind.

Ask the wind to rise all around you.
Use the wind to shape your world.
How does your world transform
as you release the wind?

Let the wind die down.

Look all around you.
Discover what is new and different
in the world
and in yourself.

Breathe out and open your eyes.

Chapter 3:11 · *Mem:* Water

המליך אות מם במים
וקשר לו כתר
וחתם בו
ארץ בעולם
וקור בשנה
ובטן בנפש

God made the letter *Mem*
rule over water
and tied a crown to it
and sealed with it
earth in the world
the cold in time
and the belly in the body.

Mem is the lower level of the world-temple. Located "below" the *Aleph*, *Mem* is water-earth below the air, belly below the chest. Its watery depths are the *tehom*, the great deep, that lies beneath existence. *Mem* is groundwater running beneath the earth. *Mem* is the undergirding of the ordered realm. In placing *Mem* before *Shin* in the sequence of mother-letters, *Sefer Yetzirah* again tells us that earth comes before heaven. The undergirding must be stable before the ceiling can be built.

Mem shapes and seals the entities in space, time, and body that connect to water: the earth underfoot, which *Sefer Yetzirah* sees as "mud" formed from water; the cold and rainy season of winter; and the belly. The "belly" or *beten* can mean abdomen, but can also mean "womb."[73] (The Bible speaks of the "fruit of the belly.")[74] *Sefer Yetzirah* uses this term that is gender neutral or even weighted toward the feminine, but likely means to include the phallus as well, and to associate *Mem* with the human reproductive capacity. Similarly, *Shin*, head, is associated with the tongue and language. This brings us back to 1:3 and the connection between *milah* (word) and *milah* (circumcision, i.e., phallus). If the *rosh*/head sustains life through speech and the *gaviah*/chest sustains life through breath, the *beten* sustains life through conception and birth.

The femininity of the *Mem*, and its connection to birth, is emphasized through the language of "belly." One has the strong sense that the belly is connected to *tehom*, the underwaters, the primordial ocean and its life-giving yet chaotic powers of creation. In Jonah 2:3, Jonah refers to the *beten She'ol*, the belly of the underworld. So too, the *beten* here is connected to the underworld, the waters under the earth. *Mem* has a rounded shape like a hill of earth that embodies womb, well, or cave.[75] *Mem* holds empty space within itself. The sound of *Mem* comes from down low in the belly: the *mmm* of a satisfied stomach or a feeling deep in the gut.

It is interesting to relate *Mem* to the gut. Scientists now know that the gut is lined with millions of nerve cells, as well as a nerve circuit that can rapidly communicate with the brain.[76] There is a way that the gut is a kind of second mind, letting us know of deep feelings and body sensations. And of course, humans knew this long before modern neuroscience— we speak of a "gut feeling." In the Bible, someone's "guts are moved" when they have strong feelings.[77] Not only this, but the heart has "cardiac ganglia" or groups of neurons that influence processing, perceptions, and emotions.[78] Thinking of the *Aleph*, *Mem* and *Shin* (belly and head) as three thought/feeling centers is one way to understand the relationship of these powers in the body.

In the spell that is *Sefer Yetzirah*, this passage is the only one that focuses specifically on the *Mem* as an independent entity. The passage seems meant to invoke and summon the *Mem* by naming its powers. We could imagine reciting it as part of the larger ritual of *Sefer Yetzirah*, or as a particular invocation of the *Mem*'s tehomic powers.

Practice: *Mem*

Close your eyes and breathe out.

See the *Mem* before you:
מ
Breathe in the gift of *Mem*:
water, earth, depth.
Feel *Mem* in your belly.

As you breathe,
let the shape of *Mem*—
the shape of a cave or a womb—
move through your body.

Sound the sound of *Mem*:
M*mm*.
Let the sound vibrate and resonate through you,
enlivening, nourishing, healing.

Let this sound hold a blessing:
of flowing, deepening, life-giving.
Envision the impact of this blessing
inside your body.

Breathe out and open your eyes.

Practice: Rule over Water

Close your eyes and breathe out.

You are sitting by the edge of a body of water,
wearing the *Mem* as a ring.
This ring appears exactly as you imagine it.

The ring allows you to summon the power of water.

Ask the water to flow all around you.
Use the water to shape your world.
How does your world transform
as you release the water?

Let the water return to its place.

Look all around you.
Discover what is new and different
in the world
and in yourself.

Breathe out and open your eyes.

Chapter 3:12 · *Shin:* Fire

המליך אות שין באש
וקשר לו כתר
וחתם בו
שמים בעולם
וחום בשנה
וראש בנפש

God made the letter *Shin*
rule over fire
and tied a crown to it
and sealed with it
sky in the world
the heat in time
and the head in the body.

Last in the sequence of mother-letters is the *Shin*. *Sefer Yetzirah* typically includes heaven as an aspect of the earthly realm, and here, as in Chapter One, heaven seems to come last rather than first. Yet the fire of *Shin* holds something of the awe and wonder of heaven. Fire is both bright and untouchable, just as heaven is both illuminating and inaccessible to human beings.

As the letter governing the element of fire, *Shin* shapes and seals the entities in space, time, and body that connect to fire: the sky overhead, the hot season of summer, and the head. *Shin* typically manifests "above" the other mother letters: sky is above earth; head is above chest and belly. We might think of *Shin* as the top layer of the world: the celestial dome with its bright lights. Sky and fire occupy the "up" direction; David Cavill has noted that in the Bible, divine fire typically comes "down" from heaven,[79] and the fires on biblical altars seem meant to send sustenance and prayer "up" to God's dwelling. *Shin* is the ceiling of the human realm, from which descend the fiery entities: angels, divine voices, and light.

The head is closest to the sky of all the body parts, and the head lifts us upright to stand closer to heaven. The head connects to heat, as there is a sense of heat in the head when one is excited or enlivened. One's face can become flushed, one's eyes can "light up." The head is the primary seat of consciousness, thought, and feeling, and also the place where speech emerges. The face is the site of verbal creativity: words, song, meaning. *Sefer Yetzirah* portrays the head as connected to the fires of heaven because, through language, human beings access the creative powers of God.

In the spell that is *Sefer Yetzirah*, this passage is the only one that focuses specifically on the *Shin* as an independent entity. The passage seems meant to invoke and summon the *Shin* by naming its powers. We could imagine reciting it as part of the larger ritual of *Sefer Yetzirah*, or as a particular invocation of the *Shin*'s fiery gifts.

It makes sense that we seal Chapter 3 with *Shin*, fire, the element of sky. In some sense, the mothers give us an intimation of the ways of heaven. Like divine fire descending to the altar, the three mothers channel God's energy into our world. They are the most powerful of the twenty-two letters of Wisdom.

Practice: *Shin*

Close your eyes and breathe out.

The *Shin* is before you:
ש
Breathe in the *Shin*:
fire, flame, light.
Feel the *Shin*
as a flame at the crown of your head.

As you breathe,
let the flame of *Shin*
radiate through your body.
Sound the sound of *Shin*:
Shhh.
Let the sound vibrate and resonate through you,
igniting, awakening, invigorating.

Let this sound hold a blessing:
of inspiration, energy, illumination.
Envision the impact of this blessing
inside your body.

Breathe out and open your eyes.

Practice: Rule Over Fire

Close your eyes and breathe out.

You are sitting in the sunlight or under a bright moon,
wearing the *Shin* as a ring.
This ring appears exactly as you imagine it.

The ring allows you to summon the power of fire.

Ask the fire to flow all around you.
Use the fire to shape your world.
How does your world transform
as you release the fire?

Let the fire subside.

Look all around you.
Discover what is new and different
in the world
and in yourself.

Breathe out and open your eyes.

Chapter 4:1 · The Seven Double Letters

Seven double letters:	שבע כפולות
bet gimel dalet kaf peh reish tav	בגד כפרת
Expressed in two manners:	מתנהגות בשתי לשונות
life	חיים
peace	ושלום
wisdom	וחכמה
wealth	ועשר
grace	חן
seed	זרע
sovereignty	ממשלה
and pronounced in two manners:	ומתנהגות בשתי לשונות
bet vet	בי בי
gimel jimel	גימל גימל
dalet thalet	דלת דלת
kaf khaf	כף כף
peh feh	פי פי
reish hreish	ריש ריש
tav thav	תיו תיו
soft and hard	רך וקשה
strong and weak	גיבור וחלש
Doubles that are transformations:	כפולות שהן תמורות
the transformation of life is death	תמורת חיים מות
the transformation of peace is evil	תמורת שלום רע
the transformation of wisdom is foolishness	תמורת חכמה אולת
the transformation of wealth is poverty	תמורת עשר עוני
the transformation of seed is desolation	תמורת זרע שממה
the transformation of grace is ugliness	תמורת חן כיאור
the transformation of sovereignty is slavery	תמורת ממשלה עבדות

Chapter 4 now opens the door to a new set of letters: the double letters. This set of letters is unique in that each letter manifests in two ways. This is true grammatically: double letters manifest in two different sounds depending on placement in a word. It is also true metaphysically: each letter manifests two opposing qualities or states of human experience. One state is beneficial, the other detrimental. The double letters are a series of seven dualities that create diversity and polarity in our experience.

The seven double letters do not deal with elemental forces like water and air, but with the experiences of human beings: life and death, abundance and lack. We might name these seven states "societal elements," as distinct from the mothers which are "natural elements." Just as the core expressions of the mothers are air, water, and fire, the core expressions of the seven double letters are the seven dual states.

Seven Double Letters, Expressed in Two Manners   שבע כפולות מתנהגות בשתי לשונות

The seven beneficial states are: life, peace, wisdom, wealth, grace (beauty), seed (fertility), and sovereignty. The seven detrimental states are the opposite: death, evil, foolishness, poverty, ugliness, desolation, and slavery. All seven states relate to the circumstances of humankind: one can be alive or dead, at peace or at war, wise or foolish, wealthy or poor, beautiful or ugly, fertile or infertile, free or enslaved.

In some versions of the *Sefer Yetzirah*, we see direct correspondences between the seven letters and the seven states: *bet* corresponds to life, *gimel* to peace, *dalet* to wisdom, *kaf* to wealth, *peh* to grace, *reish* to seed, and *tav* to sovereignty.[1] However, in Aryeh Kaplan's text (the Gaon of Vilna's version), *bet* corresponds to wisdom, *gimel* to wealth, *dalet* to seed, *kaf* to life, *peh* to sovereignty, *reish* to peace, and *tav* to grace.[2] The correspondences between the letters and the states are difficult to sort out, since the earliest strata of the text do not directly make these correspondences. However, we can provisionally assume that the order of the letters corresponds to the order of the states.[3]

What is the nature of the seven states? One can sometimes make an impact on one's health, wealth, wisdom, beauty, or power, but one can also come into such circumstances with no choice at all. Whether we live or die has to do as much with external factors as with any choices we make. The seven states are partly a result of our actions, but also partly beyond our control. Therefore, the seven states cannot properly be labeled as human faculties: rather, they are our circumstances.

We might adopt an attitude of equanimity toward these circumstances. Things like wealth, peace, and life come and go, and we may experience all of them in the course of our lives. In this view, the best way to relate to this ephemerality is to observe these states without attachment. Or we might adopt an attitude of agency: we might use the power of the letters to change these states, turning poverty to wealth, foolishness to wisdom, etc. In this view, we are meant to try to transform our lives and the world. The double letters could become tools for changing our circumstances.

We might understand Chapter 4 as offering both of these approaches: meditative and magical. We could imagine a contemplative practice in which we reflect on opposing qualities until their differences melt away and we see them as equal. As the Muslim mystic poet Agahi Dede wrote: "Leave all your hopeless duality... I don't care if I live in ruins or hold the whole world in my hand."[4] We also could imagine a practice in which the seven double letters, in their beneficent form, become allies that manifest our desires in the world. In a similar vein, the ancient poet Sappho cries to Aphrodite, the power of love: "What my heart most hopes will happen/make happen; you yourself join forces on my side!"[5] The creative tension of these two "opposite" approaches enriches the narrative of *Sefer Yetzirah*—and extends the theme of Chapter 4, which is "opposites."

While later kabbalists made efforts to link the seven states of *Sefer Yetzirah* to the lower seven *sefirot* of the Zohar,[6] the two lists do not easily map onto one another. For example, in the Zohar, "wisdom" is one of the three upper *sefirot*, not one of the lower seven *sefirot*, yet Wisdom is associated with one of the seven double letters. Interestingly, in the Long and Saadyan Recensions, *tav*, the final letter of the *aleph-bet* and the seventh of the double letters, corresponds to *memshalah* or sovereignty. It could be that this text influenced later kabbalists to understand their final *sefirah* as *Malkhut*—kingship or sovereignty.

Pronounced in Two Manners   מתנהגות בשתי לשונות

The phrase *mitnahagot b'shtei leshonot* (pronounced in two manners) appears twice in our passage, and it means different things in its different locations. The first time, it means that the letters metaphysically express particular qualities and their opposites. In that case, it's been translated "expressed in two manners." The second time, the phrase clearly means "pronounced in two manners" and refers to the linguistic qualities of the seven double letters.

It is a well-known attribute of the Hebrew language that certain letters have two forms of pronunciation, depending on where they are placed in a word. The shift in pronunciation is generally marked by a *dagesh* (dot) placed within the letter. Bet with a *dagesh* is pronounced "b;" bet without a *dagesh* is pronounced "v." The dot at the center appears or disappears, but everything else about the letter's form remains the same. These two forms are the physical manifestation of the letters' metaphysical "double" quality.

Not all of the double letters are pronounced differently by all Jewish communities: for example, Sephardic Hebrew does not distinguish between the two forms of *tav* (though Yiddish does—*tav* and *sav*—and Iraqi Hebrew does—*tav* and *thav*). Nor do many Hebrew speakers distinguish among the two forms of *Gimel*, though Yemenite and Iraqi Jewish speakers do, and Yemenite Jews distinguish the two forms of *Dalet* as well.[7] Nevertheless, the intention of our passage seems to be that the dualities inherent in the letters have a physical expression in their sound as well as their shape.

The passage describes the sound-forms of the letters as *rakh vekashe*, "soft and hard." Christian Syriac literature of the period uses similar terms to describe the two forms of particular Aramaic letters: *rukhakha* (soft) and *qushshaya* (hard). Jews in other contexts of the time period don't generally use the terms "soft" and "hard" to describe pronunciation. Tzahi Weiss believes this is a support for the Syriac (Mesopotamian) context of *Sefer Yetzirah*.[8]

Generally Hebrew understands there to be only six double letters (*bet, gimel, dalet, kaf, peh, tav*)—the *reish* is not included in the list. Scholars have debated whether *Sefer Yetzirah* added the *reish* out of the need to complete a list of seven, or whether it was written in a Jewish ethnic context where the *reish* actually has two forms of pronunciation.[9]

Doubles That Are Transformations   כפולות שהן תמורות

Our passage names the dualities or oppositions inherent in each of the seven double letters *temurot* (singular *temurah*). The word *temurah* in its biblical context means "substitution" or "exchange." If one donates an animal to the Temple and wishes to donate a different animal instead, one is not permitted to do so; but if one did make such an exchange (*temurah*), both animals become holy.[10] In the Talmud, the term is also used for other kinds of exchange (for example, hostage exchange).[11]

As a word referring to ritual sacrifice, *temurah* evokes Temple practice, as if the pairs of double letters are offerings in the temple of the world.

To say that life is a *temurah*, an exchange, for death seems to imply that both are holy—just as in the biblical text, when one offering is switched for another, both become holy. The instruction to the practitioner may be that when we work with the pairs of opposites, we may find one member of the pair more desirable than the other, but we must understand the holiness in both.

But in *Sefer Yetzirah*, *temurah* can also mean permutation. Aryeh Kaplan translates it as "transposition," which means switching letters. This translation recalls the book's practice of arranging letters in different combinations. In a sense, the rearranging of reality is simply a rearranging of letters. Similarly, *temurah* becomes a word kabbalists use for the permutation of letters or the rearranging of words and sentences in the Bible to derive deeper meaning.

Exchanging one form of a letter for another is a mundane grammatical procedure, yet this passage seems to indicate that there is a deep power to the shifting of the sounds and shapes of letters. Therefore, one appropriate translation for *temurah* is "transformation." For *Sefer Yetzirah*, the rearranging of letters is the rearranging of elements. Changes in the letters become changes in the physical world.

There is perhaps a hint to the practitioner in the word *temurah*: within the disciplined mind, one state can shift to another. Death can be exchanged for life; foolishness for wisdom. The temple that is consciousness allows for such exchanges, such shifts in being. Perhaps the intimation is that one who opens to the paths of wisdom can pull grace out of ugliness, fecundity out of stagnation. We only need to "return to the place."

The Transformation of Life is Death   תמורת חיים מות

It is unclear from the text of *Sefer Yetzirah* which form of the letter is meant to represent the good quality and which form is meant to represent the bad quality. One could assume that the "dot" (or *dagesh*) in the center of the letter signifies fullness or completion, and thus represents the "full" quality: life, seed, wealth, etc. The form of the letter without a dot at the center would thus embody the "empty" quality: death, poverty, desolation, etc.

However, one could make the opposite case. The "blank" letter could be the "pure" form, while the letter with the mark could represent a blemished form. While we can provisionally assume the letter with the dot/*dagesh* is the "positive" version, we should bear in mind that the text doesn't confirm this.

In creating a duality that shifts with the placement of a single dot, one cannot help but feel that *Sefer Yetzirah* is noting the ephemerality of these phenomena: wealth and poverty, life and death, can come and go with abrupt ease. We may not even be clear which one we are experiencing: do we always know if we've been wise or foolish? If we've acted under compulsion or with free choice? The doubles—opposite qualities framed through a grammatical duality—point back to *Sefer Yetzirah*'s larger vision that dualities can be reframed as multiplicity-within-singularity. Ultimately, the book suggests, both positive and negative experiences arise from the dynamic creative process of a single cosmic Creator. Both are part of the cosmic temple that is the world.

The list of dualities begins with life and death, establishing that the quality of our experience begins with being alive. The letter of life is *bet*, the letter that begins creation. Once we come into the world, then the other factors of our experience begin to matter. But the most important thing, from the point of view of the mortal reader, is life—the quality of having been created at all.

The Transformation of Wisdom is Foolishness

תמורת
חכמה אולת

We began our journey with thirty-two wondrous paths of Wisdom, so it is interesting to suddenly come upon Wisdom as a humble double letter, with an opposite like all the other doubles. Nothing on the surface in this passage singles out Wisdom as unusual. Yet the term Wisdom also refers to the mediating web of channels that the Creator uses to channel the energies of being.

Wisdom pairs with the letter *dalet*, and the name of this letter means "doorway." In Proverbs 6, Wisdom cries out "near the gates, at the entrance of the city, at the coming in of the doors."[12] In *Sefer Yetzirah*'s Chapter 2, the practice of combining letters has to do with opening gateways: creating openings through which God's creative intention can come. Indeed, Proverbs indicates that Wisdom stands "where the paths meet," which in the cosmic architecture of *Sefer Yetzirah* would mean the sacred center of all the doorways.[13] The quality of Wisdom, then, is associated with the spiritual work of *Sefer Yetzirah*, which is to trace Wisdom's paths.

In Proverbs 14, we read "the wisest of women builds her house, but the foolish tears it down with her own hands."[14] This is clearly related to the opposition of wisdom and foolishness in our text. In Exodus, *Chochmah* or Wisdom is one of the qualities of Betzalel, builder of the tabernacle. So we might see Wisdom here, not only as a quality of intellect, but as the quality of being able to form the doorways of the letters, to build the structures of the universe in one's mind and imagine them into being. Whether a person has (or can develop) Wisdom may relate to their ability to do the ritual/visionary work that is the subject of the Book of Creation.

Practice: Seven Gifts

Close your eyes and breathe out.

Before you is a tree.

Approach the tree
and observe that it has a branch with seven blossoms.
Each blossom contains a gift.

The seven gifts are:
life
peace
wisdom
wealth
grace
seed
and sovereignty.

Observe the seven blossoms.

As you do so,
one of the blossoms falls into your hand
and reveals to you its gift.
Welcome this gift into your life.
See how your life is transformed
by the presence of this gift.

Breathe out and open your eyes.

Practice: Seven Transformations

Close your eyes and breathe out.

Before you are seven archways.

Each archway leads to two opposing truths:
life and death
peace and evil
wisdom and foolishness
wealth and poverty
grace and ugliness
seed and desolation
sovereignty and slavery.

Look through one of the archways.

See one half of the truth it reveals.
Then see the other half of that truth.

Now, look through the archway
and see that truth
integrated into a whole.

What happens in your heart
as you witness the whole truth?

Breathe out and open your eyes.

Chapter 4:2 · The Seven Directions

שבע כפולות
בגד כפרת
שש קצוות
והיכל הקדש מכוון באמצע
והוא נושא את כולם

Seven double letters:
bet gimel dalet kaf peh reish taf
Six directions:
and the holy shrine
set in the center—
it bears them all.

The seven double letters embody not only the societal elements but also the seven directions (up, down, north, south, east, west, and center). The text names this center explicitly as the *heichal hakodesh*, the holy shrine.[15] Just as in 1:7, where the ten *sefirot* together form a cosmic structure with God's dwelling at the center, the seven double letters also have a cosmic temple at their center.

As we have noted, Tzahi Weiss notes that the term *otiyot yesod*—foundation letters—can be translated "letter-elements"—a direct translation of the Greek *stoicheon* (which means both letters and elements).[16] As we have noted, both the elements and the directions are a language for multiplicity within unity. When one ritually names the elements, one is invoking discrete substances that together add up to an entire world. When one ritually names the directions, one is invoking multiple orientations that together create a single world-space. The elements and the directions are the structure of the cosmic temple, the multiplicity-within-unity that makes for a diverse creation.

Ronit Meroz points out that the center has a special function: "joining or bridging together the other elements."[17] The sacred shrine at the center of the universe unifies the diversity of the directions. It provides a fulcrum to balance the many entities that make up the architecture of the cosmos.

If we put together 1:7, 1:13, and 4:2, the last six of the *sefirot and* the first six of the seven double letters embody the six directions. 4:2 adds a new layer: the directional forces have an internal duality. If the seven letters are the directions of the universe, and each letter contains both a positive and a negative state, then the universe itself contains good and evil, abundance and lack, life and death, by its nature. Suffering therefore is not a mistake, but built into the system. Even though the Creator has made a sealed space within which life can thrive, that sealed space still contains both life and death.

Humans, via their choices, can sometimes shift a negative state to a positive one, or vice versa, but both possibilities are inherent within the system.

This is not an insignificant point. *Sefer Yetzirah* doesn't seem to posit humanity as the source of death and evil (as, for, example, Genesis 3 does in the story of the eating of the forbidden fruit) or any outside force (such as Satan, or the "other side" named in the kabbalah) as the root of evil. Good and evil are part of the dimension of *nefesh*, the body or person. Whatever impact humans can have on life and death, good and evil, we must have in a world where both things naturally exist. No wonder *Sefer Yetzirah* will state in Chapter 6 that the human heart is like a "king in war"—the tension of opposite states is an ongoing and organic part of life in the world.

This is a point where *Sefer Yetzirah* differs from the incantation bowls. The magical bowls made by Jews of Babylonia name various demons that cause plague and pestilence. *Sefer Yetzirah* names no such demonic forces (unless we are to assume that the detrimental states somehow constitute demons). For *Sefer Yetzirah*, God reigns supreme over a morally and experientially diverse world.

Six Directions   שש קצוות

Every chapter thus far has come to a moment where the entities it describes form a whole. In Chapter 1 the *sefirot* form the "depths" of the universe; in Chapter 2 the letters form a single name of God. In Chapter 3, the mother letters form heaven, earth, and everything in between. Here in Chapter 4, the double letters form the six directions within which the Creator dwells. (In Chapter 5, we'll see that the twelve simple letters form the cosmic boundaries, and in Chapter 6, all the categories are named as a whole.) This invocation and re-invocation of the whole is a primary theme of the text.

These repetitions of the structure of the cosmos may also be part of the ritual of the book. In many magical systems, magic strengthens by repetition. Repeating the components of the whole over and over again, with slight variations, may be a way of strengthening the whole. If we read *Sefer Yetzirah* as a ritual to be performed, it seems that one component of the ritual is an incantation for the cohesion of all things.

The Holy Shrine Set in the Center— It Bears Them All[18]

והיכל הקדש
מכוון באמצע
והוא נושא את כולם

The Temple at the center supports all the directions, and is the underpinning for the whole cosmos. As Ronit Meroz says, "The Holy Temple serves as the axis mundi."[19] Meroz translates *ketzavot*, directions, as "ends" or "edges."[20] This particular word for the directions (distinct, for example, from *arba ruchot*/the four winds) suggests that the cosmic structure is supported not from the edges, but from the center, as if it is a treehouse built around a single tree trunk. The Temple "lifting" the cosmos offers us an image of the world hanging in space, with the Temple holding it up.

The word *nosei* (bear or carry) conjures up the angelic chariot-bearers in the first chapter of Ezekiel. These heavenly beings are said to be borne above the earth (the Hebrew is a form of the same verb: *hinasei*) along with the wheels of the divine chariot, which also are borne in the air. The word "bear" or "carry" implies movement of some kind. It is possible that in choosing this verb—to "carry" the six directions—the passage hints at a chariot flying in space, with the divine as its engine.

We might actually translate the last line—"it bears them all"— somewhat differently. The Hebrew says *hu nosei et kulam*—"he bears them all." Hebrew does not have a gender-neutral "it" pronoun. The most obvious reading is that "he/it" here refers to the Holy Temple. But the text could also mean that the Creator bears all of this: the Temple and the six directions.

Practice: Holy Temple

Close your eyes and breathe out.

You are in a cube-shaped chamber.
Each wall has a window.
as does the ceiling and floor.
Look through the windows
to north, south, east, west,
up, and down.

What do you see, hear, and feel
as you look through the windows?

Now come to stillness
at the center of the room.

At this moment,
you are in the Holy Temple
at the center of the universe.
Feel the harmony and blessing
that this place offers.

Breathe out and open your eyes.

Figure 4. The seven double letters positioned in the seven directions.

Practice: The Holy Temple Bears Them All

Close your eyes and breathe out.

From a place outside yourself,
see yourself.
Zoom out.

See your town,
your region,
your country,
your continent.
Now see the Earth,
the solar system,
the Milky Way galaxy,
the Andromeda cluster of galaxies,
the universe.

Now see the holy temple,
set in the center of the universe,
holding up all of being.
See the nature of this holy temple.
It is holding up
the universe
your galaxy
your solar system
your planet
your continent
your town
you
at this very moment.

Breathe out and open your eyes.

Chapter 4:3 · The Seven Stars, Days, and Gates

שבע כפולות
בגד כפרת
חקקן חצבן צרפן
וצר בהן
כוכבים
ימים
ושערים

Seven double letters:
bet gimel dalet kaf peh reish tav
The Creator engraved them
carved them, combined them
and with them made

stars

days

and gates

To form the "sevens" of the world, the Creator once again goes back to the divine workshop to engrave, carve, and combine letters. The engraved channels of the seven double letters now become specific forms: the "sevens" of creation. These "sevens," like the "threes" of the previous chapter, form diverse yet unified systems and structures within creation.

In Chapter 3, we saw that each of the three mothers has an inherent nature (air, water, or fire) and also each one manifests in different forms in space, time, and soul. Now, in Chapter 4, we learn that the seven doubles have an inherent nature (the seven states of life, wealth, wisdom, etc.), and each one also manifests in space, time, and soul. In space, the seven doubles manifest as seven planets or "stars." In time, the seven doubles manifest as days of the week. In the body, the seven doubles manifest as sensory apertures within the human being.

The number seven is a number beloved by the Hebrew Bible and by later Jewish tradition. The seven days of the week, the seven branches of the menorah, the seven days of Passover and Sukkot, the seven years of the sabbatical cycle, the seven circles of Jericho, all testify to the attachment the Bible has to this number. Seven is often associated with the powers of creation. In Leviticus 16, when the high priest enters the Holy of Holies on the Day of Atonement, he sprinkles the blood of the offering seven times, as if completing and restarting the world.

Later, seven is a popular number in Jewish magic, used in incantations and amulets. (Elsewhere, we've mentioned the seven seals invoked in the words of a Jewish incantation bowl.)[21] When the number seven is doubled (or even tripled), as in this passage, it takes on even more power. The number seven (*sheva*) is similar in its sound to words like "sit" (*shevet*) and "return" (*shuv*) as in "return the Creator to His/Her dwelling place." *Sheva*, seven, perhaps has the intimation of "return"—placing the Creator at the center. *Sefer Yetzirah*, by reciting the three "sevens" (in space, time, and soul) is performing an incantation, bringing new creations into being.

Stars   כוכבים

In the realm of space, the seven letters manifest as seven *kochavim* or stars. The more common Hebrew word for "planets" is *mazalot*. However, it is clear that by *kochavim*, *Sefer Yetzirah* means "planets"—the seven heavenly bodies, including the sun and the moon, that determined fate according to astrology. In the Babylonian Talmud, we see a similar usage, where *kochavim* refers to planets in their orbit, while *mazalot* means signs of the Zodiac.[22]

Tzahi Weiss suggests that the connection between the planets and the letters is an adaptation of the Greek idea that the seven Greek vowels correspond to the seven planets. Weiss theorizes that *Sefer Yetzirah* shifts this idea, moving away from vowels (since the book does not dwell on the Hebrew vowels) and suggesting instead that the seven planets embody the seven double letters.[23]

As we will see in 4:5 and 4:6, expanded versions of *Sefer Yetzirah* list the seven planets as the sun, moon, Mercury, Venus, Mars, Jupiter, and Saturn (the known solar system bodies at that time).[24] Given that the seven letters each have a quality (life, wisdom, etc.), it seems that the seven planets are in some way related to the qualities of the letters that give rise to them. Thus, the planets are tied into the "societal elements" of human experience. As astrologists might suggest, the fate of the human appears tied into the movements of the planets. While the text doesn't offer a full tutorial in astronomy or astrology, it certainly suggests that such knowledge may be useful for understanding and perhaps manipulating creation.

Yet the astrology of *Sefer Yetzirah* is not simply a causal connection between stars and human experiences. Human destiny and planetary movement both arise from the letters, which are channels for divine will. A human practitioner must attune to divine creative intention in order to understand the cosmos and its fate. Understanding the stars may be one tool for such attunement.

Again, word and world move together. We might explore the will of the Creator in the realm of text or in the vastness of the night sky. What is written in the letters may also be written in the stars.

Days ימים

In the realm of time, the seven letters manifest as the seven days of the week. The six ordinary days correspond to the six directions. Shabbat, the Sabbath, would thus correspond to the sacred center. This fits nicely with 4:2's depiction of the holy shrine at the center of the cosmos. Just as the Temple is a holy space, the Sabbath is a holy time.

We might also imagine that, as with the planets, each day takes on one of the dual qualities of the seven double letters. Thus, each day is connected to a particular blessing or difficulty associated with its tutelary letter. This too potentially offers humans a magical science for understanding fate: knowing the day of an event (or a birth) might help an adept understand the letter-forces at play. We will explore this possibility in 4:5 and 4:6.

As *Sefer Yetzirah* continues to unfold, we will see that the mother letters, double letters, and single letters form an entire system of time: days, months, seasons. Each of these individual cycles of time is regulated by a natural phenomenon (sunlight, phases of the moon, seasonal cycles). By understanding the cycles of time, we come to know the patterns that the Creator laid down to support life.

Gates   ושערים

The text refers to the apertures of the body-soul as "gates," just as in Chapter 2 the channels formed by letter combination were known as "gates." In *Sefer Yetzirah*, the term "gates" seems to imply openings that admit some significant input or output—such as eyes that admit light or ears that admit sound, or a mouth that admits air and food and exhales breath. Similarly, the gates made by letter combination are apertures that admit or exude divine intention or energy.

Other versions of the *Sefer Yetzirah* list the eyes, ears, nostrils, and mouth as the seven gates of the body.[25] The image of the eye or ear or mouth as a gate is striking. The body, like the world, is a house: a structure that needs gates in order to let light, sound, air, food, etc. inside. The senses are not only faculties but doorways that allow a human body-house to open itself to the larger cosmos. Without these doorways, we'd be sealed off from input from the reality outside us. And, without these doorways, we'd be unable to send our intentions into the world.

These doorways also mean that the human is like the world: as the world needs gates to let in God's creative impulse, the human needs gates for sustenance and life. The microcosm echoes the macrocosm. The later kabbalah takes this idea further, suggesting that the Creator shapes the universe in the form of a man, and naming the pattern of the cosmos Adam Kadmon: the ancient human.[26]

We should note that in spite of the book's interest in creation, nowhere in the text are the apertures in the lower body mentioned. The text might have found matters of reproduction and elimination too delicate to address. However, in using the language of gates, our text perhaps alludes to the rabbinic prayer for using the bathroom, which states that "if one opening that should be closed opens, or if one opening that should be open closes, it would be impossible to stand before You."[27] The proper functioning of all the gates is necessary to the health of the body.

Referring to the sensory organs as gateways is, perhaps, also advice about sacred practice. It is possible to turn inward and limit the input we get from our senses—this is one of the methods for entering a meditative state. Or, we can open the gates wider, being especially attentive to what we sense. This is another way to enter a contemplative state.

Practice: The Seven Days

Close your eyes and breathe out.

Think back to a week ago.

Recall the past seven days,
one at a time.

See if you can summon a memory
from each of the seven days.

When you get to the present moment,
notice how these seven memories
have led you to this time and place.

Notice also
how this time and place
are a fresh start.

Rest in this moment
without attachment to the past
or concern about the future.

Breathe out and open your eyes.

Practice: The Seven Gates

Close your eyes and breathe out.

Bring your attention to your eyes.
Think of moments of joyful experience
they have given you.
Offer gratitude.
If they don't work perfectly or at all,
offer them your blessing anyway.
Now bring your attention to your ears.
Think of moments of joyful experience
they have given you.
Offer gratitude.
If they don't work perfectly or at all,
offer them your blessing anyway.
Now bring your attention to your nose.
Think of moments of joyful experience
your nose has given you.
Offer gratitude.
If your nose doesn't work perfectly or at all,
offer it your blessing anyway.
Now bring your attention to your mouth.
Think of moments of joyful experience
your mouth has given you.
Offer gratitude.
If your mouth doesn't work perfectly or at all,
offer it your blessing anyway.
When you have brought attention to all seven apertures,
come to stillness.
Notice what you are sensing
through those apertures
right now.
Offer gratitude
for this moment.

Breathe out and open your eyes.

Chapter 4:4 · The Seven Stones

כאיזה צד צרפן
שתי עבנים בונות שני בתים
שלוש בונות ששה בתים
ארבע בונות עשרים וארבע בתים
חמש בונות מאה ועשרים בתים
שש בונות שבע מאות ועשרים בתים
שבע בונות חמשת אלפים וארבעים בתים
מיכאן ואילך צא וחשוב
מה שאין הפה יכולה לדבר
ומה שאין האוזן יכולה לשמוע

In what way did God combine them?
Two stones build two houses.
Three build six houses.
Four build twenty-four houses.
Five build one hundred and twenty houses.
Six build seven hundred and twenty houses.
Seven build five thousand and forty houses.
From here on out
go and contemplate
what the mouth cannot say
and the ear cannot hear.

As if turning the bend on a garden path, we come upon an image of the seven letters, not as gates or stars, but stones. God piles stones to build houses: first two houses out of two stones, and then more houses, and then many more, until the mind cannot calculate their number. The combined stones are combined letters; word and thing all at once.

They are *amudim gedolim*, "great pillars," carved out of air that cannot be grasped.[28] As God builds an infinity of houses out of an infinity of stones, one easily could become mesmerized, and pass out of thought into what "the mouth cannot say and the ear cannot hear."

Marla Segol sees this passage as the center of *Sefer Yetzirah*,[29] and this feels right when one reads it.[30] If letters are stones, there is no distinction between text and thing. The image of the Temple is entwined here too, since the word "house" can also mean temple. The house/temple is composed of letters that are stones. It is a house of word and world. The loss of the physical Temple is negated. The greater temple is built wherever elements come together into a whole.

The passage opens by describing the Creator (*K'eizeh tzad tzarfan?*/In what way did [he] combine them?") but ends by addressing the reader: "Go and contemplate..." The energy of the text pivots from describing God's actions to describing a human practice—the reader must take up the challenge of combining the seven letters into their myriad combinations. Via the human practice, the reader and God are joined in a single image: building a temple from stones.

Yet the passage admonishes the reader that in this act of meditation that is *imitatio dei*, the reader will reach the limits of his or her understanding. It is not possible for a human being to combine all twenty-two letters in all of their possible permutations. The numbers are simply too large for us to hold in our minds. For a person to permute even seven letters (5,040 combinations) stretches the imagination. The temple of the cosmos is so big, so complicated that a human could never duplicate the letter-combinations that created it. The numbers merge into a varied, infinite unity.

Thus the multiplication of the stones, as it approaches infinity, returns us to the oneness with which the world began. Through this practice of combination of letter-elements, we can achieve the contemplative purpose of *Sefer Yetzirah*. We can encompass all of Creation. We can move beyond the calculating mind into the power and wonder of it all.

Two Houses שני בתים

Proverbs 9:1 reads "Wisdom has built her house; she has hewn her seven pillars." This passage is a kind of commentary on that verse. For *Sefer Yetzirah*, Wisdom is the network of channels by which God brings things into being. Through combining the letters, piling the stones, we build Wisdom's house and open ourselves to Wisdom's web of channels.

We become like the letters or the *sefirot*: hollow entities for the Creator to work through.

That Wisdom's house has seven pillars helps to explain the placement of this passage in Chapter 4. While we have already discussed the combination of letters in Chapter 2, Chapter 4 deals with the number seven. The text in Proverbs suggests that "seven pillars" are crucial to Wisdom's house. So too, in our text, the seven stones are the height of the combination practice.

This passage marks the central working of the ritual that is *Sefer Yetzirah*.

The practice of combination is a movement from unity to multiplicity and from multiplicity to unity. Every time we bring diversity into unity, or unity into diversity, we are strengthening the cosmic temple. And in some way we are repairing the loss of the physical Temple that once stood in Jerusalem.

It is striking that the phrase "one stone" never appears in the passage. In the human world, we have to deduce unity from multiplicity. Only by allowing the multiplicity to grow and grow do we finally come again to oneness. The very plethora of creations are the witnesses that there is a Creator behind them all.

What the Mouth Cannot Say   מה שאין הפה יכולה לדבר

This passage uses language to try to explain an experience that is beyond language. Without advanced math, it is attempting to describe infinity: not just infinity as a concept, but infinity as a lived experience. Prophets and visionaries have such experiences: brief flashes of awareness of an All that is beyond limit and beyond description. It is the mystery of this All that causes 1:5 to say: "Stop your mouth from speaking."

We might assume that, since we are not all prophets and visionaries, this experience is closed to us. *Sefer Yetzirah* seems to suggest otherwise. The practice of *Sefer Yetzirah*—the reading and enacting of its various passages—is meant to give us an experience that approximates direct perception of the infinite. Such perceptions, if we are lucky enough to have them, will be impossible to explain to others or even to ourselves. It is this experience that "the mouth cannot say and the ear cannot hear."

The passage suggests that nature itself, physics and math, is a demonstration of the Creator's presence. That the text is using mathematical infinity to try to represent divine infinity feels post-modern somehow. The text does not reach for another world to show us the sublime nature of God. Rather, it reaches deep into this world. We don't need to fly to another dimension. We only need to start counting.

In Hayman's accounting of the earliest recoverable version, Chapter 4 ends here. The primary message of the book, encapsulated in the text/ritual of combining the stones, has been delivered. Letters have become things and things have been recognized as letters. Consciousness has reached out to the Creator, to the place beyond words.

Practice: The Stones Multiply

Close your eyes and breathe out.

You are holding a stone in your hand.
See and/or feel the stone:
its form, color, texture.
Place the stone in front of you.
The stone becomes two stones.
The two stones multiply,
becoming many stones.
As they multiply and multiply,
observe what unity emerges.
This unity is at the core of being,
at the core of your life,
at the core of this moment.

Breathe out and open your eyes.

Practice: What The Mouth Cannot Say

Close your eyes and breathe out.

Envision a shining circle
like a sun or moon.
The circle divides into two circles.
It divides and divides
until there is no more circle,
only light.
Bathe in this light.
Know that you are healed and transformed
by means of this infinite light.

Breathe out and open your eyes.

Practice: Seven Stones

Close your eyes and breathe out.

Before you is a pond.
There are seven steppingstones in the pond.
They lead across the water.
Their destination is veiled in mist.
Move from stone to stone.
As you reach each stone,
observe what is different,
how your perspective shifts,
how the mist lifts or thickens,
how sound and light change.
When you come to the final stone,
the veils are lifted,
the temple appears.
The mystery is revealed.

Breathe out and open your eyes.

Return to the Place

Chapter 4:5 · Crowning the Seven Letters

God gave rule to the letter **Bet**
and tied a crown to it and combined
one thing with another and formed with it
Saturn in the world
Shabbat in the year
and the **mouth** in the body.

המליך אות בית
וקשר לו כתר וצרפן
זה עם זה וצר בו
שבתי בעולם
ושבת בשנה
ופה בנפש

God gave rule to the letter **Gimel**
and tied a crown to it and combined
one thing with another and formed with it
Jupiter in the world
Sunday in the year
and the **right eye** in the body.

המליך אות גימל
ווקשר לו כתר וצרפן
זה עם זה וצר בו
צדק בעולם
ואחד בשבת בשנה
ועין ימין בנפש

God gave rule to the letter **Dalet**
and tied a crown to it and combined
one thing with another and formed with it
Mars in the world
Monday in the year
and the **left eye** in the body-soul.

המליך אות דלת
ווקשר לו כתר וצרפן
זה עם זה וצר בו
מאדים בעולם
ושני שבת בשנה
ועין שמאל בנפש

God gave rule to the letter **Kaf**
and tied a crown to it and combined
one thing with another and formed with it
the **Sun** in the world
Tuesday in the year
and the **right nostril** in the body-soul.

המליך אות כף
ווקשר לו כתר וצרפן
זה עם זה וצר בו
חמה בעולם
ושלישי שבת בשנה
ועף ימין בנפש

God gave rule to the letter **Peh**
and tied a crown to it and combined
one thing with another and formed with it
Venus in the world
Wednesday in the year
and the **left nostril** in the body-soul.

המליך אות פה
ווקשר לו כתר וצרפן
זה עם זה וצר בו
נוגה בעולם
ורביעי שבת בשנה
ועף שמאל בנפש

God gave rule to the letter **Reish**
and tied a crown to it and combined
one thing with another and formed with it
Mercury in the world
Thursday in the year
and the **right ear** in the body-soul.

המליך אות ראש
ווקשר לו כתר וצרפן
זה עם זה וצר בו
כוכב בעולם
וחמישי שבת בשנה
ואוזן ימין בנפש

God gave rule to the letter **Tav**
and tied a crown to it and combined
one thing with another and formed with it
the **Moon** in the world
Friday in the year
and the **left ear** in the body-soul.

המליך אות תיו
ווקשר לו כתר וצרפן
זה עם זה וצר בו
לבנה בעולם
ושישי שבת בשנה
ואוזן ימין בנפש

Chapter 4:6 · The Seven Letters in the Three Worlds

שבעה כוכבים בעולם
ואלו הן
חמה נוגה כוכב לבנה
שבתי צדק מאדים
ושבעה ימים
שבעת ימי בראשית
ושבעה שערים בנפש
שתי עיניים ושתי עזנים
ושתי נחיריים ופה

These are the seven planets in the world:
Sun, Venus, Mercury, Moon, Saturn, Jupiter, Mars.
Chamah Nogah Kochav Levanah Shabtai Tzedek Ma'dim

And the seven days:
The seven days of creation.

And the seven gates of the body-soul:
Two eyes, two ears, two nostrils, and the mouth.

These passages of *Sefer Yetzirah* are not attested in all manuscripts, and Hayman does not believe they are part of the earliest recoverable text.[31] They likely contain material that was added to explicate the text (e.g., by explaining the nature of the seven gates, planets, and days) and/or to make the text conform to rabbinic ideas.[32] Yet since these passages offer specific ways to work with each of the seven letters and their attributes, they are included here as an aid to practitioners.

The passages list the planets, days, and body parts linked with the seven double letters. This is an expansion of 4:3, which specifies that the double letters manifest as the planets in the realm of space, the days in the realm of time, and the gates in the realm of the body-soul. These texts offer us ways to work with each of the seven letters: connecting each letter with a day of the week, for example, might yield a meditational or magical practice of connecting a day of the week with its particular gift. For example, the letter *bet* connects to life, Shabbat, Saturn, and the mouth. The letter *bet* could perhaps be used to heal or open mouths, or to assist in the healing of the womb (giver of life). Or someone seeking wisdom could invoke *dalet*, Mars, Monday, or the left eye.

Scholar Lorelai Kude believes that "the planetary influence on specific body parts [described in these passages] is a cookbook-style medical manual, perhaps intended as a guide for healers. The identification of letters, planets, and constellations with body parts informs the reader as to when to effect a *segula* or remedy for a specific ailment, as well as the optimum timing of its application."[33] If this is the case, these passages were added to the text to make the book more usable for magical healing practitioners.

Hayman believes these passages were added by rabbinic Jews, perhaps partly to make the book more consistent with rabbinic thought.[34] There were in fact talmudic traditions around planets and days of the week. The planet names that appear here are exactly those that appear in a passage in the Babylonian Talmud:

> One who is born on the first day of the week will be completely for the best or completely for the worst... One who is born on the second day of the week will be bad-tempered... One who is born on the third day of the week will be wealthy and unchaste... One who is born on the fourth day of the week will be a wise and enlightened person... One who is born on the fifth day of the week will perform acts of lovingkindness. One who is born on the sixth day of the week will be a seeker, one who seeks out good deeds... One who is born on the Sabbath will die on the Sabbath, because the great day of the Sabbath was desecrated on their account...[35]

Rabbi Hanina said... It is not the constellation of the day that determines a person's nature but the constellation of the hour. One who was born under the sun will be a radiant person who eats and drinks from his own resources... one who was born under Venus (*Nogah*) will be a rich and promiscuous person... One who was born under Mercury (*Kochav*) will be an enlightened and expert person... One who was born under the influence of the moon will be one who suffers pains, who builds and destroys, and destroys and builds... One who was born under the influence of Saturn will be one whose thoughts are for naught...One who was born under Jupiter (*Tzedek*) will be a just person... One who was born under Mars (*Ma'dim*) will shed blood... A constellation makes one wise and a constellation makes one wealthy, and there is a constellation for the Jewish people. Rabbi Yochanan said: there is no constellation for the Jewish people.[36]

Some of the attributes listed in the Talmud seem consistent with the passages in *Sefer Yetzirah*. For example, *Kaf* goes with wealth, the sun, and Tuesday, and the Talmud agrees that the sun and Tuesday go with wealth. Bet goes with the Sabbath and with life and death, and the Talmud agrees that the Sabbath is associated with birth and death.

However, the qualities of the planets listed in the Talmud don't always match the qualities of the letters to which they are assigned in *Sefer Yetzirah*. For example, in *Sefer Yetzirah*, *dalet*, Mars, and Monday go with wisdom; in the Talmud, Monday goes with short-tempered people and Mars with violence. In *Sefer Yetzirah*, *reish*, Mercury, and Thursday go with seed; in the Talmud, Thursday goes with good deeds and Mercury with wisdom (not fertility or abundance). So we may not be dealing with exactly the same astrological system.

Scholar Lorelai Kude believes the correspondences in this passage between planets and days of the week in *Sefer Yetzirah* are mainly consistent with the Talmud's portrayal of the planets and days of the week. However, she notes that *Sefer Yetzirah* is not consistent with Ptolemy's system, which was a widespread astrological system in the region.[37] For example, in our passage the Moon rules over Friday, but in the Greek system it rules Monday. Jupiter rules over Sunday in this passage but Thursday in the

Greek system. The only day when the two systems agree is Saturday, which is ruled over by Saturn in both systems.

It seems the astrology offered in these passages is not exactly the same as the Greek one, and not exactly the same as the Talmudic one. Rather, it seems to offer its own unique system, consistent with its understanding of the seven double letters as planetary influences. Ultimately, this astrological system assumes, not that planets control human beings, but that both planets and humans are governed by the divine creative forces at the root of existence.

These passages, with their lists of correspondences, clarify the letters and their qualities for practitioners. They make the letter mysteries of *Sefer Yetzirah* more accessible to those who want to use them for prediction, transformation, and magic. These texts are also potentially aids for meditation, giving practitioners the opportunity to contemplate each letter carefully and consider its nature.

Practice: The Gate of *Bet*

Close your eyes and breathe out.

See the letter *Bet* ב before you.

See *Bet* as a mouth.
What does *Bet* say to you
about the mysteries of creation?

See *Bet* as a womb.
What emerges from the womb of *Bet*?

See *Bet* as Shabbat.
What does *Bet* teach
about the power of rest and stillness?

Breathe out and open your eyes.

Practice: The Gate of *Dalet*

Close your eyes and breathe out.

See the letter *Dalet* ד before you.
See *Dalet* as an elder, a wise person, pointing the way.
What is the wisdom to which *Dalet* points?
Look to where *Dalet* points
and see the wisdom you are growing into.

Breathe out and open your eyes.

Practice: The Gate of *Reish*

Close your eyes and breathe out.

See the letter *Reish* ר before you.
Reish is seed. *Reish* is a head, a beginning:
a sprout bursting from the ground, a child being born.
What is the beginning *Reish* shows you?

Breathe out and open your eyes.

Practice: The Gate of *Tav*

Close your eyes and breathe out.

See *Tav* ת before you.
Walk through the gate in the *Tav*.
The full moon is before you.
In the light of the full moon,
you see a vision of yourself in your full sovereignty.
Taking this vision of your sovereignty with you,
step back through the door.

Breathe out and open your eyes.

Chapter 4:7 · The Three Worlds as Witnesses

חיצה את העדים
והעמידן אחד אחד לבדו
עולם לבדו
שנה לבדה
נפש לבדה

God divided the witnesses
and stood each one by itself
the world by itself
the year by itself
the body-soul by itself

This passage closes Chapter 4 by naming and invoking the realms of *olam*, *shanah*, and *nefesh*—space, time, and body-soul.[38] The text refers to the three realms as "witnesses." This use of the term "witnesses" may refer back to the biblical texts in which God calls heaven and earth to be witnesses to God's declarations.[39] The three realms of *Sefer Yetzirah* seem to be witnesses to God's unfolding of the universe.

There is something unsettling about referring to dimensions of the cosmos as "witnesses." Might it be that space and time as well as all living entities are consciously witnessing creation? Of course, we could say that "witness" is used poetically here, to mean something that's been part of creation from the beginning. But we might also say that all along there have been hints that the elements of God's universe are alive. The *sefirot* running and returning, the three mothers behind their veils and seal-rings, the letters with their crowns and dominions, have an impersonal quality but also a personal quality. We are to imagine the impersonal elemental forces as conscious entities in relationship to the Creator who shapes them and us.

Each One By Itself   אחד אחד לבדו

It appears that the three "witnesses," space, time, and body-soul, were originally one entity. God had to separate them (the Hebrew verb is *chet-tzadi-heh*, to divide) in order to make them each an individual phenomenon: "the world by itself, the year by itself, the body by itself." In the end, each of the three has its own separate identity. Yet the text seems to imply that God begins with a single mass—space-time-body-soul—and divides that mass into three linked realms, in order to create the cosmos as we know it.

Sefer Yetzirah seems to be looking back to a time before God used the "paths of wisdom" (the letters and *sefirot*) to channel creative energy into the cosmos. First, God had to create the "books" or "witnesses" of space, time, and being. Only then could other creations come into being.

This text extends the book's theme of multiplicity-within-unity: the three realms are themselves both divided and connected. There is no true duality between space and time, or between time and person. Space, time, and perspective are joined at the root, and it is only by God's creative act of division that these things exist separately. The "three books" are really one book divided into three parts.

Physicist Karen Barad has formed a theory of "agential realism" or "the ontological inseparability of intra-acting agencies." In this theory, everything is inextricably entangled with everything else, to the extent that it is not meaningful to speak of "entities" outside of their inter- (or as Barad says, intra-) actions.[40] Entities co-arise, shaped by their mutual intra-actions. According to Barad, all phenomena can be linked back to a single unity. *Sefer Yetzirah* is imagining something similar. Space, time and perspective, and all related phenomena, are all intertwined and constantly affecting one another: they are "inter-being."

Chapter 4 closes with this sense of inter-being. The universe is alive and intertwined. The seven double letters, divided in two though they may be, are also one with their alternate forms, and with one another.

Practice: Three Witnesses

Close your eyes and breathe out.

Call to mind where you are in space:
in your house or under a tree,
at work or school,
on a certain continent or island.
Let the layers of where you are
unfold in your perception.

Call to mind where you are in time:
morning or night, summer or winter,
a workday or a moment of leisure,
in youth or old age or in the middle.
Let the layers of when you are
unfold in your perception.

Call to mind the sensations of your body:
ease or discomfort, excitement or calm,
energy or fatigue, fullness or hunger.
Let the layers of your body experience
unfold in your perception.

Now, try to hold these three dimensions
in your consciousness at the same time.

You exist
at the nexus of space, time, and body-soul.

Breathe out and open your eyes.

Chapter 5:1 · The Simple Letters

שתים עשרה פשוטות
ה ו ז ח ט י
ל נ ס ע צ ק
יסודן
ראיה שמיעה ריחה
שיחה לעיטה תשמיש
מעשה הילוך רוגז
שחוק הרהור שינה

Twelve simples:
heh, vav, zayin, chet, tet, yud
lamed, nun, samech, ayin, tzadi, kuf.
Their foundation
is sight, hearing, smell,
speech, taste, sexuality,
action, locomotion, agitation,
laughter, thought, and sleep.

As we continue the ritual recitation of the Hebrew letters, we move from few to many—three mothers, seven doubles, and now twelve simples. Chapter Five introduces us to the last of the three groups of letters: the *peshutot* or simple letters. Since twelve is the number of the twelve tribes of Israel (though the tribes themselves are never mentioned in the text of *Sefer Yetzirah*), we have the sense that the twelve simples constitute an entire nation of multiplicity.

Yehuda Liebes notes that the word *peshutot*, simple, seems to mean "ordinary"—not otherwise designated as special.[1] While the seven double letters embody overarching states in human experience: life/death, peace/war, etc., the twelve simple letters embody "ordinary" human faculties.

Yet these faculties, far from being insignificant, shape individual human experience and mediate human impact on the world.

There isn't one English word that describes the twelve faculties. Sight, hearing, smell, and taste are senses. Sexuality, sleep, and laughter are body functions and needs, providing renewal and release and supporting creativity. Action and walking have to do with body motion, while thought and feeling are internal experiences. Speech expresses thought and feeling and also requires body motion. And there are a few faculties (like touch or tears) that could be here, but aren't.

Together, the twelve faculties, the core expressions of the twelve simple letters, make up a human's daily life. Each faculty pairs with a letter: *heh* with sight, *vav* with hearing, and so on.[2] Later in the chapter, we'll learn about the entities these twelve letters engender: twelve constellations, twelve months, and twelve organs of the body. The twelve simple letters thus help create not only the diversity of the cosmos but the diversity of human experience.

Sexuality תשמיש

Tashmish means the act of sex (and presumably implies the human capacity for erotic response as well as reproduction). It is notable that *Sefer Yetzirah* identifies sex as a body function like any other, and doesn't set it apart, either positively or negatively, from other senses and capacities. As with many Jewish texts, there is no sense here that sexuality is problematic or to be avoided. It is simply one of the human faculties, to be engaged when appropriate. This matter-of-fact treatment of sexuality fits with the rest of *Sefer Yetzirah*'s attitude toward the body, as well as its attitude toward gender relations. The diversity and depth of human experience is to be acknowledged, even celebrated.

Action מעשה

The Hebrew word *maaseh* means "deed" or "physical act." In this context, it seems to refer to any sort of "doing"—the work one does with one's hands. A Talmudic saying goes: "The world is judged with lovingkindness, and yet all depends on the majority of one's deeds (*rov hamaaseh*)."[3] *Maaseh* also implicitly refers to good deeds—actions that improve the world. The Hebrew phrase *maasim tovim* means "good acts" or righteous deeds. *Maaseh* can also refer to practice or practical experience: *halakhah l'maaseh* means Jewish law as it is practiced in the real world.

Locomotion　　　　　　　　　　　　　　　　　　　　　　　　　　　הילוך

The word *hiluch* comes from the Hebrew verb *halakh*, to walk. The text identifies the ability to move from place to place as a unique faculty: locomotion. We might include movement on a scooter, in a wheelchair or on a bike (or in a car or a plane) in the category of *haloch*. "Walking" or "locomotion" could also imply ritual behaviors; *halakhah* (literally, "the way" or "the walking") is a common Hebrew term for Jewish law and practice.

Agitation　　　　　　　　　　　　　　　　　　　　　　　　　　　　רוגז

The Hebrew *rogez* is often translated as "anger," and this is indeed one of the meanings of the word *rogez*. However, the biblical *rogez* means "quivering," and can denote agitation, excitement, rage, fear, or disturbance.[4] In the Talmud, *rogez* generally conveys anger, but can also mean agitation or commotion; for example, Jacob's feelings after the disappearance of Joseph are called *rogez*.[5] It may be that *rogez* is intended to cover a number of negative emotion-states from anger to fear to sorrow. (If this is the case, then *rogez* might also include tears, which are otherwise obviously missing from the list. Why include laughter and not tears?)

It is possible that *rogez* is meant to mean the body-state of excitement. Psychologists have learned by experimentation that when people experience physical excitement (as a result of exercise, for example), they will name that excitement as different emotions depending on context: as anger, or as happiness. This is called misattribution of arousal.[6] This misattribution occurs because the arousal state in the body is similar even when the underlying emotions are different. *Rogez* may indicate generalized agitation, such as an increased heart rate, which manifests as anger, grief, fear, etc.—but also as elation. Reading the word *rogez* this way suggests that there are more human faculties in 5:1 than might otherwise be apparent.

Thought　　　　　　　　　　　　　　　　　　　　　　　　　　　　הרהור

Sefer Yetzirah does not use the abstract Hebrew word for thought, which is *machshavah*. Instead, the text uses *hirhur*, which can mean thinking, conception, perseveration, or meditation.[7] *Hirhur* refers not to a single thought but to internal monologue. In rabbinic literature, *hirhurim* or internal thoughts can refer to planning, sexual fantasies, or unresolved anxiety—all are thought-activities that transpire over time.[8] Similarly, *hirhur* in our passage means the sustained process of thinking.

In general, the twelve faculties are body experiences. Thought is the hardest one to establish as a body experience, since we usually think of thought as internal and invisible. *Sefer Yetzirah* lists it, not as some separate more godly function, but among other body faculties like smell, taste, laughter, and sleep. *Sefer Yetzirah* understands the body as the site of consciousness.

Sleep שינה

Sleep, the last body faculty on the list, also stands out for its connections with mystical experience. The Bible frequently considers dreams to be divine messages,[9] and the Talmud suggests sleep is "one-sixtieth of prophecy."[10]

Practice: The Twelve Faculties

This practice offers gratitude for the twelve faculties. If any of these faculties are absent for you, or impaired, you can skip them, or contemplate any ways in which they have mattered to you. Or, you can substitute a sense; for example, touch instead of sight, or vibration instead of hearing.

Close your eyes and breathe out.

Remember a moment when...

the gift of sight has mattered to you.
the gift of hearing has mattered to you.
the gift of smell has mattered to you.
the gift of speech has mattered to you.
the gift of taste has mattered to you.
the gift of sexuality has mattered to you.
the gift of action has mattered to you.
the gift of walking or locomotion has mattered to you.
the gift of strong feelings—tears, anger, grief, joy—has mattered to you.
the gift of laughter has mattered to you.
the gift of thought has mattered to you.
the gift of sleep has mattered to you.

Offer gratitude for all these moments.

Now, choose a sense-gift that is inspiring to you in this moment.

Commit to use this gift in a special way today.

Breathe out and open your eyes.

Practice: The Circle

Close your eyes and breathe out.

Visualize a circle.

Within this shape,
place whatever feeling or sensation
you are experiencing right now:
contentment or anger, grief or joy,
pain, discomfort, pleasure, sleepiness,
love, excitement, or terror.

Watch the feeling you've summoned
move within the circle.
Does it have a color or texture or shape?

Observe whether the feeling
strengthens or dissipates or stays the same.

What do you learn
by observing this feeling?
When you are ready,
release the circle.

Breathe out and open your eyes.

Chapter 5:2 ·
The Borders of the Cosmic Temple

שנים עשר גבולי אלכסון
גבול מזרחית צפונית
גבול מזרחית דרומית
גבול מזרחית רומית
גבול מזרחית תחתית
גבול צפונית תחתית
גבול צפונית מערבית
גבול צפונית רומית
גבול מערבית תחתית
גבול מערבית דרומית
גבול מערבית רומית
גבול דרומית תחתית
גבול דרומית רומית

Twelve diagonal borders:
the east-north border
the east-south border
the east upper border
the east lower border
the north lower border
the north-west border
the north upper border
the west lower border
the west-south border
the west upper border
the south lower border
the south upper border

Just as Chapter 4 invokes the double letters as the six "walls" of the cosmic temple, Chapter 5 invokes the simple letters as the twelve "borders" that define those walls. The three mother letters complete the picture, comprising the "zones" of the cosmic temple: sky, air, and earth. Each Hebrew letter has a role to play in the building of this massive temple.

Each letter is a structural element in a carefully built universe. The letters work together as a group, channeling God's creative power to build the sacred space of reality. By invoking the components of the cosmic temple in every chapter, *Sefer Yetzirah* continues to unfold its ritual of making and re-making creation.

The *peshutot*, the twelve simple letters, establish the lines (*gevulei alechson*) that form the cube of the cosmic temple. The word *alechson* is a Greek-derived word that means crosswise or diagonal,[11] though these lines aren't exactly diagonal—they are the twelve lines that surround the faces of a cube—*gevulei alechson* or "boundaries of the diagonal." Each of the boundary lines of the sacred cube is labeled with a combination of two directions (east-north, or south lower, or west upper) in order to explain its exact position within the cosmic structure. This is another example of the cooperation of multiple forces (in this case, the directions) in creating the world's architecture.

The tracing of the borders of the cosmic cube is clearly meant to be a meditative focus for the seeker. Just as the reader must imagine the seven directions of the double letters, or the three elements and realms of the three mothers, the reader is invited to trace the lines of the cosmic cube, identifying each line with the appropriate Hebrew letter. This thought exercise may be intended to have magical power: a practitioner might draw these twelve lines around her or himself as a protective structure, just as God uses this structure to protect the whole world.

If we look back to 5:1, we notice that each of these lines of the cosmic cube also represents a human faculty like smell or sexuality or sleep. This implies that the sacred cube is intimately related to the human body. The world-temple is a body-temple. We created beings, made up of a variety of faculties and senses, hold cosmic forces within us.

The East-North Border   גבול מזרחית צפונית

Conducting the ritual of tracing the borders according to the text of *Sefer Yetzirah* is slightly difficult, because there is manuscript variation in the order of the twelve boundaries. Some, for example, begin with the south-east border rather than the north-east border.¹² However, all manuscripts agree that the order of the boundaries starts in the east. The direction of the rising sun signifies beginnings.

One can imagine God, the magician, turning to the east to begin sketching the lines of the sacred cube that is to contain the world. Starting in the east, the cosmic sorcerer inscribes the borders of each face of the cube, moving through all the directions and returning to the starting point. The human reader/practitioner is implicitly invited to copy the Creator and speak the names of the borders as well. The reader perhaps might do this as a personal protection. Or, the reader might perhaps do this to reinforce the cosmic boundaries that already exist.

Border   גבול

The word "border" (*gvul* in Hebrew) has resonance within the Jewish imagination, particularly with the concept of holy space. For example, in the book of Exodus, God commands that Moses "set bounds around the mountain" (*hagbel et hahar*) to keep people from approaching.¹³ The book of Exodus and the book of Joshua both set the "border" (*gvul*) of the land of Israel, using certain physical features of the land.¹⁴ In the book of Jeremiah, God promises Rachel that her children will return to "their border" (*ligvulam*).¹⁵ The word "border" has inevitably to do with land, frequently with the land of Israel, and sometimes (as in the case of Sinai) land occupied by God.

That is why the use of the term "border" here has a radical implication. The borders here are not of any specific land, but rather the borders of the whole world. *Sefer Yetzirah* is re-imagining the "holy land" to mean "everywhere." Sacred space can be found in any place, not only in the land that originated the Jewish people.

The one who draws these lines in the imagination is setting the borders of a "land," a sacred space, simply by willing that it be so. We might see this as a reclamation (even in exile) of sacred space. One can own one's own space and declare it holy, merely by using one's consciousness to draw a line in the sand.

Practice: Twelve Diagonal Lines
Close your eyes and breathe out.

You are holding a rod or twig or feather—
any kind of implement for sketching lines in the air.

Form an intention
to protect or bless someone or something
within a sacred space.

With your implement, draw a vertical line.
This is the first line
of the cube of energy you are making.
Put your intention into this line as you draw it.
Sketch another three lines
so that you complete a square, a face of a cube.
Continue to hold your intention.
Now, turning to your left, sketch another three lines
so that you have a second face of the cube.
Continue to hold your intention.
Turn to your left again and sketch another three lines
to make a third face of the cube.
Continue to hold your intention.
Turn to your left.
You will need to draw only two more lines
to make a fourth face of the cube
and connect all the cube's sides together.
When the cube is complete,
feel its lines glow with your intention.
Now, bring into the cube,
simply by intending to do so,
anyone or anything
you want this intention to reach.

Visualize the impact of your intention
on this person or entity.

Breathe out and open your eyes.

Practice: Twelve Diagonal Lines with the Hebrew Letters

Close your eyes and breathe out.

You are holding a rod or twig or feather—
any kind of implement for sketching lines in the air.
Form an intention to protect or bless
someone or something within a sacred space.

You are about to sketch a cube of energy
(an illustration appears on the following page).

Facing east, draw a letter *heh* ה at eye level to your left.
This creates a vertical line, like a column.
Put your intention into this line as you draw it.

Sketch *vav* ו at eye level to your right.
This forms another vertical line, parallel to the first.

Write a *zayin* ז above you
and a *chet* ח near the ground.
These create horizontal lines that join with the vertical ones
to complete one face of a cube that faces east.

Continue to hold your intention.

Now, turning to your left (north),
sketch *yud* י to your left.
This forms a new vertical line.

Sketch a *lamed* ל above you
and a *tet* ט near the ground.
These create horizontal lines that join with the vertical ones
so that you now have a second north-facing side of the cube.

Continue to hold your intention.

Figure 5. The twelve simple letters marking the boundaries of the cosmic cube.

Turn left once again so you are facing west.
Draw a *samech* ס to your left.
This creates a vertical line, like a column.

Sketch a *nun* נ near the ground
and an *ayin* ע higher up.
These create horizontal lines that join with the vertical ones
so that you now have a third west-facing side of the cube.

Continue to hold your intention.

Turn left once more to face south.
Draw a *tzadi* צ close to the ground
and a *kuf* ק higher up.
These create horizontal lines that join with the vertical ones
so that you now have the southern face,
finishing the entire cube.

When the cube is complete,
see that its lines glow with your intention.

From your place within the cube,
feel the intention you have drawn into its lines.
How do you feel or appear different
within this space?

Now, bring into the cube,
simply by intending to do so,
anyone or anything
you want this intention to reach.
Feel the impact of the cube you have drawn
on this person or entity.

Breathe out and open your eyes.

Practice: Setting the Borders

Close your eyes and breathe out.

You are sitting on a beach.
A wave comes toward you.
Reach out and draw a line around you in the sand.
Draw the line with the intention
to hold your space.
See that this line holds.
The wave breaks around you
but does not touch you.

No matter how many waves come,
they do not cross the line.

Feel the open space
that surrounds you.
Feel the freedom of this open space.

Now release the line,
and let the waves touch you once more.

Feel the surrender
of opening to the waves.

Breathe out and open your eyes.

Chapter 5:3 · Constellations, Months, and Organs

שתים עשרה פשוטות
חקקן צרפן חצבן
שקלן והמירן
וצר בהם
מזלות וחדשים ומנהיגים

Twelve simple letters:
God engraved them, transmuted them, carved them,
weighed them, exchanged them,
and created with them
constellations, months, and organs.

ואילו הן שנים עשר מזלות
טלה שור תאומים סרטן
אריה בתולה מעזנים עקרב
קשת גדי דלי דגים

ושנים עשר חדשים
ניסן אייר סיון תמוז
אב אלול תשרי מרחשוון
כסליו טבת שבט אדר

ואילו הן שנים עשר מנהיגים בנפש
שתי ידים שתי רגלים שתי כליות
כבד ומרה טחול
המסס קרקבן וקיבה

> These are the twelve constellations in the world:
> Aries, Taurus, Gemini, Cancer,
> Leo, Virgo, Libra, Scorpio,
> Sagittarius, Capricorn, Aquarius, Pisces.
>
> The twelve months in the year are:
> Nisan, Iyar, Sivan, Tamuz,
> Av, Elul, Tishrei, Marcheshvan,
> Kislev, Tevet, Shevat, Adar.
>
> The twelve organs in the body-soul are:
> Two hands, two feet, two kidneys
> The liver, the gall, the spleen,
> The gullet, the intestines, and the stomach.

The simple letters, like the mothers and doubles, manifest as different entities in the realms of space, time, and body. In space, the twelve simple letters become the constellations of the Zodiac. In time, the simples become months of the year. In the body, the twelve simple letters become limbs and organs. The Hebrew word is *manhigim* or "directors"—organs that guide the functioning of the body. The organs guide the body, just as the stars and months guide the destiny of a person.

The phrase "engraved and carved" returns us again and again to the divine workshop, inviting us to imagine God hewing lines and pathways in the raw materials of the cosmos. These pathways are the reason why, in the conception of *Sefer Yetzirah*, the planet under which one is born can connect to one's destiny. The world is full of subtle connections between seemingly disparate things.

The twelve simple letters combine into many, many possible permutations, yielding myriad creations. When discussing the three mothers and the seven doubles, the text spells out the number of possible combinations. Chapter 5 does not—presumably because the number is too large to contemplate.

Constellations   מזלות

The Hebrew phrase *mazalot* means stars, planets, constellations, or astrological signs. Though some texts assert that astrology is forbidden to

Jews—such as the famous *"ain mazal b'yisrael"* ("astrology does not apply to the people Israel")—others assert that even a blade of grass has a "planet" that tells it to grow.[16] The Talmud states that "anyone who knows how to calculate the astrological seasons and the planetary movements and does not do so, the Torah says about him that "they do not take notice of the movements of God..."[17]

Synagogue floors in Beit Alpha, Yafia, and Tiberias depict the twelve zodiac signs. The synagogue floor at Tiberias pictures the sun (Helios) in the center—or, this image may be intended to symbolize the divine.[18] This suggests that for Jews of that period, astrology was not controversial, or else it would not have been depicted in sacred places. Bernard Goldman writes that for the Jews of those synagogues, the zodiac was a "symbol of the heavens and constellations under whose aegis the destinies of nature and of men were ordered."[19]

Sefer Yetzirah seems to stand firmly in a Jewish tradition where astrology plays a role in history. Marla Segol writes that "the power of the letters is embedded in astrological forces."[20] Segol adds that later kabbalists believed the letter combination practices of *Sefer Yetzirah* could bring about "the reconstruction and restoration of broken constellations"[21] that would hasten the messianic age: "The *Sefer Yetzirah* posits that the manipulation of letters was intended to produce practical, messianic effects."[22] This is Segol's reading based on later understandings of *Sefer Yetzirah*. We can only see the vaguest outline of such beliefs in the passage before us. However, it does seem clear that *Sefer Yetzirah* connects the letters to the stars, and both stars and letters have the power to control destiny.

Months וחדשים

The Hebrew for months is *chadashim*—the singular is *chodesh*. This word is from the root *chadash* which means "renewal." The Jewish calendar has twelve months (though one month, Adar, repeats itself in leap years for a total of thirteen). The months begin at the new moon and last 29-30 days.

According to *Sefer Yetzirah*, each month matches with a particular constellation, just as they do in classical astrology. It is possible that *Sefer Yetzirah* intends to indicate that those born under certain zodiac signs will have particular strengths and weaknesses in their faculties and organs. This would give Chapter 5 a diagnostic use—magical practitioners could diagnose certain problems or prescribe healing practices based on when and under what sign the patient was born.

Organs   ומנהיגים

In rabbinic Hebrew, a *manhig* is a community leader.[23] There is a rabbinic usage of a similar word to mean the stars as directing agencies of the heavens.[24] *Sefer Yetzirah* uses the word to mean "organ."

We should note that the word *manhig* is connected to Hebrew word *minhag*, which generally refers to a custom, often a binding custom that has become community practice. A *minhag* is the way something is done, as per community tradition. The *manhigim* or guiding organs provide the internal environment of the body and constitute its pathways: they are the way the body does things.

In the earliest recoverable version, the text ends here, having invoked the faculties, borders, constellations, months, and organs as aspects of the twelve simples. The accounting of the twenty-two letters is now complete. The pathways have all been carved and activated for use. The stones have been combined, and the temple has been built. We now await the conclusion of our ritual.

Twelve Constellations in the Cosmos

Hayman notes that the passage ending with "constellations, months, and organs" is then compounded by additions, one version of which has been included here in italics.[25] Presumably, readers needed to know which constellations, months, and organs corresponded to one another, for magical and healing purposes as well as meditative purposes, and so this section of *Sefer Yetzirah* expanded over time. The chapter thus came to end, not with a brief statement about "constellations, months, and organs," but with extensive lists pertaining to those three categories.

The first list is of the constellations. The names of the constellations match the Greek astrological system, but use Hebrew terms (*Taleh*, the Ram, Aries; *Shor*, the Bull, Taurus, etc.). The tenth-century philosopher Maimonides mentions these Hebrew terms for the signs of the Zodiac, as does the midrashic commentary by Pirkei deRabbi Eliezer.[26] The second list, of the months, lists the Jewish months developed during the Babylonian exile, the same months we find in other Jewish sources.[27] The third list is of the organs. We can see that in the list of organs, classical "organs" are included but also other body-soul parts, such as hands and feet. There is considerable debate about which organs are indicated by some of these words; this translation has followed Hayman's version.

There is a significant Talmud-era tradition of associating the twelve constellations and months (as well as the human faculties like speech, sleep, etc.) with the twelve tribes of Israel. Neusner notes a fourth or fifth century CE text in which Judah, Issachar, and Zebulun correspond with Aries, Taurus, and Gemini; Reuben, Simeon, and Gad correspond with Cancer, Leo, and Virgo; Ephraim, Manasseh, and Benjamin correspond with Libra, Scorpio, and Sagittarius; and Dan, Asher, and Naphtali correspond with Capricorn, Aquarius, and Pisces.[28] Commentators on *Sefer Yetzirah*, medieval and contemporary, often include tribal correspondences in their commentaries.[29]

The Gullet, the Intestines, and the Stomach

המסס
קרקבן
וקיבה

These are Hayman's translations for *hamses*, *korkeban*, and *kivah*. However, *hamses* could mean "first stomach of ruminants," *korkeban* could mean "the thick muscular stomach of birds, or craw," and *kivah* could mean "maw," as in the maw of a livestock animal.[30] It is fascinating that this layer of *Sefer Yetzirah* seems to be naming body parts that go with animals, not humans. Kaplan notes this and theorizes that perhaps the organs are human after all and the terms are being used in some idiosyncratic way, or perhaps "by making use of these organs, one may create an animal or a bird rather than a human"—in other words, one can use this text to make a *golem* of an animal kind.[31]

This last reading suggests that when *Sefer Yetzirah* says *nefesh*, it means not only body, but being, as in any living being. It may be that the book is not as human-centric as it appears, but that multiple kinds of life are included in the cosmic dimensions of "body-soul." Indeed, the Hebrew word *nefesh* can be used for non-human beings, as in the Hebrew phrase *nefesh chaya*, a living being, which appears often in Genesis.[32]

Contemporary scientists have shown that consciousness does not only belong to human beings but to many creatures. Similarly, David Seidenberg, author of *Kabbalah and Ecology: God's Image in the More-than-Human World*, notes that in many kabbalistic texts, not only are humans made in the "divine image" but all of creation is as well.[33] Seidenberg quotes the Zohar Chadash as saying: "In the secret of Shekhinah [the divine presence] were arrayed all these lower beings... All these that are existing below are united in Her, in Her image, in actuality."[34] It may be that *Sefer Yetzirah* also understands all life as emanated from and inhabited by the Divine.

Practice: The Star

Close your eyes and breathe out slowly.

You are lying beneath a night sky.
Stars shine above you.
One particular star catches your attention.
Its light falls on you
and permeates your body.
Healing and cleansing
from the light of this star
reaches all the limbs and organs of your body.

Perhaps one particular part
needs healing
and receives it from the light of this star.

The star recedes
but its light now shines within you,
illuminating all your cells, organs, and limbs,
all of your body and soul.

Breathe out and open your eyes.

Practice: Circle of Twelve

Close your eyes and breathe out.

Around you are twelve figures.
Perhaps they are the twelve simple letters,
the signs of the Zodiac,
or the months of the year.
Turn in a circle
and see all twelve figures.

One of the figures comes to life
and comes to stand with you.
This being has come to share with you
wisdom you need for healing and growth.
Listen to what this being has to tell you.
The being steps back into place.

Turn in a circle
and again see all twelve beings.
Notice what, if anything, is different now.

Breathe out and open your eyes.

Chapter 5:4 · Crowning the Twelve Letters

המליך אות **הי** וקשר לו כתר
וצרפן זה עם זה
וצר בו **טלה** בעולם
וניסן בשנה
וכבד בנפש

המליך אות **ויו** וקשר לו כתר
וצרפן זה עם זה
וצר בו **שור** בעולם
ואייר בשנה
ומרה בנפש

המליך אות **זיין** וקשר לו כתר
וצרפן זה עם זה
וצר בו **תאומים** בעולם
וסיון בשנה
וטחול בנפש

המליך אות **חית** וקשר לו כתר
וצרפן זה עם זה
וצר בו **סרטן** בעולם
ותמוז בשנה
והמסס בנפש

המליך אות **טית** וקשר לו כתר
וצרפן זה עם זה
וצר בו **אריה** בעולם
ואב בשנה
וכוליה ימין בנפש

המליך אות **יוד** וקשר לו כתר
וצרפן זה עם זה
וצר בו **בתולה** בעולם
ואלול בשנה
וכוליה שמאל בנפש

Chapter 5:4 · Crowning the Twelve Letters

המליך אות **למד** וקשר לו כתר
וצרפן זה עם זה
וצר בו **מאזנים** בעולם
ותשרי בשנה
וקרקבן בנפש

המליך אות **נון** וקשר לו כתר
וצרפן זה עם זה
וצר בו **עקרב** בעולם
ומרחשוון בשנה
וקיבה בנפש

המליך אות **סמך** וקשר לו כתר
וצרפן זה עם זה
וצר בו **קשת** בעולם
וכסליו בשנה
ויד ימין בנפש

המליך אות **עין** וקשר לו כתר
וצרפן זה עם זה
וצר בו **גדי** בעולם
וטבת בשנה
ויד שמאל בנפש

המליך אות **צדי** וקשר לו כתר
וצרפן זה עם זה
וצר בו **דלי** בעולם
ושבט בשנה
ורגל ימין בנפש

המליך אות **קוף** וקשר לו כתר
וצרפן זה עם זה
וצר בו **דגים** בעולם
ואדר בשנה
ורגל שמאל בנפש

God gave rule to **Heh** and tied a crown to it
and combined one thing with another and formed with it
Aries in the world
Nisan in the year
and the **liver** in the body.

God gave rule to **Vav** and tied a crown to it
and combined one thing with another and formed with it
Taurus in the world
Iyar in the year
and the **gall bladder** in the body.

God gave rule to **Zayin** and tied a crown to it
and combined one thing with another and formed with it
Gemini in the world
Sivan in the year
and the **spleen** in the body.

God gave rule to **Chet** and tied a crown to it
and combined one thing with another and formed with it
Cancer in the world
Tamuz in the year
and the **gullet** in the body.

God gave rule to **Tet** and tied a crown to it
and combined one thing with another and formed with it
Leo in the world
Av in the year
and the **right kidney** in the body.

God gave rule to **Yud** and tied a crown to it
and combined one thing with another and formed with it
Virgo in the world
Elul in the year
and the **left kidney** in the body.

God gave rule to **Lamed** and tied a crown to it
and combined one thing with another and formed with it
Libra in the world
Tishrei in the year
and the **intestines** in the body.

God gave rule to **Nun** and tied a crown to it
and combined one thing with another and formed with it
Scorpio in the world
Marcheshvan in the year
and the **stomach** in the body.

God gave rule to **Samech** and tied a crown to it
and combined one thing with another and formed with it
Sagittarius in the world
Kislev in the year
and the **right hand** in the body.

God gave rule to **Ayin** and tied a crown to it
and combined one thing with another and formed with it
Capricorn in the world
Tevet in the year
and the **left hand** in the body.

God gave rule to **Tzadi** and tied a crown to it
and combined one thing with another and formed with it
Aquarius in the world
Shevat in the year
and the **right foot** in the body.

God gave rule to **Kuf** and tied a crown to it
and combined one thing with another and formed with it
Pisces in the world
Adar in the year
and the **left foot** in the body.

Return to the Place

This section is also not part of the earliest recoverable version. Hayman describes this section as part of "the major expansion of *Sefer Yetzirah* that produced the Long Recension." We include a version of it here[35] so we can get a further sense of how the scribes and readers of *Sefer Yetzirah* understood the constellations, months, and organs. There is an even more expansive version of this section in which the twelve faculties are listed with the constellations, months, and organs (such that Aries/Nisan is associated with speech, Taurus/Iyar with thought, etc.).[36]

As we noted in Chapter 4, this passage may have been included as a guide to healing practitioners, showing which constellations and times of year could impact the healing of various organs and limbs.[37] Perhaps the text might also have suggested the body strengths and/or weaknesses of those born in various months, under various signs of the Zodiac. *Sefer Yetzirah* seems to suggest that just as the body is a microcosm of the world (containing elements of air, water, and fire), so too the body is a microcosm of the night sky, representing all of the zones of the zodiac. This sends the message that the human being is intrinsically connected to the larger creation.

The human and the cosmos are also connected in the later kabbalah. For example, the *sefirot* (divine facets) of the kabbalah have their expression in particular human beings. Abraham, for example, embodies *chesed* or divine love, while Isaac is paired with *gevurah* or limitation, Leah is *binah* or the divine womb (also a form of divine understanding), and Rachel embodies *malkhut* or Shekhinah/divine presence.[38] The *sefirot* also manifest in human body parts: *chesed* in the right arm, *gevurah* in the left, *tiferet* in the heart, and so forth.[39] These extrapolate the approach already present in *Sefer Yetzirah*: that each part of the human body is connected to a particular cosmic force, and that the whole human is linked with the whole of creation.

Sefer Yetzirah's belief that the universe and the human share a pattern could be seen as humans making God and/or the world in our image. But if we look at it a different way, we can see this idea as an acknowledgment that everything in us comes from the stars and the water and the earth, and everything in the stars and the water and the earth stems from the underlying patterns of the cosmos. In Chapter 5, *Sefer Yetzirah* lays out before us the nature of our existence.

Practice: Letter of Healing

Before you begin, you can choose a letter from among the twelve simple letters, corresponding to a body part that wants healing. The example below will use the letter nun, but you can use any of the simple letters.

Close your eyes and breathe out.

The *nun* appears before you.

נ

See, hear, and touch the *nun*.
Notice any feelings or associations you have.
The *nun* now becomes transparent
and able to pass through any substance.
Allow the *nun* to enter your body
and go to your stomach,
which is its natural space within the body.
Feel the healing power of *nun*
as it rests in your stomach.
Notice what happens in your stomach.
Does it become less sore or tight?

Allow the *nun* to dissolve
and become part of you.

Breathe out and open your eyes.

Repeat with as many letters as you wish.

Practice: Blessings of the Months

Before you begin, note the Hebrew month and the letter of that month, according to 5:4. The examples below will use the month of Nisan, the spring month of Passover, and Tishrei, the fall month of Rosh haShanah, but you can use any month and letter.

Nisan

Close your eyes and breathe out.

Allow Nisan,
month of spring
to arise in your thoughts.
What feelings arise
as you contemplate this month?
Notice what is good or hard for you
about this moment in time.

Visualize *heh*, the letter
connected to this month.

ה

The quality of *heh* is "sight."
Allow your sight or perception to deepen and expand
as you contemplate this month.
What can you see or perceive now
that you could not before?
See how the month is filled with this blessing of sight.

Keep this blessing with you
in the days ahead.

Breathe out and open your eyes.

Tishrei

Close your eyes and breathe out.

Allow Tishrei,
month of autumn and the new year,
to arise in your thoughts.
What feelings arise
as you contemplate this month?
Notice what is good or hard for you
about this moment in time.

Visualize *lamed*, the letter
connected to this month.
ל
The quality of *lamed* is "action."
Seek within yourself
for the knowledge that you can act
to improve the world and your life.
See that the *lamed*,
tall like a shepherd's crook,
strengthens this place.
Allow your capacity for action
to deepen and expand.
To what action
will you commit this month?
See how the month is filled with this blessing of action.

Keep this blessing with you
in the days ahead.

Breathe out and open your eyes.

Table of Letter Correspondences

	Letter	Type	Space	Time	Body-Soul
א	Aleph	Mother	Sky	Spring	Chest
ב	Bet	Double	Saturn	Shabbat	Mouth
ג	Gimel	Double	Jupiter	Sunday	Right Eye
ד	Dalet	Double	Mars	Monday	Left Eye
ה	Heh	Elemental	Aries	Nisan	Liver
ו	Vav	Elemental	Taurus	Iyar	Gall Bladder
ז	Zayin	Elemental	Gemini	Sivan	Spleen
ח	Chet	Double	Cancer	Tamuz	Gullet
ט	Tet	Elemental	Leo	Av	Right Kidney
י	Yud	Elemental	Virgo	Elul	Left Kidney
כ	Kaf	Double	Sun	Tuesday	Right Nostril
ל	Lamed	Elemental	Libra	Tishrei	Intestines
מ	Mem	Mother	Middle World	Winter	Belly
נ	Nun	Elemental	Scorpio	Marcheshvan	Stomach
ס	Samech	Elemental	Sagittarius	Kislev	Right Hand
ע	Ayin	Elemental	Capricorn	Tevet	Left Hand
פ	Peh	Double	Venus	Wednesday	Left Nostril
צ	Tzadi	Elemental	Aquarius	Shevat	Right Foot
ק	Kuf	Elemental	Pisces	Adar	Left Foot
ר	Reish	Double	Mercury	Thursday	Right Ear
ש	Shin	Mother	Earth	Summer	Head
ת	Tav	Double	Moon	Friday	Left Ear

Table of Letter Correspondences

			Foundation	Kaplan's Foundations*
א	Aleph	Mother	Air	Air
ב	Bet	Double	Life	Wisdom
ג	Gimel	Double	Peace	Wealth
ד	Dalet	Double	Wisdom	Seed
ה	Heh	Elemental	Sight	Speech
ו	Vav	Elemental	Hearing	Thought
ז	Zayin	Elemental	Smell	Locomotion
ח	Chet	Double	Speech	Sight
ט	Tet	Elemental	Taste	Hearing
י	Yud	Elemental	Sexuality	Action
כ	Kaf	Double	Wealth	Life
ל	Lamed	Elemental	Action	Sexuality
מ	Mem	Mother	Water	Water
נ	Nun	Elemental	Locomotion	Smell
ס	Samech	Elemental	Agitation	Sleep
ע	Ayin	Elemental	Laughter	Agitation
פ	Peh	Double	Grace	Sovereignty
צ	Tzadi	Elemental	Thought	Taste
ק	Kuf	Elemental	Sleep	Laughter
ר	Reish	Double	Seed	Peace
ש	Shin	Mother	Fire	Fire
ת	Tav	Double	Sovereignty	Grace

* Please note there are different traditions regarding the foundation or essence of the double and simple letters. This chart was created by matching the lists of letters in each chapter with the lists of essences (the first listed letter matching with the first listed essence, etc.) Aryeh Kaplan's translation and commentary use a later version of the text.

Chapter 6:1 · The Conclusion

אילו עשרים ושתים אותיות
שבהן חקק יה וה צבאות
אלוהים חיים אלוהי ישראל
רם ונשא
שוכן עד וקדוש שמו

These are the twenty-two letters
through which
the Becoming One who Holds Many
the living God
God of Israel
lofty and exalted
dwelling in eternity
of holy name
engraved
the cosmos

Having journeyed through the ten *sefirot* and the twenty-two letters, we are now winding toward the end of our incantation. As we come to the end, we circle back to the beginning.[1] In 1:1, *YHWH Tzeva'ot* engraved the thirty-two paths; here in 6:1, *YHWH Tzeva'ot* (God of Hosts, translated here as the Becoming One who Holds Many) again engraves the paths. *Sefer Yetzirah* is an unfolding ritual process in which the reader, by reading, engages the ritual: the invocation at the beginning and the benediction at the end frame the ritual work.

Yet there is something not quite right. The text mentions the twenty-two letters, but there is no mention of the ten *sefirot* from Chapter 1. The benediction does not perfectly reflect the invocation. The word "Wisdom" also does not appear in our passage, so Wisdom in the opening passage does not receive an echo. This shows us, perhaps, some of the "seams" between the texts: they do not all come from the same author. Hayman is

Chapter 6:1 · The Conclusion

not even certain whether this paragraph belongs in the earliest recoverable version, yet ultimately he places it there in brackets.[2]

The paragraph contains a verb describing what God does with the twenty-two letters. The manuscripts disagree about what verb this is. Some manuscripts indicate the verb is *yasad* (founded) while others say the verb is *chakak* (engraved).[3] Hayman speculates that later editors may have chosen the word *yasad* to reflect Proverbs 3:19—"With Wisdom, God founded the earth" or Psalms 104:5—"God founded the earth on its foundations."[4] Ultimately Hayman chooses *yasad* for his version, but *chakak* is parallel with 1:1 and therefore we will use it here.

Yasad implies the setting of a building on a firm foundation, and evokes the image of God as builder. *Chakak* presents the image of God as scribe, or stoneworker. Throughout the book, *chakak* suggests that God creates world and text by the same means: inscription. The word *chakak* reifies the theme of the book: that the universe and the text are fundamentally the same.

By returning to the word *chakak*, the book comes full circle. The "engraving" is at the same time God's engraving of the letters/elements, the human "engraving" of words as the book is recited and practiced, and the ritual's "engraving" into the cosmos as it is performed over and over again. The book draws toward its conclusion by re-invoking God's process of engraving, echoed and reified by our speaking and enacting of it.

In 1:1, God engraves the letters into the three books. In 6:1, it is unclear into what substance God engraves the letters. Hayman suggests "the cosmos" as a possible object for the verb, even though the word is not in the text.[5] Or, we might reconsider Marla Segol's reading of 1:1 in which *chakak Yah*, "God engraved," may also mean "engraved out of God." That is, the thirty-two paths of Wisdom are engraved or hollowed within God's substance. We might then suggest that here, *chakak* means "engraved within Godself" and that the word "universe" is missing because God already contains the universe.

We might also say that by avoiding the word for "universe," the text refuses to limit itself to a particular word. It is almost as if we should end the passage with an ellipsis: "These are the twenty-two letters through which the Infinite One engraved…" It is as if the "everything" that God engraved is too vast and multiple to have a name, just as we learned in 4:4 that the number of God's creations are "what the mouth cannot say and the ear cannot hear." In this sense, the book can never really conclude. The creative process goes on into infinity.

The Becoming One Who Holds Many יה וה צבאות

The list of divine names in this passage echoes the divine names invoked at the beginning of *Sefer Yetzirah*. The invocation of God's name is a kind of seal on the book: just as in Chapter 1, God's name was used to open the book and also to seal the six directions of the universe. The book requires a protective closure, which this paragraph provides. One can easily imagine the reader chanting these names out loud—utilizing the act of speech to seal the creative work that has been done with the twenty-two letters. In fact, there are six God-names/phrases listed in the earliest recoverable manuscript, and this could constitute a seal for the six directions.

As we noted in the commentary to 1:1, the name *Yah Tzeva'ot* (God of Hosts) was not chosen by accident. The entire purpose of *Sefer Yetzirah* is to establish an unbroken link between the unity of God and the diversity of creation. The name *Yah Tzeva'ot*, God of the many hosts, reiterates this purpose. God is a deity of oneness and also of countless stars, creatures, stones. God's engraved and living hosts now arise and give glory to their creator.

Practice: The Engraver

Close your eyes and breathe out.

You are watching one who engraves letters into stone.

Maybe this is God, or another creator-being,
or maybe it is you or someone you know.
It is not easy to see what is being engraved.
Go closer until you are able to see
the engraved stone.

Engraved into the stone
is the primary wisdom of creation.
Take in this wisdom.

Breathe out and open your eyes.

Practice: Dwelling in Eternity

Close your eyes and breathe out.

Rays of light
extend from the universe
into your body:
twenty-two rays of light.

Through these lines,
you feel a potent energy—
the power of eternity—
come into your body.

Allow yourself to fill
with the energy of the rays.

Allow yourself to know what you must do
with the energy that fills you.

Let the answer come
in whatever form it comes.

Breathe out and open your eyes.

Practice: Twenty-Two Letters

Close your eyes and breathe out.

You are in a place of treasures:
a king's counting room,
a dragon's hoard,
or a museum of priceless antiquities.

All around you are precious things.

Among the treasures,
you discover the twenty-two Hebrew letters.

Pick up one of the letters.

This letter has been given to you
so you may carry out your mission in the world.

Promise it that you will do your best
to use the letter well.

Now, with the letter's help,
see the beginning of your task.

Breathe out and open your eyes.

Chapter 6:2 · The Road Map, Revisited

שלושה אבות ותולדותיהן
ושבעה כבשים וצבאותיהן
ושנים עשר גבולי אכלסין
וראיה לדבר
עדים נאמנים
עולם שנה ונפש

Three fathers and their generations
seven conquerors and their hosts
twelve diagonal boundaries
and the proof of the matter:
faithful witnesses,
the world, the year, and the body-soul.

As the first passage of Chapter 6 echoes the first passage of Chapter 1, the second passage of Chapter 6 echoes the second passage of Chapter 1. The narrative returns to the "road map" of three, seven, and twelve, and also invokes the realms of space, time, and body-soul (which are also the *sefirot*: beginning and end, up, down, east, west, north, south, good and evil). These concepts have accompanied us throughout our reading of the book. Returning to them and naming them completes our ritual journey.

And, as with Chapter 1, the parallel isn't perfect. The mothers are called "fathers." The august tenth-century commentator Saadya Gaon is so nonplussed by this that he simply translates the phrase as "three mothers," explaining that for the text's purposes, "mothers" and "fathers" imply the same thing (i.e., origins or elements).[6] We know "diagonal boundaries" are an attribute of the twelve simples—but why call the twelve simples "diagonal boundaries" instead of the twelve simples? "Conquerors" as a word for the seven doubles doesn't appear elsewhere, and "proof of the matter" (as opposed to "a sign of the matter" is a rabbinic phrase that doesn't appear anywhere else in the book. The passage is speaking in a voice we aren't quite used to. And this chapter has no tagline—no repeated phrase that indicates the theme of Chapter 6. This is a strange departure from the carefully formulated structure of the rest of the book.

It feels as if the passages in Chapter 6 are different somehow—and one way they are different is that they consistently offer biblical allusions or prooftexts for their insights. Maybe the author(s) of the passages in Chapter 6 is hoping to integrate the wisdom of *Sefer Yetzirah* into normative Judaism by showing the relationship between the secrets of this book and the ideas and images of the Bible itself. In a way, this is an understandable anxiety that arises at the end of the book's process: how will the reader integrate and absorb this wisdom into their community and daily life?

Three Fathers   שלושה אבות

It is probable that at some point in the recension of the text, some editors found the partnership between the Creator and the three mothers uncomfortable, and thus added (or in this case substituted) the three fathers. This passage may be trying to offer "proof" for the primacy of *Aleph, Mem,* and *Shin* by relating them to the three patriarchs. The phrase "generations," used often in Genesis, further links the "father letters" to the patriarchs of the Bible. The "fathers" do seem like they might be more palatable to normative Jews of the period than the "mothers."

Yet in all of the early manuscripts, the phrase *toldoteihen*, "their generations" is feminized, where it should be masculine because "fathers" is masculine. It could be that the passage once referenced mother letters rather than father letters—or that a scribe or editor who copied the text understood "fathers" as another word for mothers (just as Saadya Gaon later did).

Seven Conquerors   ושבעה כבשים וצבאותיהן

We've noted that the seven doubles receive a new name in this passage: "seven conquerors." *Kovshim*—those who conquer or subdue—apparently refers to the seven double letters. Since the seven doubles are linked to powerful planets and determine human fate, they may well be said to be conquerors.

However, there is another implied meaning here. The word *kevasim* (lambs) is spelled with the letter *sin*, which is written identically to *Shin* except for a change in the placement of one dot. In a manuscript without vowels, the two words would be identical. We wouldn't think of calling the seven doubles "lambs" except that the phrase *shivah kevasim*, "seven lambs," occurs in the book of Numbers and is written exactly the way the phrase is written here.[7] In Genesis, Abraham makes a non-aggression pact with his neighbor Abimelech by setting aside seven ewes (*sheva kivshot*)—a very similar phrase to *shivah kevasim*.[8] The author of the passage, in naming the doubles as *kovshim*, may be suggesting that the Torah itself alludes to the seven doubles.

Twelve Diagonal Boundaries ושנים עשר גבולי אכלסין

In 5:2, the simple letters are named "twelve diagonal boundaries"— the twelve lines that makes up the cube of the cosmic Temple. The text could have chosen other terms—the human faculties, organs, months, or constellations. "Boundaries" may have been chosen for its biblical resonance. According to Numbers, each of the twelve Israelite tribes received a particular allotment of land. The land would of course have been divided by boundaries, as is noted in Deuteronomy.[9] 6:2 may imply that the twelve boundaries of the cosmic Temple—and thus the twelve simple letters—are linked to the twelve boundaries of the tribes. This too constitutes a subtle biblical proof.

The parallel between the boundaries of tribal land and the boundaries of the cosmic cube is fascinating. Where the land is physical and specific, the cosmos is metaphysical and general. David Abram suggests that the experience of alienation from land and place leads to more abstract mythmaking:

> The land itself, stripped of the particularizing stories that once sprouted from every cave and streambed and cluster of trees, begins to lose its multiplicitous power. The human senses, intercepted by the written word, are no longer gripped and fascinated by the expressive shapes and sounds of particular places. The spirits fall silent. Gradually the felt primacy of place is forgotten, superseded by a new, abstract notion of "space" as a homogeneous, placeless void.[10]

Abram's words would seem to apply to *Sefer Yetzirah*'s abstraction from the real land of Israel to a "cosmic space" that does indeed appear to be a homogeneous void. Yet in building the void out of letters that are distinct and unique, *Sefer Yetzirah* points us back toward what Abram calls "the expressive shapes and sounds of particular places." Even when the connection to a specific land is compromised, the human being can turn to the universe, in order to be at home anywhere s/he happens to be—and from that place, we can begin again to notice the specificity of the world around us.

Faithful Witnesses עדים נאמנים

6:2, like 4:6, uses "faithful witnesses" as synonyms for the realms of space, time, and body-soul. This too is a biblical allusion, as God tells the prophet Isaiah to call "faithful witnesses" to witness a written prophecy.[11] In Deuteronomy, God invokes heaven and earth as witnesses, and asks the heavens and earth to hear God's words.[12] We can see that 6:2 connects the "fathers," "conquerors," and "diagonal boundaries" as well as the "faithful witnesses" to biblical texts, and thus perhaps attempts to provide biblical legitimacy for *Sefer Yetzirah*'s ideas.

In general, a witness is a conscious entity that can attest to some event. For example, in Deuteronomy, two witnesses are required to convict someone of a crime.[13] In the Book of Ruth, Boaz asks the town elders to witness his marriage.[14] Elizabeth Roberts writes: "One of the most basic modern separations, especially within modern science, is that between animated spirit and inert matter."[15] The language of *Sefer Yetzirah* consistently comes down on the side of eliding this distinction by treating the characteristics of the universe as animate.

So in our passage, the cosmic witnesses of space, time, and body-soul are observers of all of our experiences, for they are the playing field upon which the drama of being and consciousness can unfold. We might say they watch over that playing field and the entities that play upon it. In 1:8, the cosmic dimensions are fiery angels who bow before God's throne. Perhaps this passage invites us to imagine space, time and perspective as angels holding and witnessing the world.

Practice: Faithful Witnesses
Close your eyes and breathe out.

Three angels appear before you:
the angel of space,
the angel of time,
the angel of the body-soul.
You may ask one question
of each of these angels:
the angel of space
the angel of time
the angel of the body-soul.
Ask your three questions
and receive the answers.
Each of the angels
now has a gift for you.
As the gifts pass to you,
the angels vanish.

Breathe out and open your eyes.

Practice: Three, Seven, Twelve
Close your eyes and breathe out.

Facing you are three ancestors.
Behind them are the generations.
Where is your place
among the ancestors and their generations?
Facing you are seven conquerors.
Behind them are their hosts.
Where is your place
among the conquerors and their hosts?
Facing you are twelve boundaries.
Within them are twelve lands,
twelve tribal territories.
Where is your place
in these twelve lands?

Breathe out and open your eyes.

Chapter 6:3 · The Three Kings

חק עשרה שלשה ושבעה ושנים עשר
פקודים
בתלי וגלגל ולב
תלי בעולם כמלך על כסאו
גלגל בשנה כמלך במדינה
לב בנפש כמלך במלחמה

An engraved rule
of ten and three and seven and twelve
entrusted to
the Dragon, the Wheel, and the Heart.

The Dragon in the World
is like a king on his throne.

The Wheel in the Year
is like a king in the countryside.

The Heart in the Body
is like a king in war.

Like 6:2, 6:3 invokes the book's core sets of numbers: three, seven, ten, and twelve. The passage calls these numbers a *chok*, an "engraved rule" of the cosmos. In that sense, this passage too is a summary and benediction, invoking the fundamental structures of the universe and reiterating God's engraving of these structures.

Yet this passage also introduces new characters: the Dragon, the Wheel, and the Heart. Each of these entities rules one of the three realms: the Dragon directs space, the Wheel directs time, and the Heart directs the body-soul. One might say that each entity is a genius or a guiding spirit for its realm. By introducing these guiding spirits, the text gives us a key to the three "books" of space, time, and human experience.

Each realm can be better understood if we understand the way its guide functions.

The Hebrew used here for "entrusted with" or "appointed over" is *pekudim. Pekudim* can also mean "records," as in "records of the Tabernacle"—records that describe and define all of the sacred vessels and the artists who made them.[16] By using this word, this passage too alludes to the building of the cosmic shrine—by the Creator and by the creators who come after.

The Dragon in the World   תלי בעולם

The Hebrew word *T'li* does not appear in the Bible or Talmud, but seems to come from the root *taleh*, to hang. Some translate it "the Hook,"[17] but many others understand *T'li* to mean "Dragon."[18] It is generally agreed that the *T'li* is an astrological phenomenon: a central force around which all of space organizes itself. The nature of a dragon is power, and the Dragon of *Sefer Yetzirah* exercises power over all six directions.

Aryeh Kaplan defines *T'li* as "the invisible axis around which the heavens rotate," and indicates that this axis is also sometimes called the "ecliptic pole." The constellation Draco surrounds the ecliptic pole, and Jewish commentators have identified Draco with the "Pole Serpent," a mythic dragonlike entity mentioned in the Book of Job.[19] Hence, one view of the "Dragon" in our text is that it is the axis mundi, the central pole of the world.

Jewish astrologer Lorelai Kude writes: "The undulating coils of the cosmic dragon mark the path of the eclipses across the earth over time."[20] Kude understands the *T'li* as identical to the "lunar nodes"—points in space where the orbit of the moon crosses the ecliptic. She notes that this image does not correspond to the rigid Ptolemaic axis mundi.[21] Rather, it looks like a serpent snaking among the constellations.

Similarly, the medieval commentator Shabbetai Donnolo comments:

> When God created the firmament above us, which is divided into seven heavens, He created the *T'li* from water and fire in the shape of a great dragon, like a twisted serpent, and made for it a head and a tail and put it in the fourth heaven, which is the middle heaven, the abode of the sun...

> The T'li...darkens the light of the two luminaries and the five planets, it moves the luminaries forward and backward and the planets and constellations from east to west and from west to east; it draws the planets back and holds them in one place, preventing them from straying either forwards or backwards...it cannot be seen with the naked eye but rather it is by the study of ancient texts transmitted to us that we gain knowledge of the Dragon...and how the twelve constellations are attached to it.
>
> The dragon upon whose undulating scales the starry universe is hung, holds the fate and destiny of all creation between head and tail.[22]

Tenth-century philosopher Saadya Gaon understands the T'li differently: as an embodiment of the place where the two orbits of the sun and moon intersect. (He is careful to note that he defines the T'li as a purely astrological term, not as a constellation or an actual "dragon."[23]) Other commentators understand the T'li as the Milky Way.[24] Marla Segol defines T'li as "a circular entity motivating the circular orbits of the constellations and planets."[25] And some understand the T'li as the "imaginary line from which the celestial sphere hangs, very much like a hook from its line."[26] However we define the T'li, we can see it is an organizing principle for the dimension of space: a sacred center, guiding force, or focal point.

The T'li stands in a long line of mythic world-forming dragons. We see a dragon who shapes the world in Babylonian myth, where the body of Tiamat, the dragon-like sea-goddess, is used to build the world.[27] We also see such an image in the primordial sea-monsters who are part of creation in Genesis 1, and in the biblical myth of Leviathan, God's sea-monster opponent and playmate.[28] While these ancient dragons dwell in the sea, the T'li of *Sefer Yetzirah* dwells among the stars. From the depths of the galaxies, the Dragon guides the world.[29]

A King on His Throne   כמלך על כסאו

As king of the world, the T'li is like a "king on his throne"— as opposed to a king in the countryside or at war. A king on a throne is a powerful, centralized force. From the throne, orders and directives go forth to realize the king's will. So too, the Dragon occupies a central point in space and exercises control from that central point.

In other texts from *Sefer Yetzirah*, letters "rule" over particular entities: for example, Aleph is king over air, etc. To "rule" or "be king" seems to mean "to initiate and govern the energies of particular entities." As Aleph initiates and governs the entities that arise from air, or Mem the entities that arise from water, the Dragon initiates and governs the entities that exist in the dimension of space: all physical phenomena "hang" from the Dragon. Perhaps, just as one might invoke the Aleph or the Mem to affect air or water energies within the world, one might invoke the Dragon to affect all of space. Marla Segol believes that adepts who learn how to work with the letters are supposed to then be able to shift the stars.[30]

In *Sefer Yetzirah*, diversity always begins with oneness—and here, the great diversity of matter hangs on a single dragon. From that single "hook" dangle all the celestial spheres. One is reminded of the cosmic Dragon as imagined by the writer A. A. Attanasio, a companion of the creator goddess, who sings matter into being:

> The Dragon's dreamsongs accompanied Her music, the boisterous polyphony of energy chilling to matter, atoms compressing to stars and fusing in the stellar interior to heavy elements, building larger, more complex harmonies of molecules, densities, starfields, and galaxies—all of it expanding faster and faster into the void...[31]

The Wheel in the Year גלגל בשנה

The nature of the wheel is movement. The Hebrew word for "wheel" is *galgal*, from a word for "circle" or "roll."[32] While the Dragon is a king on a throne (*melekh al kiso*), the Wheel is a *melekh bamedina*—a king in the provinces, or a king in the countryside. A king on a throne stays still while everyone comes to him. A king in the countryside makes his home in different places as he moves around inspecting every aspect of his realm. So too, the Wheel, which is governor of Time, moves constantly.

The Wheel appears to be the sphere of stars and constellations that revolves around the earth. Medieval commentator Shabbetai Donnolo, imagining the Wheel, writes:

The sphere turns the planets, the constellations, and the luminaries. This sphere is set within the depths of the firmament, and the constellations are permanently attached to it, never straying from their fixed position. This sphere supports the firmament to the south, the north, the east, and the west, and the Dragon stretches within it from end to end like a crossbeam."[33]

As the Wheel of Time moves through the months of the year, the constellations in the sky change. The wheel cycles again and again through months and seasons, yet it moves forward through the years as well. In this respect, it is similar to the "wheel" of letters that we encountered in Chapter 2—the wheel that "cycles forward and back" and "repeats in a cycle." The image of repetitive cycles that nevertheless move forward suggests that time is cyclical and linear, seasonal and progressive.

The wheels of the divine chariot in Ezekiel 1 may also be in the background of this text. The mysterious chariot wheels in Ezekiel are generally called *ofan*, but sometimes they are called *galgal*.[34] One wonders if our passage here, in naming the *Galgal*/Wheel, intends to evoke the divine wheels that bear God's throne. The wheels of the chariot have a *ruach chaya*, a living spirit to direct them,[35] and so too the Wheel seems to have a spirit that propels it onward.

The Dragon provides a central axis or crossbeam, and the Wheel a sphere surrounding that crossbeam. Thus, space and time interrelate. The Heart provides the third, and far less predictable, component in this complex weaving.

The Heart in the Body-Soul   לב בנפש

The Heart is the ruler of the body-soul. While we tend to associate the heart with feelings, in the Bible and throughout much of Jewish history, the heart is associated with thinking as well as feeling. The heart is the seat of consciousness in the body.

Our passage compares the Heart to a king at war. A king at war is dealing with opposing forces on a battlefield. The king must assert his power in order to be victorious. So too, the Heart must assert its power in opposition to evil. The Heart governs the human choices that make up a life. The Heart is also the site of good and bad experiences: pain, pleasure, and everything in between.

This view of the human heart as a battleground is consistent with Jewish views of the *yetzer hatov* (good inclination) and *yetzer hara* (evil inclination), which inform the actions of the human being. One rabbinic text asks "Who is strong? One who overcomes his [evil] inclination."[36] A passage from the Talmud explains the verse "you shall love your God with all your heart" by commenting: "with your two inclinations: your good inclination and your evil inclination."[37] Tendencies toward generosity and selfishness, reverence and cynicism, exist naturally in every human heart. So too, joy and sorrow, contentment and anger war in every being.

The heart is ever engaged in decision-making, questioning, regret, repentance, and renewal. The sixteenth century mystic St. John of the Cross called his inner struggle "the dark night of the soul."[38] When we sit quietly with ourselves, we become aware of the ways the heart is struggling on the inside. When we observe this struggle for what it is, rather than becoming caught up in the individual conflicts, we can slowly learn to disengage from the battle and find equilibrium. Contemplative quiet can help us to get distance from our difficult feelings, and make better decisions when we return to active engagement with life.

As we learned in Chapter 1, the Heart of the Body-Soul acts in relationship to the two *sefirot* of Good (*tov*) and Evil (*ra*). Similarly, the Wheel of Time works in relationship to the two *sefirot* of Beginning and End, and the Dragon of Space asserts its power in relationship to the six *sefirot* of North, South, East, West, Up, and Down. Opposites play a structural role in the realms of space and time, but the realm of the Body-Soul is different. The opposition of Good and Evil is not only a structural tension but a moral battle. The Heart is a "king at war"—always engaged in a battle for the good.

Kaplan, citing the twelfth-century kabbalistic work *Sefer haBahir*, associates the Shin (Fire) with the Dragon, the Mem (Water) with the Wheel, and the Aleph (Air) with the Heart.[39] We can easily see why fire and dragons go together, and why the breath—which gives rise to the chest—might be associated with the heart. And a wheel, like water, is always moving. If these associations are correct, the mother letters, the realms, and their directors can all be unified into a coherent structure.

The purpose of this passage in the ritual of *Sefer Yetzirah* seems to be to exhort the human reader, now an adept in the creative forces of the Hebrew letters, to return to the world prepared to do good. Even though we face a world in which good and evil exist, we also face a world that is coherently structured and full of God's presence. These factors support us in acting on behalf of creation, not destruction.

Practice: Throne of the Dragon

Close your eyes and breathe out.

You are gazing up at a vast sky of stars.
Above you,
a throne appears.
On the throne is a dragon.
The dragon guides and knows all space.
Ask the dragon to show you
the precise space in the universe
assigned to you.
Find and occupy your space in the universe
fully, without reservation.
From your place,
look up and thank the dragon
on its throne among the stars.

Breathe out and open your eyes.

Practice: The Wheel of Time

Close your eyes and breathe out.

Before you is a revolving wheel.
As the wheel revolves,
see that everything changes
with the passage of time.
Perceive that a change is unfolding
at this very moment.
See that this change
is a loss and a gain.

Breathe out and open your eyes.

Practice: The Heart at War

Close your eyes and breathe out.

Listen carefully to your heart.
Perceive the war that your heart is fighting.

Let your heart know
that you hear the pain of this war,
that you feel its suffering.

As you listen,
become aware of what must happen
for the heart to be at peace.

Let the transformation happen.

Let peace unfold.
Sit in the peace
of your heart.

Breathe out and open your eyes.

Chapter 6:4 · The Opposites

גם כל חפץ
זה לעומת זה
עשה אלהים
טוב לעומת רע
רע מרע וטוב מטוב
טוב מבחין את רע
ורע מבחין את טוב
טובה גנוזה לטובים
ורעה שמורה לרעים

Every experience,
one against the other,
God has made:
good opposite evil.
Evil from evil, good from good.
Good tests the evil
and evil tests the good.
Good is stored up for the good
and evil kept for the evil.

This passage picks up where the last one left off: with the heart at war, wrestling with the two alternatives of good and evil. This passage and the next one are a kind of subsection dealing with the conflict of opposites. In the dimensional version of the *sefirot*, six *sefirot* constitute space (north, south, east, west, up, down); two constitute time (beginning, end); and two constitute human experience/body-soul (good, evil). This passage zeroes in on the human experience of good and evil, building on the idea that the heart is a battleground.

The paragraph in 6:4 begins with a somewhat altered quote from Ecclesiastes 7:14.

> On a good day enjoy the good, and on a bad day, observe that one opposite the other God has made (*gam et zeh le'umat zeh asa Elohim*)...

This verse seems to offer the advice that when one is suffering, one should consider that God has made both good and evil in the world and therefore we are bound to experience both at some point. 6:4 subtracts the first part of this verse ("on a good day enjoy the good") and substitutes another phrase from Ecclesiastes: *kol hefetz*, which translates to something like "every experience," and which comes from Ecclesiastes 3:1.

> There is a season for everything, and a time for every experience (*lechol hefetz*) under heaven.

Now we have the amalgamated phrase *kol hefetz zeh le'umat zeh asa Elohim*, "every experience, one opposite the other, God has made." The text adds an introductory *gam* ("also") drawn from the second phrase in Ecclesiastes 7:14, so that the text now reads:

> Also every experience, one opposite the other, God has made...

The passage now continues with an Ecclesiastes-esque poem: "good opposite evil, evil opposite good" and so forth. In speaking of the good and the evil, our *Sefer Yetzirah* passage also seems to be integrating ideas from Ecclesiastes 3:17.

> I said in my heart: God will judge both righteous and wicked, for there is a time for every experience...

It is not an accident that these words about good and evil are quoted, or extrapolated, not from Genesis or Deuteronomy but from Ecclesiastes: a wisdom book that describes complex realities and evinces a certain fatalism about the vagaries of human experience. *Sefer Yetzirah* generally speaks in the voice of wisdom literature rather than law. It does not offer clear and easy answers about how to be good. It is not even clear that "good" and "evil" here solely means ethical good and evil—the text equally may be referring to experiential good and evil—i.e., pleasure and suffering.

What the passage does say is that the polarities of good and evil are inevitable in this world. God, the creator of multiplicity, has made them both. There is no satanic force in *Sefer Yetzirah*: there are only the opposites God has built into reality. God has made one (good) opposite the other (bad), and a wise person will accept that both must occur in the course of a life. Yet human actions matter: good gives rise to more good, while evil gives rise to more evil.

One Opposite the Other זה לעומת זה

In several places in *Sefer Yetzirah*, pairs of opposites characterize the diversity of existence.[40] In 1:3, the *sefirot* are described as two "hands" whose fingers oppose one another—in other words, each *sefirah* has an opposite. In 1:7, each *sefirah* is a depth that opposes another depth: north vs. south, beginning vs. end, good vs. evil. And in 4:1, the double letters represent opposing states: life and death, wealth and poverty, etc. Here in 6:4, the world contains opposing states of good and evil.

Yet a third entity resolves the opposites. In 1:7, God "rules over all of [the opposing *sefirot*] from God's holy place" and provides a balancing center. In 4:2, the six directions each have an opposite (east/west, etc.), but "the holy shrine bears them all." In 3:1, the opposing mother letters Mem and Shin find resolution in the third "balancing" mother letter, Aleph. The Gnostics called opposing pairs of cosmic qualities syzygies.[41] In the Gnostic understanding of syzygies, the opposites are "pacified and equalized by the unity, God."[42] Gnosticism may well have influenced *Sefer Yetzirah*'s view of opposites.

6:4 leaves the tension between the opposites without obvious resolution. Yet there is a hint here that God will resolve even this dichotomy, since God is the one who made good and evil. Although the war between good and evil takes place within the human heart, the ultimate resolution of the two opposites is ultimately in God's hands—perhaps postponed to some future redemptive time.

Good Tests the Evil and Evil Tests the Good טוב מבחין את רע ורע מבחין את טוב

The text asserts that good and evil can be used to probe and define one another. One cannot know one without knowing the other. This seems like an instruction to the practitioner: one must use one's knowledge of good to know what bad is, and use one's knowledge of bad to understand what good is. One should compare one's pleasure and suffering, one's compassion and selfishness, in order to distinguish between them, and note how consuming (and fleeting) they both are.

The word "test" or "examine" (*mavchin*) can specifically mean "to prove or examine a text" to determine its accuracy; it can also mean to test a metal that has been forged. The passage may be intimating that one function of evil/suffering is to "test" the righteous. The practitioner must be on guard against evil in order to prove worthy when "tested."

The word *mavchin* beautifully brings together the idea of "testing" words with "testing" in the physical world. "Good" and "evil" are words— and they are also human experiences, lived out in the relationship of our bodies to one another. Again, word and world are bound up together.

Good Is Stored Up for the Good   טובה גנוזה לטובים

Tovah genuzah latovim: good is hidden away for the good ones. The term *genuzah*, stored or hidden away, is related to *genizah*: a repository for sacred texts that are no longer usable. The term "hidden away for the righteous" also appears in rabbinic texts—in Genesis Rabbah, for example, we read:

> The light by which the world was created—the first human being could look from one end of the world to the other by its light. When the Holy One of Blessing saw the corrupt actions of the generations of Enosh and the Flood and the Tower of Babel, He hid the light from them... and stored it away for the righteous in the future.[43]

The implication of *Sefer Yetzirah*'s words that good is "stored up" or "hidden away" is that this passage accepts the "world to come"—a future messianic redemption (or paradise) where righteous souls will be rewarded. The ultimate answer to the resolution of good vs. evil thus seems to be postponed to some future time, whether a messianic redemption or an afterlife. *Sefer Yetzirah* here uses a rabbinic legend of some theological importance, which means that either the author of this passage knew some rabbinic lore on this topic, or that this passage was added to the original text at an early stage of development. There's little indication elsewhere in the book of any concern with eschatology.

Kaplan is convinced that the "good" stored up for the righteous is God's presence: "the ultimate good is therefore to partake of God... The ultimate goal of creation is that we should come close to God."[44] Yet in this book, God tends to exist at the center of dichotomies rather than on one side or the other, and this may perhaps mitigate against Kaplan's understanding. The "good" that the righteous receive, while it may reflect the best humans can achieve and experience, is part of God's creation, not the whole.

And Evil is Kept for the Evil ורעה שמורה לרעים

This phrase, although it appears in most manuscripts, does not make it into Hayman's earliest recoverable version.[45] It does seems an obvious corollary to the phrase "good is stored up for the good." Hayman does not include it because there is one early manuscript where the phrase "good is stored up for the good" appears without the corollary phrase "evil is kept for the evil."[46] Hayman opines that "the weight of the evidence" suggests the phrase "evil is kept for the evil" should be included in the text, though there is a possibility it was added later.[47]

If we do include this phrase in the text, it seems to imply that those who act wickedly will receive punishment at some future date. As we've noted, this is a typical Jewish belief of the time. Again, the text seems to imply a hidden place in the divine realm, within which "evil" (punishment and suffering) can be stored until it is needed. Again, recourse to a hidden or future world is unusual within the text as a whole.

Yet a contemporary reader could put aside metaphysical speculation, and imagine that "good is stored up for the good and evil is kept for the evil" is an observation about consciousness. The actions we take and the memories we create affect us. The impact of practicing righteousness is "stored up" in the consciousness we develop over time. So too, the impact of selfish actions also accrues over time. The text thus could be read to advise us that each action we take will have a lasting impact on us as well as others. We must take care about every action we perform, for these actions add up in time, creating habits that may influence our doings in the future.

This seems like a crucial message to place near the end of *Sefer Yetzirah*. The book offers creative power to human beings: a godlike ability to manipulative the forces of being. It only makes sense that, as it winds toward its conclusion, the book would remind us to use these powers in compassionate and righteous ways.

Practice: Good Opposite Evil
Close your eyes and breathe out.

On one side of you is good.
On the other side is evil.
Perceive them both clearly:
how they look, sound, feel, smell.
How does each one look and feel?
Which one is more approachable?
Which one is scarier?
Which one is tempting,
which one off-putting?
What does each one say to you?
Now, good and evil approach one another.
What happens?
What happens when they touch one another?
Now, breathe out
and perceive that evil is no longer present.
See the good that has been stored up for you.

Breathe out and open your eyes.

Practice: Treasury of Good
Close your eyes and breathe out.

You are in a place where good is hidden.
You know where it is hidden
and can find it.
Seek out the good
and release it
so that it is now visible and available to all.
See what happens in the world
and in you
when the good that is hidden
enters the world.

Breathe out and open your eyes.

Chapter 6:5 · The Battle

עשאן כמין מריבה
וערכן כמין מלחמה
גם את זה לעומת זה עשה האלהים

God formed them like a kind of quarrel;
God arranged them like a kind of war;
God has made them
one opposite the other.

Chapter 6:6 · Letters, Joined and Divided

שלשה
אחד אחד לבדו עומד
שבעה
שלושה חלוקין על שלשה
ואחד חוק מכריע בינתיים
שנים עשר עומדים במלחמה
שלשה אויבים ושלשה אוהבים
שלשה מחיים ושלשה ממיתים
וכולן אדוקין זה וזה

Three:
each one stands alone.

Seven:
three divided against three.

Chapter 6:5 · The Battle

> And one is an engraved law
> balancing between them.
>
> Twelve stand in battle:
> three are enemies and three are friends;
> three give life and three kill
> and each is joined to the other.

In 6:5 and 6:6, we have somehow moved from a universe where north's opposition to south is a crucial structural support for creation, to a universe in which cosmic forces battle one another. It is as if we have shifted books somehow—almost as if, as we approach the end of the book, the mundane world is about to break through with its conflicts and petty quarrels. The letters become, not only a series of opposites, but a series of violent oppositions, a quarrel, a war. The letters are suddenly set up as combatants: three against three, six against six. Only the three mothers "stand alone," refusing to battle one another.

The placement and location of these passages differs from one manuscript to another, though Hayman does include them near the end of Chapter 6 in his earliest recoverable version.[48] The content of the passages is hard to reconcile with the rest of the book. In Chapter 3, we don't see the three mothers standing alone: they oppose one another with a third force balancing between them. In Chapter 4, six doubles do stand opposite one another, but there isn't conflict between them, and the seventh is presented as a sacred center rather than as "a law balancing between them." In Chapter 5, the twelve simple letters don't seem to be opposed to one another (indeed, if all the organs and constellations were in battle with one another, the human body—and the planet—wouldn't last long.) In most of *Sefer Yetzirah*, dualities support and define one another (e.g., north/south; beginning/end) rather than fighting one another. 6:5 depicts the world's components in a more conflictual mode than does the rest of the text.

The text repeats the phrase from 6:4, borrowed from Ecclesiastes: "God has made them one opposite the other." This continues the chapter's emphasis on biblical prooftexts, and also suggests that the author of these passages sees the conflicts in the world as divinely ordained. The tensions between the letters and the entities that arise from them are part of the Creator's architecture.

The passage here also echoes *Sefer Yetzirah* 1:11, where God engraves and carves chaos, void, mud, and clay in the waters. "God formed them like a kind of garden, carved them like a kind of wall, wove them like a kind of ceiling." "Formed them like a kind of quarrel" in 6:4 parallels "formed them like a kind of garden" in 1:11. The images are quite different: a war and a garden. In a way, the two passages frame how we experience the world: sometimes as a place of perpetual struggle, and sometimes as Eden. Humans are pulled between *tov* and *ra*, between goodness and suffering. The elemental forces don't always feel benign, and God, their source, becomes remote and mysterious. And yet, "each is joined to the other." God has connected these forces, suggesting a oneness that transcends the various conflicts. There is an ultimate unity even in a world of disparate needs and actions. As we prepare to end the ritual of reading the *Book of Creation*, we recount both the world's harsh realities, and the beauty of its oneness.

Twelve Stand in Battle   שנים עשר עומדים במלחמה

The text as Hayman constructs it doesn't tell us which organs and limbs are friends and enemies, or which are lifegivers and killers. In other versions of the text, the lovers/friends are listed as the heart and the ears, while the haters/enemies are listed as the liver, the gall bladder and the tongue. The givers of life are the two nostrils and the spleen, while the killers are the two "lower orifices" and the mouth.[49]

This recounting imagines the organs that remove toxins (e.g., liver and gall bladder) as "killers." The tongue is probably included because of its tendency to speak gossip—a common rabbinic concern.[50] The heart and ears would be the entities that can listen and respond to the divine, and the nostrils would be the providers of breath. The two "lower orifices" (*nekavim tachtonim*) are presumably the vagina (or phallus) and anus, and these orifices may be labeled as "killers" because of their association in the rabbinic mind with sexuality, childbirth, sin, and illness—though to label the vagina or phallus a "killer" seems counterintuitive. The mouth, again, is condemned because it is the gossip-speaker. And, of course, all of these organs are absolutely necessary for life, no matter how they are labeled.

Sefer Yetzirah tends to focus on how diverse forces add up to a living and vibrant world, even if those forces are in tension. This passage has a tendency to demonize one half of each pair, a thought pattern that diverges from much of the rest of the book. However, this section does conform to the previous section, in which good and evil battle with one another for the human heart. This section seems to extend that idea, suggesting that the whole world is composed of various battles that God has set in motion.

Each Is Joined to the Other   וכולן אדוקין זה וזה

Ve'chulan adukin zeh b'zeh—"all are joined to one another." The verb *adak* means "to cleave, stick to, or fasten to." In other words, all of these conflicting forces God has set in motion cleave to one another. This phrase conveys the multiplicity-within-unity that is the primary theme of *Sefer Yetzirah*. Cosmic forces that conflict still cannot be separated; all of them are necessary for the body, time, and space to function. All of them are wondrous paths of wisdom, conveying divine energy into creation.

Individuals and societies have conflicts. Political and social ideas contradict one another. Conflict in family life and intimate relationships, tensions in our work or creative endeavors, inner conflicts about choices and values—all these can be painful. Yet a life fully lived can't be lived without conflict. What would it mean to see these conflicts as a necessary part of our experience, yet also know that in the end, we must all cling to one another? Would we look at one another differently during conflicts if we remembered the ways we are connected? What a powerful life-tool it would be to borrow the wisdom of this passage: "Each is joined to the other."

The book is almost at an end. It has laid out for us the deepest structures of God's creative work: elements, directions, time, space, person. We have journeyed on God's path through the steps of creation, and have lent our own will and energy to the oneness of what God has created. Now we remember that even as we inhabit the profound magic of the letters, their powers cannot fix everything. We will be pulled again and again away from oneness. The only answer is: *shuv lamakom*. Return to the Place.

Practice: One Opposite the Other

Close your eyes and breathe out.

See before you a conflict in your life.
See the sides of the conflict.
Perceive that the opposing sides of the conflict
are joined together.
What new perspective on this conflict
arises from what you see?

Breathe out and open your eyes.

Practice: Each is Joined to the Other

Close your eyes and breathe out.

Become aware of the conflicts in yourself,
your immediate circle,
your community,
your society,
your world.
See how you contribute
to those conflicts.
Now, see the unity in yourself,
your immediate circle,
your community,
your society,
your world.
See how you contribute
to the unity.
Commit within yourself
to strengthening the unity.
Notice what changes
in the images before you
as you make this commitment.

Breathe out and open your eyes.

Chapter 6:7 · The Revelation

כשהבין אברהם אבינו
וצר וצרף
חקק וחצב
חקר וחשב
ועלתה בידו
נגלה עליו יי
עשאו אוהבו
וכרת לו ברית ולזרעו
עד עולם ועד עלמי עד

When Abraham our father understood
formed and transmuted
engraved and carved
delved and reflected
power arose in his hand
and God appeared to him
and made him God's friend
and made a covenant with him and his seed
forever and ever
throughout all the worlds

The ritual of *Sefer Yetzirah* is not meant to be performed only once, but many times, by many readers. It is fitting, therefore, that the ending is also a beginning. *Sefer Yetzirah* ends with a surprise: Abraham, the patriarch of Genesis, suddenly becomes a character in the story. Abraham encounters the magical verbs of the book: to form, to engrave, to delve deep. As he discovers the creative mysteries God has laid down at the dawn of time, Abraham becomes the reader, the seeker, the adept who follows in God's footsteps—and as he follows God's path, God appears to him. The final text of *Sefer Yetzirah* describes a direct encounter between a person and the Creator.

The end goal of *Sefer Yetzirah*, this implies, is not mere creative power but experience of God's presence. Thus, the very end of the book ties together the magical with the contemplative: finding our own spiritual power leads to direct experience of the Divine. Presumably, if Abraham can use the *Book of Creation* to create worlds and encounter God, so can we.

The writer(s) could have picked Moses as the exemplar who ends the story. Indeed, Moses, who wrote down the letters of the Torah for God, would have been a more natural fit. The writer could also have picked Solomon, builder of the Temple, known for his magical wisdom.[51] Yet Abraham, the ancestor of the Jewish people, is recognized also by Christians and later by Muslims as a spiritual forebear. He is a more universal character than Moses or Solomon. Abraham's presence in the text may signal that while the wisdom of *Sefer Yetzirah* is a Jewish wisdom, its authors believe it extends beyond tribe.

Also, Moses is the leader of a large group. The Bible primarily presents Abraham as an individual in relationship with God. *Sefer Yetzirah* seeks to address the individual. Its verbs are second- and third-person singular, directed toward a single God and a single human. In choosing Abraham as its exemplar, the book reinforces the power of the individual to forge a relationship with the Divine.

Abraham's near-sacrifice of his son Isaac occurs on Mount Moriah, which according to the book of Chronicles as well as long-established legend is the same site where the Temple will one day be built.[52] So there is a way that Abraham is the first to dedicate the space of the earthly Temple. *Sefer Yetzirah* now connects him to the cosmic Temple through his mastery of the Hebrew letters and their power. Abraham is the first human to connect text with Temple, word with world.

Abraham's presence at the end of the text invites us to feel that the *Book of Creation* is ancient and timeless. It is a part of the earliest quests for God. When we read the passages of the book, we become part of a long lineage of seekers of the Creator, part of an unending line of creator-contemplatives who support the unity, stability, and goodness of creation.

When Abraham our Father Understood   כשהבין אברהם אבינו

The initial verb for the process Abraham starts changes from manuscript to manuscript. Sometimes the phrase is "Abraham understood," sometimes "Abraham came" or "Abraham looked/peered."[53] According to Hayman, we cannot know which of these verbs is the original. The next set of verbs ("formed and transmuted, delved and reflected") also changes from manuscript to manuscript, though it is clear we are dealing with a list of verbs that relate to the shaping and combining of letters, a list we have seen in various forms throughout the book.

The verbs "engraved and carved," so fundamental to *Sefer Yetzirah*, appear in most but not all manuscripts, and Hayman does not even include them in his earliest recoverable version of this passage. They are included here because of the words' centrality to the book as a whole. It is impossible to imagine Abraham's actions here without the seminal image of engraving: hollowing out the letters, the self, to be a vessel for divine intention.

It is notable that these verbs contain hints of the magical (formed and transmuted) and the contemplative (delved and reflected). For *Sefer Yetzirah*, the process of creation has both components. It requires introspection and also ritual action.

Power Arose in His Hand   ועלתה בידו

"There arose in his hand..." is a Hebrew idiom for "he became capable." Yet the text leaves off without explaining exactly what Abraham's new capability was. What arose in Abraham's hand? At no point in this passage does *Sefer Yetzirah* explain what exactly Abraham was able to do using the letters of the Hebrew alphabet, just as the book never explains exactly what the reader should be able to do with the practices that appear within the book.

This cannot be an accident. While scholars have speculated that the book's magical powers include the making of a golem (a synthetic human being), or perhaps the manipulation of the stars to bring about the messianic age, the book does not directly make such claims.[54] We might perhaps attribute this to the book's intention that only true adepts should discover the book's real powers. We might imagine the central secrets, the true powers, are withheld so that no one will learn them without first seeking out a teacher who knows how to use the book properly. Alternatively, this vagueness may be an effort to maintain the book's mystery while not making magical claims that will turn out to be unprovable.

I choose to understand the passage's ambiguity differently—as an admission that the book's creative powers manifest internally rather than externally. The "creation" the book allows us to shape is our imaginal relationship to the cosmos. The powers we thus acquire are subtle. They don't manifest as the ability to make artificial people or move stars. They manifest as the ability to quiet the mind, center the spirit, and connect to the vastness of all things. They manifest as the ability to be grounded in space, time, and self: to return to the Place. Psychologist and storyteller Sharon Blackie relates: "The most important thing about the imagination is that we ground it where our feet are planted. The act of imagining is a way of connecting to this world."[55]

There is real power in these quieter capabilities. They do allow us to build worlds. When we are attuned to realities much larger than ourselves, we have a deeper perception of all that is around us. We feel connected to the Source of Life and to one another. We are inspired to create, nurture, and sustain. And that, to me, is magic.

Yehuda Liebes makes the radical suggestion that what "arises in Abraham's hand" is God—"the God who breaks through, and proceeds from, multiplicity."[56] Abraham's creative power lies in his awareness of divine presence. This powerful assertion leads us into the next radical revelation of this passage.

God Appeared to Him   נגלה עליו יי

The Hebrew reads *niglah alav Adonai*: God was revealed upon him. This is the last phrase Hayman includes in the earliest recoverable version, so we might treat it as the end of the book. And it's an extraordinary end.

The sentence is extraordinary because up until this point, we have seen God's works but never God. The book has walked us through God's creative actions (engraving, combining, etc.) and through God's channels: the letters, the *sefirot*, and so on. Yet there has been no portrayal of the God behind all of these actions and channels. The text has shown us the infinite dimensions of the universe with God's dwelling at the center, without explicitly depicting the God we might meet there. So in a sense, "God was revealed to him" is a surprise ending, one that indicates all of this magical and meditative work will in fact bring us to divine revelation. More expansive manuscripts often include that God kisses Abraham's head—suggesting an affectionate intimacy between God and the seeker. This is the ultimate reconciliation of unity and multiplicity: the personal bond between Creator and every single creation.

The book has pushed us to see word and thing as the same, and this final sentence seals that process. Revelation can occur through words, and it can occur through manifest presence. It can happen on Mount Sinai through the giving of the Torah—written with Hebrew letters—and it can happen in the sacred space of the Tabernacle as God physically manifests in cloud and fire.[57] The final words of the book, in Hayman's version, evoke both kinds of revelation: the word and the thing itself.

There is another reason this sentence is extraordinary. While *niglah alav Adonai* does clearly mean "God was revealed to him," it could also be read "God was revealed upon him"—that is, God appeared, revealed in Abraham. The immanent God of the universe now dwells in the human disciple. The concluding hope of the book is that we can manifest the divine in our own lives.

What exactly does this mean? What does it feel like? I can only describe what it means for me. When I meditate on the images of *Sefer Yetzirah*, I have the experience of attuning to the elements in my world and also to a deeper landscape where God's presence is manifest. Water, fire and air interact all around me, and within me, and I feel part of them. This gives me that experience of multiplicity-within-unity that is so central to *Sefer Yetzirah*'s worldview. And that experience of multiplicity-within-unity gives me a feeling of being an integral part of a larger reality—a reality I choose to call God.

And Made Him His Friend, and Made a Covenant with Him and His Seed

עשאו אוהבו
וכרת לו ברית
ולזרעו

The feeling of being part of something isn't solely a momentary phenomenon—it is an ongoing commitment. As one seeks out this feeling over time, it becomes a daily ritual, a way of being—a friendship, one might say, or even a covenant. The promise of *Sefer Yetzirah* that its practices lead to friendship and covenant—an ongoing relationship with the Source of Life.

This description of God and Abraham's friendship and covenant, placed here, does not appear in every early manuscript of *Sefer Yetzirah*.[58] However, it does appear in most, and so belongs to an early layer of the text.[59] These phrases are included here in italics, though Hayman does not include them in his "earliest recoverable manuscript." Covenantal language is consistent with the earliest layers of the text.[60]

Let's look back at the beginning of the book. In 1:3 we encounter the ten *sefirot*, the ten ethereal inscriptions, as a set of five opposite five, with a single covenant set in the center (i.e., the ten fingers and the speaking mouth at the center). In 1:5, we encounter the instruction that if our heart runs, we must return to the Place, and that "regarding this matter a covenant was made." The radical assertion of *Sefer Yetzirah* is that the divine-human relationship created via the meditative/magical practices of the *Book of Creation* is worthy of the language of covenant.

This narrative turns normative Jewish tradition virtually on its head. Covenant is not (only) a matter of law or faith or circumcision or national commitment to Torah; it is an individual relationship born out of a person's internal sacred practice. God loves Abraham because Abraham learns how to play with creative magic and contemplation the way God does.

It is Abraham's engagement with the cosmic mystery that God admires and rewards. Just as *Sefer Yetzirah* redefines the Temple as the cosmos, it redefines covenant as the development of cosmic consciousness. This covenant extends, by implication, to the reader of the text, who now has also conducted the ritual of letter combination and world-temple visualization. The conclusion of the book, by implication, grants covenant to the one who has just read and practiced it.

We are in covenant with the divine when we orient properly within the temple that is the universe, exercising our powers of imagination for the benefit of the larger structure—in other words, when we live a multiplicity-within-unity.

Like the letters, we are channels of the life-force, for life or for death, for good or for evil. Therefore the responsibility for Creation falls, not only on a transcendent deity, but on us.

Forever and Ever Throughout All the Worlds — עד עולם ועד עלמי עד

Ad olam ve'ad almei ad means "forever"[61] but can also mean "until the world and until worlds without end." This Hebrew phrase evokes endless time and endless space at the same time, and echoes 1:7, where we learned that, at the center of the cosmos, the Creator dwells and rules *ad adei ad*, out to eternity. It is as if the Creator speaks this phrase while looking out from the central sacred place into all the depths of the universe. With this phrase, *Sefer Yetzirah* collapses space and time and perspective into a single continuum. "Forever and ever" is also a specific reference to God's promise to Abraham *ad olam*, "forever."[62] This includes *nefesh*, the human perspective, in this vast picture. *Ad adei ad* hints at the three worlds.

Longer versions of the passage end the book with a more ornate passage:

> The Holy One revealed to him the secret. He drew them out into water, he burned them in fire, he blew them into the wind, he flamed them into the seven, he guided them into the twelve constellations.

Here, the twenty-two letters—three mother-letters (water, fire, wind), plus the double letters (planets) and the simple letters (constellations)—return for one last magical moment before the end of the book. Abraham opens the elemental channels, the paths of Wisdom. God's friend becomes a creator, a worker of the life-force.

But there is something powerful about ending a book that seeks to express all of Reality with "*ad almei ad*," until worlds without end. We began with the three books of space, time, and body. We end with *ad almei ad*—all these worlds, all these facets of reality, and many more. The Text that is World cannot be fully expressed. It is infinite—"go and contemplate what the mouth cannot say and the ear cannot hear."[63] We can never reach its end. We can only open the book, and follow Wisdom's paths.

Practice: Power in the Hand

Close your eyes and breathe out.

Before you is a teacher,
however you imagine that teacher.
The teacher places a sacred and immense power in your hand.
What is this power?
What is its nature?
Now, feel that the power you hold in your hand
has been within you all along.
What will you do
with this sacred power?

Breathe out and open your eyes.

Practice: God's Friend

Close your eyes and breath out.

You are journeying along a path.
As you walk, you encounter the Book of Creation,
however it appears to you.

Open the Book of Creation
to the page meant for you.

On that page, you see yourself
becoming God's friend.

Allow this truth to arise from the page
and weave itself into your life.

Breathe out and open your eyes.

Practice: Sealing the Three Books

Close your eyes and breathe out.

You are journeying on a path.
You come to a crossroad
where many paths meet.
At the crossroad, you find three gates.

Pass through the first gate:
the gate of space.

Pass through the second gate:
the gate of time.

Pass through the third gate:
the gate of the body and soul.

As you pass through the third gate,
you find the path
that is right for you at this moment.

Look back through the three gates
and see that the same inscription
is carved above each one.

What is the inscription?
A word, an image? Both?
What is the final seal
on your journey through the Book of Creation?

Breathe out and open your eyes.

Appendix I · Correspondences with Other Translations

This appendix will indicate the correspondences of this version with Peter Hayman's earliest recoverable version, Hayman's paragraph numbering within his manuscript, and with the sections of Aryeh Kaplan's *Sefer Yetzirah*, a popular translation of the Short Recension. This information is provided so readers can compare one translation with another if desired.

Throughout this book, passages of *Sefer Yetzirah* are numbered by chapter and section (e.g., 1:1, 1:2). This translation and commentary is based on the text and paragraph order of Hayman's "earliest recoverable version," which does not include all of the sections in the Short, Long, or Saadyan Recensions. Sometimes, there are also texts added from other versions in order to clarify the book's basic structures or specify further the nature of particular Hebrew letters. The sections are numbered consecutively, so as not to confuse readers. Therefore, the chapter and sections numbers here will not always match the numbering in other translations or in Hayman's version.

Sections or phrases that are not in Hayman's earliest recoverable version are noted below in Chart 1 and also in the commentary to the text, and are marked with an asterisk in Chart 2.

Chart 1

Sections included in *Return to the Place* that are not in Hayman's earliest recoverable version:	Sections where one or more lines are not included in Hayman's earliest recoverable version:
1:2	2:2
3:5-9	5:3
4:5-6	6:4
5:4	6:6

Return to the Place

Chart 2

	Hayman	Kaplan		Hayman	Kaplan
1:1	1	1:1	**3:10**	32	3:7
1:2	2*	1:2	**3:11**	33	3:8
1:3	3	1:3	**3:12**	34	3:9
1:4	4	1:4			
1:5	5	1:8	**4:1**	37	4:1-4:3
1:6	6	1:7	**4:2**	38	4:4
1:7	7	1:5	**4:3**	39	4:6
1:8	8	1:6	**4:4**	40	4:16
1:9	10	1:9	**4:5**	41*	4:8-4:14
1:10	12	1:10	**4:6**	43a	4:15
1:11	13	1:11	**4:7**	43c	absent
1:12	14	1:12			
1:13	15	1:13	**5:1**	45	5:1
1:14	16	1:14	**5:2**	47	5:2
			5:3 pt. 1	49a	5:3
2:1	9	2:1	**5:3 pt. 2**	49b*	5:4-6
2:2	17	2:3	**5:4**	52*	5:7-9
2:3	18	2:4			
2:4	19	2:5	**6:1**	56a	6:6
2:5	20	2:6	**6:2**	58a	6:1
			6:3	59	6:3
3:1	23	3:1	**6:4**	60b	6:4
3:2	24	3:2	**6:5**	48a	6:5
3:3	25	3:4	**6:6**	48b	6:5
3:4	26	part of 1:1	**6:7**	61	6:7
3:5	27*	part of 3:2			
3:6	28*	3:4			
3:7	29*	3:5			
3:8	30*	3:6			
3:9	31*	3:3			

* not in Hayman's earliest recoverable version

Appendix II · Translation without Commentary

שלשים ושתים	1:1 Wisdom's thirty-two
נתיבות פלאות חכמה	marvelous paths
חקק יה	Yah engraved—
יהוה צבאות	the Becoming One who holds many—
בשלש ספרים	within three books:
בספר וספר וסיפור	tome, tally, and tale.
עשר ספירות בלימה	1:2 Ten inscriptions of the void
ועשרים ושתים אותיות יסוד	and twenty-two foundation-letters,
שלוש אמות	three mothers,
שבע כפולת	seven doubles,
ושתים עשרה פשוטות	and twelve simples.
עשר ספירות בלימה	1:3 Ten inscriptions of the void:
מספר עשר אצבעות	the number of ten fingers,
חמש כנגד חמש	five opposite five
וברית יחיד מכוונת באמצע	and a single covenant set in the center:
במילה ולשון ופה	in word and language and speech
	(in the genitals and tongue and mouth).
עשר ספירות בלימה	1:4 Ten inscriptions of the void:
עשר ולא תשע	ten and not nine,
עשר ולא אחת עשרה	ten and not eleven
הבן בחכמה	understand in Wisdom
וחכם בבינה	be wise in Understanding
בחון בהם וחקור מהם	examine them, delve into them
העמד דבר על בוריו	stand each thing on its clarity on its absence
והשב יוצר	and return the Creator
על מכונו	to Their Dwelling Place.
עשר ספירות בלימה	1:5 Ten inscriptions of the void:
בלום פיך מלדבר	Stop your mouth from speaking,
בלום לבך מלהרהר	stop your heart from murmuring,
ואם רץ לבך	and if your heart runs
שוב למקום	return to the Place

Return to the Place

שׁכך נאמר	for scripture says:
רצוא ושוב	"running and returning."
ועל דבר זה	Regarding this matter.
נכרת ברית	a covenant was made.

1:6 עשר ספירות בלימה Ten inscriptions of the void:
נעוץ סופן בתחילן	Their end is imbedded in their beginning
ותחילתן בסופן	and their beginning in their end
כשלהבת בגחלת	like a flame in a fiery coal
שהיוצר אחד	for the Creator is one
ואין לו שני	and has no second and before one,
ולפני אחד מה אתה סופר	what are you counting?

1:7 עשר ספירות בלימה Ten inscriptions of the void:
ומדתן עשר שאין להם סוף	their measure is ten, yet they are infinite:
עומק ראשית ועומק אחרית	A depth of beginning and a depth of end
עומק טוב ועומק רע	A depth of good and a depth of evil
עומק רום ועומק תחת	A depth of above and a depth of below
עומק מזרח ועומק מערב	A depth of east and a depth of west
עומק צפון ועומק דרום	A depth of north and a depth of south
ואדון יחיד	and a singular Master—
אל מלך נאמן	a faithful Divine ruler—
מושל בכולם	rules over them all
ממעון קדשו	from God's holy dwelling
ועד עדי עד	and out to eternity.

1:8 עשר ספירות בלימה Ten inscriptions of the void:
צפיתן כמראה הבזק	their appearance has the look of lightning
ותכליתן אין להם קץ	and their end—they have no end.
ודברו בהן	God's word in them
כרצוא ושוב	is like "running and returning."
ולמאמרו	They chase after God's utterance
כסופה ירדופו	like a whirlwind
ולפני כסאו הם משתחוים	and bow before God's throne.

1:9 עשר ספירות בלימה Ten ethereal inscriptions.
אחת רוח אלוהים חיים	One: Breath of the Living God—
זו היא רוח הקדש	She is the Holy Spirit.

שתיים רוח מרוח	1:10 Two: Breath from Breath.
חקק וחצב בה	He engraved and carved within Her
ארבע רוחות השמים	the four winds of heaven.
שלש מים מרוח	1:11 Three: Water from Wind.
חקק וחצב בהם	He engraved and carved in Them
תוהו ובוהו רפש וטיט	chaos and void, mud and clay—
חקקן כמין ערוגה	engraved Them like a kind of garden,
הציבן כמין חומה	carved Them like a kind of wall,
סיככן כמין מעזיבה	wove Them like a kind of ceiling.
ארבע אש ממים	1:12 Four: Fire from Water.
חקק וחצב בה	He engraved and carved in Her
כסא הכבוד	the Throne of Glory
וכל צבא מרום	and all the heavenly hosts,
שכך כתוב	for so it is written:
עשה מלכיו רוחות	He makes the winds His messengers,
משרתיו אש לוהט	flaming fire His ministers.
חמש חתם רום	1:13 Five: God sealed Above
פנה למעלה	and faced upward
וחתמו ביהו	and sealed it with Yud Heh Vav.
שש חתם תחת	Six: God sealed Below
פנה למטה	and faced downward
ויחמו ביוה	and sealed it with Yud Vav Heh.
שבע חתם מזרח	Seven: God sealed East
פנה לפניו	and faced front
וחתמו בהוי	and sealed it with Heh Vav Yud.
שמנה חתם מערב	Eight: God sealed West
פנה לאחריו	and faced behind
וחתמו בהיו	and sealed it with Heh Yud Vav.
תשע חתם דרום	Nine: God sealed South
פנה לימינו	And faced to the right
וחתמו בויה	and sealed it with Vav Yud Heh.
עשר חתם צפון	Ten: God sealed North
פנה לשמאלו	and faced to the left
וחתמו בוהי	and sealed it with Vav Heh Yud.

1:14 These are the ten inscriptions in the void: אלו עשר ספירות בלימה
breath of the living God רוח אלהים חיים
wind, water, fire, above and below, ורוח מים אש מעלה מטה
east, west, north and south. מזרח מערב צפון ודרום

2:1 Twenty-two foundation-letters: עשרים ושתים אותיות יסוד
three mothers, seven doubles, שלש אמות שבע כפולות
and twelve simples. ושתים עשרה פשוטות

2:2 Twenty-two letters עשרים ושתים אותיות
engraved in the voice חקוקות בקול
hewn in the breath חצובות ברוח
fixed in the mouth קבועות בפה
in five places: בחמש מקומות

Aleph Chet Heh Ayin in the throat א ח ה ע בגרון
Bet Vav Mem Peh in the lips ב ו מ פ בשפתים
Gimel Yud Kaf Kuf in the palate ג י כ ק בחיך
Dalet Tet Lamed Nun Tav in the tongue ד ט ל נ ת בלשון
Zayin Samech Shin Reish Tzadi in the teeth ז ס ש ר צ בשינים

2:3 Twenty-two letters עשרים ושתים אותיות
fixed in a wheel קבועות בגלגל
that cycles forward and back. פנים ואחור
A sign of the matter: סימן לדבר
No good higher than thrill. אין לטובה למעלה מענג
No evil lower than ill. ואין ברעה למטה מנגע

2:4 Twenty-two letters עשרים ושתים אתיות
engraved, carved, חקקן חצבן
permuted, weighed and exchanged. צרפן שקלן והימירן
How did God weigh and exchange them? כיצד שקלן והימירן
Aleph with them all אלף עם כולם
and all of them with Aleph וכולם עם אלף
Bet with them all בית עם כולם
and all of them with Bet וכולם עם בית
and they all repeat in a cycle. וכלן חוזרות חלילה

נמצאו יוצאות	Thus they emerge
במאתים ושלושים ואחד	from 231
שערים	gates.
נמצא כל היצור	And so it is that all creation
וכל הדיבור	and all speech
יוצא בשם אחד	emerges from one name.

יצר מתהו ממש	2:5 The Divine formed substance out of void
ועשאו באש וישנו	and worked it in fire,
וחצב עמודים גדולים	and it became, and carved great pillars
מאויר שאינו נתפס	out of air that cannot be grasped.

שלש אמות א מ ש	3:1 Three mothers: Aleph, Mem, Shin.
יסודן	Their foundation is
כף זכות וכף חובה	a palmful of merit, a palmful of guilt
ולשון חוק	and a tongue of engraved law
מכריע בינתיים	balances between them.

שלש אמות א מ ש	3:2 Three mothers: Aleph, Mem, Shin.
סוד גדול מכוסה ומופלא	A great secret veiled and mysterious,
וחתום בשש טבעות	sealed by six seal-rings.
וממנו יוצאין אש מים רוח	From them come fire, water, and air
ומחותל בזכר ונקבה	enveloped in male and female.

שלש אמות	3:3 Three mothers:
אש למעלה	Fire above,
מים למטה	water below,
ורוח בנתיים	and wind in the middle.

שלש אמות א מ ש	3:4 Three mothers: Aleph, Mem, Shin.
מם דוממת	Mem hums,
ש שורקת	Shin hisses,
אלף רוח	Aleph is the breath,
חוק מכריע בינתיים	the engraved law balancing between them.

שלש אמות א מ ש	3:5 Three mothers: Aleph, Mem, Shin
ומהן נולדו אבות	And from them were born three fathers
שמהם נבראו הכל	from whom everything was created.

Return to the Place

שלש אמות א מ ש בעולם רוח ומים ואש שמים נבראו מאש וארץ נבראת ממים ואויר נברא מרוח מכריע בינתיים	3:6 Three mothers Aleph, Mem, Shin in the world: air, water, fire. Sky was created from fire, earth from water, and air was created from breath balancing between them.
שלש אמות א מ ש בשנה אש מים ורוח חום נברא מאש וקור נברא ממים ורויה מרוח מכריע בינתיים	3:7 Three mothers Aleph, Mem, Shin in the year: fire, water, air. Heat was created from fire, cold from water, and the overflowing from the air balancing between them.
שלש אמות א מ ש בנפש ראש נברא מאש ובטן ממים וגויה מרוח מכריע בינתיים	3:8 Three mothers Aleph, Mem, Shin in the body-soul: the head was created from fire, the belly from water, and the chest, from air, balancing between them.
שלש אמות א מ ש חקקן חצבן צרפן וחתם בהם שלש אימות בעולם ושלש אימות בשנה ושלש אימות בנפש זכר ונקבה	3:9 Three mothers—Aleph, Mem, Shin— God engraved them, carved them, combined them, and sealed with them three mothers in the world three mothers in the year and three mothers in the body-soul, male and female.
המליך אות אלף ברוח וקשר לו כתר וחתם בו אויר בעולם רויה בשנה וגויה בנפש	3:10 God made the letter Aleph rule over wind and tied a crown to it and sealed with it air in the world the overflowing in time and the chest in the body-soul.

Appendix II · Translation without Commentary

3:11 הִמְלִיךְ אוֹת מֵם בְּמַיִם	3:11 God made the letter Mem rule over water
וְקָשַׁר לוֹ כֶּתֶר	and tied a crown to it
וְחָתַם בּוֹ	and sealed with it
אֶרֶץ בָּעוֹלָם	earth in the world
וְקוֹר בַּשָּׁנָה	the cold in time
וּבֶטֶן בַּנֶּפֶשׁ	and the belly in the body.
3:12 הִמְלִיךְ אוֹת שִׁין בָּאֵשׁ	3:12 God made the letter Shin rule over fire
וְקָשַׁר לוֹ כֶּתֶר	and tied a crown to it
וְחָתַם בּוֹ	and sealed with it
שָׁמַיִם בָּעוֹלָם	sky in the world
וְחוֹם בַּשָּׁנָה	the heat in time
וְרֹאשׁ בַּנֶּפֶשׁ	and the head in the body.
4:1 שֶׁבַע כְּפוּלוֹת	4:1 Seven double letters:
בג"ד כפר"ת	Bet Gimel Dalet Kaf Peh Reish Tav
מִתְנַהֲגוֹת בִּשְׁתֵּי לְשׁוֹנוֹת	Expressed in two manners:
חַיִּים	life
וְשָׁלוֹם	peace
וְחָכְמָה	wisdom
וְעֹשֶׁר	wealth
חֵן	grace
זֶרַע	seed
מֶמְשָׁלָה	sovereignty
וּמִתְנַהֲגוֹת בִּשְׁתֵּי לְשׁוֹנוֹת	and pronounced in two manners:
בִּי בִי	bet vet
גִּימֶל גִימֶל	gimel jimel
דָּלֶת דָלֶת	dalet thalet
כַּף כַף	kaf khaf
פִּי פִי	peh feh
רִישׁ רִישׁ	reish hreish
תָּיו תָיו	tav thav
רַךְ וְקָשֶׁה	soft and hard
גִּבּוֹר וְחַלָּשׁ	strong and weak
כְּפוּלוֹת שֶׁהֵן תְּמוּרוֹת	Doubles that are transformations:
תְּמוּרַת חַיִּים מָוֶת	the transformation of life is death
תְּמוּרַת שָׁלוֹם רַע	the transformation of peace is evil
תְּמוּרַת חָכְמָה אִוֶּלֶת	the transformation of wisdom is foolishness
תְּמוּרַת עֹשֶׁר עֹנִי	the transformation of wealth is poverty

תמורת זרע שממה	the transformation of seed is desolation
תמורת חן כיאור	the transformation of grace is ugliness
תמורת ממשלה עבדות	the transformation of sovereignty is slavery

שבע כפולות	4:2 Seven double letters:
בגד כפרת	bet gimel dalet kaf peh reish tav
שש קצוות	Six directions:
והיכל הקדש	and the holy shrine
מכוון בעמצא	set in the center—
והוא נושא את כולם	it bears them all.

שבע כפולות	4:3 Seven double letters:
בגד כפרת	bet gimel dalet kaf peh reish tav
חקקן	The Creator engraved them
חצבן צרפן	carved them, combined them
וצר בהן	and with them made
כוכבים	stars
ימים	days
ושערים	and gates

כאיזה צד צרפן	4:4 In what way did God combine them?
שתי עבנים בונות שני בתים	Two stones build two houses.
שלוש בונות ששה בתים	Three build six houses.
ארבע בונות	Four build
עשרים וארבע בתים	twenty-four houses.
חמש בונות	Five build
מאה ועשרים בתים	one hundred and twenty houses.
שש בונות שבע מאות	Six build seven hundred
ועשרים בתים	and twenty houses.
שבע בונות חמשת אלפים	Seven build five thousand
וארבעים בתים	and forty houses.
מיכאן ואילך	From here on out
צא וחשוב	go and contemplate
מה שאין הפה יכולה לדבר	what the mouth cannot say
ומה שאין האוזן	and the ear
יכולה לשמוע	cannot hear.

Appendix II · Translation without Commentary

הִמְלִיךְ אוֹת בֵּית	4:5 God gave rule to the letter Bet
וקשר לו כתר וצרפן	and tied a crown to it and combined
זה עם זה	one thing with another
וצר בו	and formed with it
שבתי בעולם	Saturn in the world
ושבת בשנה	Shabbat in the year
ופה בנפש	and the mouth in the body.

הִמְלִיךְ אוֹת גִימֶל	God gave rule to the letter Gimel
וקשר לו כתר וצרפן	and tied a crown to it and combined
זה עם זה	one thing with another
וצר בו	and formed with it
צדק בעולם	Jupiter in the world
ואחד בשבת בשנה	Sunday in the year
ועין ימין בנפש	and the right eye in the body.

הִמְלִיךְ אוֹת דלת	God gave rule to the letter Dalet
וקשר לו כתר וצרפן	and tied a crown to it and combined
זה עם זה	one thing with another
וצר בו	and formed with it
מאדים בעולם	Mars in the world
ושני שבת בשנה	Monday in the year
ועין שמאל בנפש	and the left eye in the body-soul.

הִמְלִיךְ אוֹת כף	God gave rule to the letter Kaf
וקשר לו כתר וצרפן	and tied a crown to it and combined
זה עם זה	one thing with another
וצר בו	and formed with it
חמה בעולם	the Sun in the world
ושלישי שבת בשנה	Tuesday in the year
ועף ימין בנפש	and the right nostril in the body-soul.

הִמְלִיךְ אוֹת פה	God gave rule to the letter Peh
וקשר לו כתר וצרפן	and tied a crown to it and combined
זה עם זה	one thing with another
וצר בו	and formed with it
נוגה בעולם	Venus in the world
ורביעי שבת בשנה	Wednesday in the year
ועף שמאל בנפש	and the left nostril in the body-soul.

Return to the Place

המליך אות ראש	God gave rule to the letter Reish
וקשר לו כתר וצרפן	and tied a crown to it and combined
זה עם זה	one thing with another
וצר בו	and formed with it
כוכב בעולם	Mercury in the world
וחמישי שבת בשנה	Thursday in the year
ואוזן ימין בנפש	and the right ear in the body-soul.
המליך אות תיו	God gave rule to the letter Tav
וקשר לו כתר וצרפן	and tied a crown to it and combined
זה עם זה	one thing with another
וצר בו	and formed with it
לבנה בעולם	the Moon in the world
וששי שבת בשנה	Friday in the year
ואוזן ימין בנפש	and the left ear in the body-soul.

4:6 שבעה כוכבים בעולם — These are the seven planets in the world:
ואלו הן חמה נוגה כוכב לבנה שבתי צדק מאדים — Sun, Venus, Mercury, Moon, Saturn, Jupiter, Mars.
Chamah Nogah Kochav Levanah Shabtai Tzedek Ma'dim

ושבעה ימים — and the seven days:
שבעת ימי בראשית — the seven days of creation.
ושבעה שערים בנפש — and the seven gates of the body-soul:
שתי עיניים ושתי עזנים — two eyes, two ears,
ושתי נחיריים ופה — two nostrils, and the mouth.

4:7 חיצה את העדים — God divided the witnesses
והעמידן אחד אחד לבדו — and stood each one by itself
עולם לבדו — the world by itself
שנה לבדה — the year by itself
נפש לבדה — the body-soul by itself

5:1 שתים עשרה פשוטות — Twelve simples:
ה ו ז ח ט י — heh, vav, zayin, chet, tet, yud
ל נ ס ע צ ק — lamed, nun, samech, ayin, tzadi, kuf
יסודן — Their foundation
ראיה שמיעה ריחה — is sight, hearing, smell,
שיחה לעיטה תשמיש — speech, taste, sexuality,

מעשה הילוך רוגז	action, locomotion, agitation,
שחוק הרהור שינה	laughter, thought, and sleep.
שנים עשר גבולי אלכסון	5:2 Twelve diagonal borders:
גבול מזרחית צפונית	the east-north border
גבול מזרחית דרומית	the east-south border
גבול מזרחית רומית	the east upper border
גבול מזרחית תחתית	the east lower border
גבול צפונית תחתית	the north lower border
גבול צפונית מערבית	the north-west border
גבול צפונית רומית	the north upper border
גבול מערבית תחתית	the west lower border
גבול מערבית דרומית	the west-south border
גבול מערבית רומית	the west upper border
גבול דרומית תחתית	the south lower border
גבול דרומית רומית	the south upper border
שתים עשרה פשוטות	5:3 Twelve simple letters:
חקקן צרפן	God engraved them, transmuted them,
חצבן	carved them,
שקלן והמירן	weighed them, exchanged them,
וצר בהם	and created with them
מזלות וחדשים ומנהיגים	constellations, months, and organs.
ואילו הן	These are
שנים עשר מזלות	the twelve constellations in the world:
טלה שור תאומים סרטן	Aries, Taurus, Gemini, Cancer,
אריה בתולה מאזנים עקרב	Leo, Virgo, Libra, Scorpio,
קשת גדי דלי דגים	Sagittarius, Capricorn, Aquarius, Pisces.
ושנים עשר חדשים	The twelve months in the year are:
ניסן אייר סיון תמוז	Nisan, Iyar, Sivan, Tamuz,
אב אלול תשרי מרחשוון	Av, Elul, Tishrei, Marcheshvan,
כסליו טבת שבט אדר	Kislev, Tevet, Shevat, Adar.
ואילו הן	The twelve organs
שנים עשר מנהיגים בנפש	in the body-soul are:
שתי ידים שתי רגלים	Two hands, two feet,
שתי כליות	two kidneys

Return to the Place

כבד ומרה טחול	the liver, the gall, the spleen,
המסס קרקבן	the gullet, the intestines,
וקיבה	and the stomach.

5:4

המליך אות הי	God gave rule to Heh
וקשר לו כתר	and tied a crown to it
וצרפן זה עם זה	and combined one thing with another
וצר בו טלה בעולם	and formed with it Aries in the world
וניסן בשנה	Nisan in the year
וכבד בנפש	and the liver in the body.

המליך אות ויו	God gave rule to Vav
וקשר לו כתר	and tied a crown to it
וצרפן זה עם זה	and combined one thing with another
וצר בו שור בעולם	and formed with it Taurus in the world
ואייר בשנה	Iyar in the year
ומרה בנפש	and the gall bladder in the body.

המליך אות זיין	God gave rule to Zayin
וקשר לו כתר	and tied a crown to it
וצרפן זה עם זה	and combined one thing with another
וצר בו תאומים בעולם	and formed with it Gemini in the world
וסיון בשנה	Sivan in the year
וטחול בנפש	and the spleen in the body.

המליך אות חית	God gave rule to Chet
וקשר לו כתר	and tied a crown to it
וצרפן זה עם זה	and combined one thing with another
וצר בו סרטן בעולם	and formed with it Cancer in the world
ותמוז בשנה	Tamuz in the year
והמסס בנפש	and the gullet in the body.

המליך אות טית	God gave rule to Tet
וקשר לו כתר	and tied a crown to it
וצרפן זה עם זה	and combined one thing with another
וצר בו אריה בעולם	and formed with it Leo in the world
ואב בשנה	Av in the year
וכוליה ימין בנפש	and the right kidney in the body.

המליך אות יוד	God gave rule to Yud
וקשר לו כתר	and tied a crown to it
וצרפן זה עם זה	and combined one thing with another
וצר בו בתולה בעולם	and formed with it Virgo in the world
ואלול בשנה	Elul in the year
וכוליה שמאל בנפש	and the left kidney in the body.

המליך אות למד	God gave rule to Lamed
וקשר לו כתר	and tied a crown to it
וצרפן זה עם זה	and combined one thing with another
וצר בו מעזנים בעולם	and formed with it Libra in the world
ותשרי בשנה	Tishrei in the year
וקרקבן בנפש	and the intestines in the body.

המליך אות נון	God gave rule to Nun
וקשר לו כתר	and tied a crown to it
וצרפן זה עם זה	and combined one thing with another
וצר בו עקרב בעולם	and formed with it Scorpio in the world
ומרחשוון בשנה	Marcheshvan in the year
וקיבה בנפש	and the stomach in the body.

המליך אות סמך	God gave rule to Samech
וקשר לו כתר	and tied a crown to it
וצרפן זה עם זה	and combined one thing with another
וצר בו	and formed with it
קשת בעולם	Sagittarius in the world
וכסליו בשנה	Kislev in the year
ויד ימין בנפש	and the right hand in the body.

המליך אות עין	God gave rule to Ayin
וקשר לו כתר	and tied a crown to it
וצרפן זה עם זה	and combined one thing with another
וצר בו גדי בעולם	and formed with it Capricorn in the world
וטבת בשנה	Tevet in the year
ויד שמאל בנפש	and the left hand in the body.

המליך אות צדי	God gave rule to Tzadi
וקשר לו כתר	and tied a crown to it
וצרפן זה עם זה	and combined one thing with another

וצר בו דלי בעולם	and formed with it Aquarius in the world
ושבט בשנה	Shevat in the year
ורגל ימין בנפש	and the right foot in the body.

המליך אות קוף	God gave rule to Kuf
וקשר לו כתר	and tied a crown to it
וצרפן זה עם זה	and combined one thing with another
וצר בו דגים בעולם	and formed with it Pisces in the world
ואדר בשנה	Adar in the year
ורגל שמאל בנפש	and the left foot in the body.

אילו עשרים ושתים אותיות	6:1 These are the twenty-two letters
שבהן	through which
חקק	the Becoming One who Holds Many
יה וה צבאות	the living God
אלוהים חיים	God of Israel
אלוהי ישראל	lofty and exalted
רם ונשא	dwelling in eternity
שוכן עד	of holy name
וקדוש שמו	engraved
	the cosmos

שלושה אבות ותולדותיהן	6:2 Three fathers and their generations
ושבעה כבשים וצבאותיהן	seven conquerors and their hosts
ושנים עשר גבולי אכלסין	twelve diagonal boundaries
וראיה לדבר	and the proof of the matter:
עדים נאמנים	faithful witnesses,
עולם שנה ונפש	the world, the year, and the body-soul.

חק	6:3 An engraved rule
עשרה שלשה ושבעה	of ten and three and seven
ושנים עשר פקודים	and twelve entrusted to
בתלי וגלגל ולב	the Dragon, the Wheel, and the Heart.
תלי בעולם	The Dragon in the World
כמלך על כסאו	is like a king on his throne.
גלגל בשנה	The Wheel in the Year
כמלך במדינה	is like a king in the countryside.
לב בנפש	The Heart in the Body
כמלך במלחמה	is like a king in war.

גם כל חפץ	6:4 Every experience,
זה לעומת זה	one against the other,
עשה אלהים	God has made:
טוב לעומת רע	good opposite evil.
רע מרע וטוב מטוב	Evil from evil, good from good.
טוב מבחין את רע	Good tests the evil
ורע מבחין את טוב	and evil tests the good.
טובה גנוזה לטובים	Good is stored up for the good
ורעה שמורה לרעים	and evil kept for the evil.
עשאן כמין מריבה	6:5 God formed them like a kind of quarrel;
וערכן כמין מלחמה	God arranged them like a kind of war;
גם את זה לעומת זה	God has made them
עשה האלהים	one opposite the other.
שלשה אחד אחד לבדו עומד	6:6 Three: each one stands alone.
שבעה שלושה חלוקין על	Seven: three divided against three
שלשה ואחד חוק	and one is an engraved law
מכריע בינתיים	balancing between them.
שנים עשר	Twelve
עומדים במלחמה	stand in battle:
שלשה אויבים	three are enemies and
ושלשה אוהבים	three are friends;
שלשה מחיים	three give life
ושלשה ממיתים	and three kill
וכולן אדוקין זה וזה	and each is joined to the other.
כשהבין אברהם אבינו	6:7 When Abraham our father understood
וצר וצרף	formed and transmuted
חקק וחצב	engraved and carved
חקר וחשב	delved and reflected
ועלתה בידו	power arose in his hand
נגלה עליו יי	and God appeared to him
עשאו אוהבו	and made him God's friend
וכרת לו	and made a covenant
ברית ולזרעו	with him and his seed
עד עולם	forever and ever
ועד עלמי עד	throughout all the worlds

Appendix III · The Two Hundred and Thirty-One Gates

Sefer Yetzirah recommends the recitation of the combinations of all of the Hebrew letters: "Aleph with them all, and all of them with Aleph, Bet with them all and all of them with Bet." This practice can be visual—"seeing" the combination of the two letters. It can be verbal—sounding the combinations of the letters. Or, it can be through writing the letters, thus "engraving" the letters just as God does in the book itself. Or, it can be all three.

As one makes all the possible combinations, one invokes the creation of all things in the cosmos. This is, in some way, a recreation of the moment of creation. We might say that we are reinforcing the universe—adding our own intention to the unfolding of creation. With each combination, we honor each part of creation and strengthen the whole. This practice is clearly meant to induce a state of deep contemplation, since it provides a focus to occupy the mind. We should note that *Sefer Yetzirah* considers the Hebrew aleph-bet to be the Divine name, so reciting the permutations of the aleph-bet is also a recitation of an expanded name of God.

This appendix sets forth the full practice of letter permutations as a practice for the individual to engage. This practice can also be engaged as a group, if one person leads and sets the pace. The method of combining the letters used here is the one Aryeh Kaplan calls the "logical method": the 22 letters are ordered and combined sequentially. There are also more complex methods of permutation attested in the kabbalah.[1]

The Mechanics of the Practice

Mishnah 2:4 of *Sefer Yetzirah* refers to the practice of letter combination as "two hundred and thirty-one gates" because there are two hundred thirty-one possible combinations of two Hebrew letters, assuming that the order of the two letters does not matter (i.e., *Aleph-Bet* is functionally treated as the same as *Bet-Aleph*). While many texts refer to "221" gates, this appears to be a scribal error, as Hayman notes.[2]

2:4 also calls the practice "a wheel that cycles forward and back." In other words, the practice can occur through the visualization of a rotating wheel containing all the letters. One can visualize this wheel as one is combining the letters.

Appendix III · The Two Hundred and Thirty-One Gates

The "wheel that cycles forward and back" can be envisioned in different ways. Aryeh Kaplan, for example, provides a diagram with 231 lines connecting all of the possible combinations of Hebrew letters.[3] As one combines more and more letters, these lines of connection form a complicated geometric shape that approximates a circle. Kaplan suggests imagining oneself in the circle's center, and seeing these lines passing over one's head like a "kind of ceiling," as *Sefer Yetzirah* says.[4]

However, Kaplan's way doesn't explain why the combinations are referred to as gates. There is another way to think of "the wheel that cycles forward and back," that does accommodate the idea of gates. This way of visualizing the wheel appears in a manuscript of Moshe Cordovero's commentary on Sefer Yetzirah.[5]

In this method, one can visualize a double wheel, one ring within another. The outer ring and the inner ring both contain all the letters. The inner and outer rings can move, so that the letters can line up as desired: *Aleph* with *Bet*, for example, or *Mem* with *Shin*.

Pictured this way, the wheel is like a combination lock. The pairs of letters, as they line up with one another, are like the combinations to the lock. When the right letters come together, they create a "key" to the lock, thus opening one of the "231 gates."

One might say that when two letters come together, they engrave a unique channel from which a singular created thing can arise. That is, each gate opens the way to a particular reality. We might note that in section 2:4, *Sefer Yetzirah* says that the letters "emerge" or "go out" (*yotzei* in Hebrew) by the 231 gates, suggesting that some entity is indeed coming forth during the process of letter permutation.

Where is God in relationship to this circle? Maybe at the center, and God's creative power passes out into the universe beyond the circle, to where creation unfolds. Or maybe energy flows from a God beyond the circle, and enters the circle of in order to create the things of this world. Whichever way the gate goes, it allows for a channel between the divine world and the human world—a "wondrous path," just as *Sefer Yetzirah* says in its first paragraph.

Then, when the necessary creative energy has emerged, the circle spins again, lining up different letters. A different gate opens, with its own unique energies. Another part of creation comes into being.

Whether one uses the "line" method that Kaplan draws from kabbalistic sources, or the "double circle" method, the goal is to permute the letters in rapid sequence, devoting one's full concentration to the work. Unlike the brief practices found throughout the rest of this book, this particular practice takes time and energy and one should make extra space and time for it. One might well listen to the advice of the thirteenth-century kabbalist Abraham Abulafia, who advises concerning the practice of letter permutation:

> Prepare yourself, unify your heart and purify your body. Choose a special place for yourself, where your voice will not be heard by anyone else. Meditate alone, with no one else present. Sit in a room or attic. Do not reveal your secret to anyone... If it is at night, light many candles, so that your eyes are well-illuminated. Then take in your hand a tablet and some ink...
>
> Transpose the [letters] and interchange them quickly, until your heart is warmed as a result of these permutations... Through the permutations, you will gain new knowledge that you would never have learned by human traditions or intellectual analysis..."[6]

One might, as one says, writes, or visualizes each pair of letters, imagine the unique door that they open, and the creative energies that thus enter the world. Perhaps the opening of these many doors is what leads to the "new knowledge" Abulafia promises.

Notes on Pronunciation

If one is using a solely visual method (i.e., imagining or writing the letters), then one has to be primarily concerned with the shapes of the letters (which one can find in this appendix). However, if one is going to utter the letters, one also has to consider how to sound them. When one combines two letters using sound, one has to add a vowel sound in order to pronounce the two letters together. The text of *Sefer Yetzirah* does not indicate which vowels to use when combining letters orally.

Abraham Abulafia has a method of voweling letters when combining them for meditation, particularly when he permutes the letters of the divine name. Abulafia uses what he calls the "natural vowel" of the first letter. For Abulafia, the natural vowel is the first vowel in that letter's name: for *Aleph*, it would be "a," for *Bet* "e," and so forth. We'll use Abulafia's method of voweling here.[7]

"*Ei*" makes the sound in "made" or "same" and ay or ai makes the long I as in "bite." "A" makes the sound "ah." The sound "*i*" is a long ee. "U" and "oo" should be read as the same sound, a long "oo."

Double letters like *Bet, Peh* and *Kaf*, when they appear at the end of a word or syllable, take their softer form, so *Bet* becomes *Vet* and makes a "v" sound, *Pei* becomes *Fei* and makes an "f" sound, and *Kaf* becomes *Khaf* and makes a "kh" sound.

Double letters like *Gimel, Dalet*, and *Tav* change sound in some Hebrew dialects, but not in all. Those changes in pronunciation have not been included here.

Ch and *kh* (the sounds made by *Chet* and also by *Khaf*, the soft sound of the letter *Kaf*) make a sound as in "blech" or the German *achtung*.

The letter *Ayin* makes a guttural sound indicated by an apostrophe, though many cannot pronounce it, in which case the *Ayin* may be treated like the *Aleph*, as silent except for its vowel.

The letter *Vav* will be treated as a consonant making the sound "v" for purposes of pronunciation, though it also serves as a vowel and can make the sounds "o" or "oo."

The letters *Kaf, Mem, Nun, Peh*, and *Tzadi* do have a final form at the end of a word, but since *Sefer Yetzirah* does not mention these forms at all, we won't use them for purposes of letter combination.

The letter *Sin* is missing from this array. *Sin* looks exactly like the letter *Shin* except that its dot is in a different place. It is not a version of the letter *Shin*. *Sin* is a separate letter. The letter *Sin* is entirely ignored by Sefer Yetzirah.

Some of the two-letter combinations form Hebrew words (such as Chen, grace). It is powerful that the final combination of letters, שת, spells *shet*, foundation," as in the foundation of the world, or *sheet*, as in *shittim*, the carved-out pits under the Temple which descend to the primordial depths. This recitation practice brings us deeply into the hollow space of creation, where the cosmic temple is eternally built and rebuilt.

Preparing for the Practice

Decide if you are visualizing, sounding, writing, or some combination of those three. If you are using writing materials, you should have these close at hand, and should also have an intention for what will be done with the writing afterward.

Return to the Place

Begin by finding a quiet place and comfortable position, focusing on the breath and centering. Once you begin, make every effort to complete the practice without interruption.

Keep some silence after the practice in order to center and ground. Journaling afterward might also be wise, in order to write down any insights. One might consider beginning with the text of 2:4:

> ים ושתים אתיות חקקן חצבן
> צרפן שקלן והימירן
>
> כיצד שקלן והימירן
> אלף עם כולם וכולם עם אלף
> בית עם כולם וכולם עם בית
> וכלן חוזרות חלילה
> נמצאו יוצאות במאתים ושלושים ואחד שערים
>
> נמצא כל היצור וכל הדיבור
> יוצא בשם אחד

> Twenty-two letters the Divine engraved, carved,
> permuted, weighed and exchanged.
>
> How did God weigh and exchange them?
> *Aleph* with them all and all of them with *Aleph*,
> *Bet* with them all and them all with *Bet*,
> and they all repeat in a cycle.
> Thus they emerge from 231 gates.

And so it is that all creation and all speech emerges from one name.

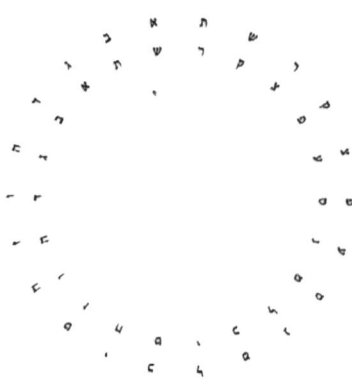

Appendix III · The Two Hundred and Thirty-One Gates

The Twenty-Two Letters

א	Aleph	ח	Chet	ס	Samech
ב	Bet	ט	Tet	ע	Ayin
ג	Gimel	י	Yud	פ	Peh
ד	Dalet	כ	Kaf	צ	Tzadi
ה	Heh	ל	Lamed	ק	Kuf
ו	Vav	מ	Mem	ר	Reish
ז	Zayin	נ	Nun	ש	Shin
				ת	Tav

The 231 Gates

1.	Aleph	Bet	Ab	אב
2.	Aleph	Gimel	Ag	אג
3.	Aleph	Dalet	Ad	אד
4.	Aleph	Heh	Ah	אה
5.	Aleph	Vav	Av	או
6.	Aleph	Zayin	Az	אז
7.	Aleph	Chet	Ach	אח
8.	Aleph	Tet	At	אט
9.	Aleph	Yud	Ay	אי
10.	Aleph	Kaf	Akh	אכ
11.	Aleph	Lamed	Al	אל
12.	Aleph	Mem	Am	אמ
13.	Aleph	Nun	An	אנ
14.	Aleph	Samech	As	אס
15.	Aleph	Ayin	A'	אע
16.	Aleph	Peh	Af	אפ
17.	Aleph	Tzadi	Atz	אצ
18.	Aleph	Kuf	Ak	אק
19.	Aleph	Reish	Ar	אר
20.	Aleph	Shin	Ash	אש
21.	Aleph	Tav	At	את
22.	Bet	Gimel	Beg	בג
23.	Bet	Dalet	Bed	בד
24.	Bet	Heh	Beh	בה
25.	Bet	Vav	Bev	בו
26.	Bet	Zayin	Bez	בז
27.	Bet	Chet	Bech	בח
28.	Bet	Tet	Bet	בט
29.	Bet	Yud	Bey	בי
30.	Bet	Kaf	Bekh	בכ
31.	Bet	Lamed	Bel	בל
32.	Bet	Mem	Bem	במ
33.	Bet	Nun	Ben	בנ
34.	Bet	Samech	Bes	בס
35.	Bet	Ayin	Be'	בע

Return to the Place

36.	Bet	Peh	Bef	בפ
37.	Bet	Tzadi	Betz	בצ
38.	Bet	Kuf	Bek	בק
39.	Bet	Reish	Ber	בר
40.	Bet	Shin	Besh	בש
41.	Bet	Tav	Bet	בת
42.	Gimel	Dalet	Gid	גד
43.	Gimel	Heh	Gih	גה
44.	Gimel	Vav	Giv	גו
45.	Gimel	Zayin	Giz	גז
46.	Gimel	Chet	Gich	גח
47.	Gimel	Tet	Git	גט
48.	Gimel	Yud	Giy	גי
49.	Gimel	Kaf	Gikh	גכ
50.	Gimel	Lamed	Gil	גל
51.	Gimel	Mem	Gim	גמ
52.	Gimel	Nun	Gin	גנ
53.	Gimel	Samech	Gis	גס
54.	Gimel	Ayin	Gi'	גע
55.	Gimel	Peh	Gif	גפ
56.	Gimel	Tzadi	Gitz	גצ
57.	Gimel	Kuf	Gik	גק
58.	Gimel	Reish	Gir	גר
59.	Gimel	Shin	Gish	גש
60.	Gimel	Tav	Git	גת
61.	Dalet	Heh	Dah	דה
62.	Dalet	Vav	Dav	דו
63.	Dalet	Zayin	Daz	דז
64.	Dalet	Chet	Dach	דח
65.	Dalet	Tet	Dat	דט
66.	Dalet	Yud	Day	די
67.	Dalet	Kaf	Dakh	דכ
68.	Dalet	Lamed	Dal	דל
69.	Dalet	Mem	Dam	דמ
70.	Dalet	Nun	Dan	דנ
71.	Dalet	Samech	Das	דס
72.	Dalet	Ayin	Da'	דע
73.	Dalet	Peh	Daf	דפ
74.	Dalet	Tzadi	Datz	דצ
75.	Dalet	Kuf	Dak	דק
76.	Dalet	Reish	Dar	דר
77.	Dalet	Shin	Dash	דש
78.	Dalet	Tav	Dat	דת
79.	Heh	Vav	Hev	הו
80.	Heh	Zayin	Hez	הז
81.	Heh	Chet	Hech	הח
82.	Heh	Tet	Het	הט
83.	Heh	Yud	Hey	הי
84.	Heh	Kaf	Hekh	הכ

Appendix III · The Two Hundred and Thirty-One Gates

85.	Heh	Lamed	Hel	הל
86.	Heh	Mem	Hem	המ
87.	Heh	Nun	Hen	הנ
88.	Heh	Samech	Hes	הס
89.	Heh	Ayin	He'	הע
90.	Heh	Peh	Hef	הפ
91.	Heh	Tzadi	Hetz	הצ
92.	Heh	Kuf	Hek	הק
93.	Heh	Reish	Her	הר
94.	Heh	Shin	Hesh	הש
95.	Heh	Tav	Het	הת
96.	Vav	Zayin	Vaz	וז
97.	Vav	Chet	Vach	וח
98.	Vav	Tet	Vat	וט
99.	Vav	Yud	Vay	וי
100.	Vav	Kaf	Vakh	וכ
101.	Vav	Lamed	Val	ול
102.	Vav	Mem	Vam	ומ
103.	Vav	Nun	Van	ונ
104.	Vav	Samech	Vas	וס
105.	Vav	Ayin	Va'	וע
106.	Vav	Peh	Vaf	ופ
107.	Vav	Tzadi	Vatz	וצ
108.	Vav	Kuf	Vak	וק
109.	Vav	Reish	Var	ור
110.	Vav	Shin	Vash	וש
111.	Vav	Tav	Vat	ות
112.	Zayin	Chet	Zach	זח
113.	Zayin	Tet	Zat	זט
114.	Zayin	Yud	Zay	זי
115.	Zayin	Kaf	Zakh	זכ
116.	Zayin	Lamed	Zal	זל
117.	Zayin	Mem	Zam	זמ
118.	Zayin	Nun	Zan	זנ
119.	Zayin	Samech	Zas	זס
120.	Zayin	Ayin	Za'	זע
121.	Zayin	Peh	Zaf	זפ
122.	Zayin	Tzadi	Zatz	זצ
123.	Zayin	Kuf	Zak	זק
124.	Zayin	Reish	Zar	זר
125.	Zayin	Shin	Zash	זש
126.	Zayin	Tav	Zat	זת
127.	Chet	Tet	Chet	חט
128.	Chet	Yud	Chey	חי
129.	Chet	Kaf	Chekh	חכ
130.	Chet	Lamed	Chel	חל
131.	Chet	Mem	Chem	חמ
132.	Chet	Nun	Chen	חנ
133.	Chet	Samech	Ches	חס

134.	Chet	Ayin	Che'	חע
135.	Chet	Peh	Chef	חפ
136.	Chet	Tzadi	Chetz	חצ
137.	Chet	Kuf	Chek	חק
138.	Chet	Reish	Cher	חר
139.	Chet	Shin	Chesh	חש
140.	Chet	Tav	Chet	חת
141.	Tet	Yud	Tey	טי
142.	Tet	Kaf	Tekh	טכ
143.	Tet	Lamed	Tel	טל
144.	Tet	Mem	Tem	טמ
145.	Tet	Nun	Ten	טנ
146.	Tet	Samech	Tes	טס
147.	Tet	Ayin	Te'	טע
148.	Tet	Peh	Tef	טפ
149.	Tet	Tzadi	Tetz	טצ
150.	Tet	Kuf	Tek	טק
151.	Tet	Reish	Ter	טר
152.	Tet	Shin	Tesh	טש
153.	Tet	Tav	Tet	טת
154.	Yud	Kaf	Yuk	יכ
155.	Yud	Lamed	Yul	יל
156.	Yud	Mem	Yum	ימ
157.	Yud	Nun	Yun	ינ
158.	Yud	Samech	Yus	יס
159.	Yud	Ayin	Yu'	יע
160.	Yud	Peh	Yuf	יפ
161.	Yud	Tzadi	Yutz	יצ
162.	Yud	Kuf	Yuk	יק
163.	Yud	Reish	Yur	יר
164.	Yud	Shin	Yush	יש
165.	Yud	Tav	Yut	ית
166.	Kaf	Lamed	Kal	כל
167.	Kaf	Mem	Kam	כמ
168.	Kaf	Nun	Kan	כנ
169.	Kaf	Samech	Kas	כס
170.	Kaf	Ayin	Ka'	כע
171.	Kaf	Peh	Kaf	כפ
172.	Kaf	Tzadi	Katz	כצ
173.	Kaf	Kuf	Kak	כק
174.	Kaf	Reish	Kar	כר
175.	Kaf	Shin	Kash	כש
176.	Kaf	Tav	Kat	כת
177.	Lamed	Mem	Lam	למ
178.	Lamed	Nun	Lan	לנ
179.	Lamed	Samech	Las	לס
180.	Lamed	Ayin	La'	לע
181.	Lamed	Peh	Laf	לפ
182.	Lamed	Tzadi	Latz	לצ

Appendix III · The Two Hundred and Thirty-One Gates

183.	Lamed	Kuf	Lak	לק
184.	Lamed	Reish	Lar	לר
185.	Lamed	Shin	Lash	לש
186.	Lamed	Tav	Lat	לת
187.	Mem	Nun	Men	מנ
188.	Mem	Samech	Mes	מס
189.	Mem	Ayin	Me'	מע
190.	Mem	Peh	Mef	מפ
191.	Mem	Tzadi	Metz	מצ
192.	Mem	Kuf	Mek	מק
193.	Mem	Reish	Mer	מר
194.	Mem	Shin	Mesh	מש
195.	Mem	Tav	Met	מת
196.	Nun	Samech	Nus	נס
197.	Nun	Ayin	Nu'	נע
198.	Nun	Peh	Nuf	נפ
199.	Nun	Tzadi	Nutz	נצ
200.	Nun	Kuf	Nuk	נק
201.	Nun	Reish	Nur	נר
202.	Nun	Shin	Nush	נש
203.	Nun	Tav	Nut	נת
204.	Samech	Ayin	Sa'	סע
205.	Samech	Peh	Saf	ספ
206.	Samech	Tzadi	Satz	סצ
207.	Samech	Kuf	Sak	סק
208.	Samech	Reish	Sar	סר
209.	Samech	Shin	Sash	סש
210.	Samech	Tav	Sat	סת
211.	Ayin	Peh	'Af	עפ
212.	Ayin	Tzadi	'Atz	עצ
213.	Ayin	Kuf	'Ak	עק
214.	Ayin	Reish	'Ar	ער
215.	Ayin	Shin	'Ash	עש
216.	Ayin	Tav	'At	עת
217.	Peh	Tzadi	Petz	פצ
218.	Peh	Kuf	Pek	פק
219.	Peh	Reish	Per	פר
220.	Peh	Shin	Pesh	פש
221.	Peh	Tav	Pet	פת
222.	Tzadi	Kuf	Tzak	צק
223.	Tzadi	Reish	Tzar	צר
224.	Tzadi	Shin	Tzash	צש
225.	Tzadi	Tav	Tzat	צת
226.	Kuf	Reish	Kur	קר
227.	Kuf	Shin	Kush	קש
228.	Kuf	Tav	Kut	קת
229.	Reish	Shin	Reish	רש
230.	Reish	Tav	Reit	רת
231.	Shin	Tav	Sheet	שת

Appendix IV · Index of Practices

See also: ReturnToThePlace.com

Aleph 152

All Creation and All Speech
    Emerges from One Name........106

Balancing Between 119

Before One 41

Blessings of the Months 222

Breath from Breath........................... 61

Circle of Twelve 215

Circle, The..200

Cycling the Wheel 99

Depths, The.. 47

Divine Throne....................................71

Dwelling in Eternity 229

Each is Joined to the Other 255

Elemental Sounds............................ 136

Engraved in the Voice......................95

Engraver, The...................................228

Engraving the Paths..........................11

Enveloped in
    Male and Female 125

Faithful Witnesses 235

Fire Above, Water Below 130

Fire from Water 73

Firelight 72

Five Opposite Five 22

Flame in a Fiery Coal......................40

Flash of Lightning, The....................5

Foundations 17

Four Winds, The...............................62

Gate of Bet, The 190

Gate of Dalet, The 191

Gate of Reish, The............................191

Gate of Tav, The 191

God Sealed Above,
    God Sealed Below........................85

God's Friend.....................................263

Good Opposite Evil 249

Heart at War, The............................243

Hewn in the Breath 96

Higher than Delight,
    Deeper than Sorrow 100

Holy Breath.. 57

Holy Temple 173

Holy Temple Bears Them All, The...174

Holy Wind..58

Letter of Healing 221

Like a Kind of Garden......................67

Mem..156

Mem Hums, Shin Hisses................ 135

Nisan 222

One Opposite the Other 254	Stones Multiply, The 184
Opening The Book 10	Stop Your Heart from Murmuring 35
Palmful of Merit, a Palmful of Guilt 118	Tapestry 91
Pillars of Breath 112	Temple of Elements 87
Power in the Hand 262	Three Breaths 148
Reed in a Whirlwind 53	Three Fathers 139
Return to the Place 36	Three Mothers 131
Returning the Creator to the Place 30	Three Witnesses 194
	Three Worlds 132
Rule Over Fire 161	Three, Seven, Twelve 235
Rule over Water 157	Throne of the Dragon 242
Rule over Wind 153	Tishrei 223
Scribing Letters 90	Treasury of Good 249
Sealing the Directions 84	Twelve Diagonal Lines 204
Sealing the Three Books 264	Twelve Diagonal Lines with the Hebrew Letters 205
Setting the Borders 208	Twelve Faculties, The 199
Seven Days, The 179	Twenty-Two Letters 230
Seven Gates, The 180	Two Beings 149
Seven Gifts 168	Until Eternity 48
Seven Stones 185	Void, The 16
Seven Transformations 169	Water from Breath 68
Shin 160	What the Mouth Cannot Say 185
Single Covenant 21	Wheel of Letters, The 107
Six Rings 124	Wheel of Time, The 242
Stand Each Thing on Its Absence ... 29	Working in Fire 111
Star, The 214	

Endnotes to the Introduction

1. Liebes, Yehuda. *The Ars Poetica of the Sefer Yetzirah* (Tel Aviv: Schocken, 2000), p. 35.
2. Midrash Tadshe, Chapter 2.
3. Wolfson, Elliot. "Text, Context, Pretext: A Review Essay of Yehudah Liebes," in *Studies in Hellenisic Judaism*, vol. 16 (2004), pp. 218-228.
4. Hayman, Peter. "Some Observations on Sefer Yesira: The Temple at the Center of the Universe," in the *Journal of Jewish Studies*, vol. 37 no. 2, p. 181.
5. Elior, Rachel. *The Three Temples: On the Emergence of Jewish Mysticism* (Oxford: The Littman Library of Jewish Civilization, 2004), pp. 69-70.
6. Schilling, Lachelle. "Desierto Divino: Messages from the Earth," https://feminismandreligion.com/2017/02/17/desierto-divino-messages-from-the-earth-by-lachelle-schilling/, accessed Nov. 9, 2017
7. Segol, Marla. *Word and Image in Medieval Kabbalah: The Texts, Commentaries, and Diagrams of the Sefer Yetzirah* (New York: Palgrave MacMillan, 2012), p. 63.
8. Turner, Victor. *The Forest of Symbols: Aspects of Ndembu Ritual* (Ithaca, NY: Cornell University Press, 1967), p. 105.
9. Honko, Lauri. "The Problem of Defining Myth," in *Sacred Narrative: Readings in the Theory of Myth*, ed. Alan Dundes (Berkeley: University of California Press, 1984), p. 49.
10. Alexander, Bobby. *Victor Turner Revisited: Ritual as Social Change* (Riga, Latvia: Scholars Press, 1991), p. 139.
11. Gruenwald, Itamar. "Some Critical Notes on the First Part of Sefer Yetzira," in *Revue des Etudes Juives*, vol. 132, (1973) p. 477.
12. Kaplan, Aryeh. *Sefer Yetzirah: The Book of Creation in Theory and Practice* (Boston: Weiser Books, 1997), xii-xiv.
13. Liebes, Yehuda. *The Ars Poetica of the Sefer Yetzirah* (Tel Aviv: Schocken, 2000), pp. 229-230.
14. Scholar Shlomo Pines has suggested an early date for the *Sefer Yetzirah* of the second century, believing that the *Sefer Yetzirah* bears a significant resemblance to the Pseudo-Clementine Homilies of the same period. (Pines, Shlomo, "Points of Similarity between the Exposition of the Doctrine of the *Sefirot* in the Sefer Yezira and a Text of the Pseudo-Clementine Homilies: The Implications of this Resemblance," in *Proceedings of the Israel Academy of Sciences and Humanities*, vol. 7 no. 3 (Jerusalem, 1989).
15. Wolfson, Elliot. "Text, Context, Pretext: A Review Essay of Yehudah Liebes," in *Studies in Hellenistic Judaism*, vol. 16 (2004), pp. 218-228.
16. Babylonian Talmud, Sanhedrin 67a

17 Segol, Marla. *Word and Image in Medieval Kabbalah: The Texts, Commentaries, and Diagrams of the Sefer Yetzirah* (New York: Palgrave MacMillan, 2012), pp. 25-26.
18 Hayman, Peter. "Was God a Magician? Sefer Yesira and Jewish Magic," in *The Journal of Jewish Studies*, vol. 41 no. 2, pp. 226-227.
19 Segol, Marla. *Word and Image in Medieval Kabbalah: The Texts, Commentaries, and Diagrams of the Sefer Yetzirah* (New York: Palgrave MacMillan, 2012), pp. 25-26.
20 Langerman, Y. Tzvi. "On the Beginning of Hebrew Scientific Literature and on Studying History through 'Maqbilot' (Parallels)," in *Aleph*, no. 2 (2002), p. 169-189.
21 Liebes, Yehuda. *The Ars Poetica of the Sefer Yetzirah* (Tel Aviv: Schocken, 2000), pp. 238.
22 Weiss, Tzahi. *Sefer Yesirah and Its Contexts: Other Jewish Voices* (Philadelphia, PA: University of Pennsylvania Press, 2018), p. 73.
23 See Babylonian Talmud, 59a, and also Lobel, Andrea, *Under a Censored Sky: Astronomy and Rabbinic Authority in the Talmud Bavli and Related Literature* (Dissertation, Concordia University, Montreal, Quebec, 2015), p. 33.
24 Babylonian Talmud, Berachot 55a
25 Hayman, Peter. "Was God a Magician? Sefer Yesira and Jewish Magic," in *The Journal of Jewish Studies*, vol. 41 no. 2, p. 225. However, Yehuda Liebes notes that the text does mention circumcision and Shabbat, so it is not completely devoid of Jewish concerns (Liebes, Yehuda. *The Ars Poetica of the Sefer Yetzirah* (Tel Aviv: Schocken, 2000), p. 225.
26 Cited in Liebes, Yehuda. *The Ars Poetica of the Sefer Yetzirah* (Tel Aviv: Schocken, 2000), p. 225).
27 Ibid.
28 Kaplan, Aryeh. *Sefer Yetzirah: The Book of Creation in Theory and Practice* (Boston: Weiser Books, 1997).
29 Hayman, Peter. *Sefer Yesira: Edition, Translation, and Text-Critical Commentary* (Tubingen, Germany: Mohr Siebeck, 2004), p. 25.
30 Ibid., pp. 1-2.
31 Meroz, Ronit. "Between *Sefer Yetzirah* and Wisdom Literature," in *Journal for the Study of Religions and Ideologies*, vol. 6 no. 18, (Winter 2007).
32 Hayman, Peter. *Sefer Yesira: Edition, Translation, and Text-Critical Commentary* (Tubingen, Germany: Mohr Siebeck, 2004), p. 60.
33 Wolfson, Elliot. "Text, Context, Pretext: A Review Essay of Yehudah Liebes," in *Studies in Hellenistic Judaism*, vol. 16 (2004), pp. 218-228.
34 Hayman, Peter. *Sefer Yesira: Edition, Translation, and Text-Critical Commentary* (Tubingen, Germany: Mohr Siebeck, 2004), pp. 5-6.
35 Ibid., p. 4.

36 However, on occasion we will deviate from Hayman's earliest recoverable text, in cases where the later material provides needed specificity for the earlier material.
37 Weiss, Tzahi. *Sefer Yesirah and Its Contexts: Other Jewish Voices* (Philadelphia, PA: University of Pennsylvania Press, 2018), pp. 74-75.
38 These chapter divisions themselves seem to have been added later in the book's development.
39 Segol, Marla. *Word and Image in Medieval Kabbalah: The Texts, Commentaries, and Diagrams of the Sefer Yetzirah* (New York: Palgrave Macmillan, 2012), p. 49.
40 Ibid., p. 45.
41 Segol, Marla. *Word and Image in Medieval Kabbalah: The Texts, Commentaries, and Diagrams of the Sefer Yetzirah* (New York: Palgrave Macmillan, 2012), p. 63.
42 Barad, Karen. *Meeting the Universe Halfway: Quantum Physics and the Entanglement of Matter and Meaning* (Durham, North Carolina: Duke University Press, 2007).
43 Meroz, Ronit. "Between *Sefer Yetzirah* and Wisdom Literature," *Journal for the Study of Religions and Ideologies*, vol. 6 no. 18, (Winter 2007), p. 112.
44 Gruenwald notes that it is indeed difficult to reconcile this rendition with the one that will follow (Gruenwald, Itamar. "Some Critical Notes on the First Part of Sefer Yetzira," in *Revue des Etudes Juives*, vol. 132 (1973), p. 495). The solution of Weinstock (Weinstock, I. *Levarer hanusach shel Sefer Yetzirah, Temirin I* (Jerusalem: Mossad haRav Kook, 1972), pp. 38, 59) is to suggest that the second rendition is a later addition by commentators, but Hayman (p. 77) points out that there is very little variation among manuscripts as to these two distinct renditions of the *sefirot*. This suggests that both versions of the *sefirot* were included in the early manuscripts. That is, the earliest editors of *Sefer Yetzirah* included two different versions of the *sefirot*, the divine dimensions of the universe.
45 Hayman, Peter. *Sefer Yesira: Edition, Translation, and Text-Critical Commentary* (Tubingen, Germany: Mohr Siebeck, 2004), p. 70.
46 Ecclesiastes 1:4-7.
47 Maimonides, *Mishneh Torah, Yesodei haTorah* 4:1
48 Shulman, David. "Is There an Indian Connection to *Sefer Yetzirah*?" in *Aleph*, vol. 2 (2000), p. 191-199.
49 Liebes, Yehuda. *The Ars Poetica of the Sefer Yetzirah* (Tel Aviv: Schocken, 2000), p. 24.
50 Zohar II, 24a
51 Zohar I, 231a
52 Scholem, Gershom, *On The Kabbalah and its Symbolism* (New York: Schocken Books, 1941), p. 75.

53 See, for example, Douglas, Mary. *Purity and Danger: An Analysis of Concepts of Pollution and Taboo* (London: Routledge, 2002), pp. 125-140.
54 Durkheim, Emile. *The Elementary Forms of the Religious Life* (Oxford: Oxford World's Classics, 1912), p. 60; cited in Segol, p. 36.
55 Harari, Yuval. *Jewish Magic before the Age of Kabbalah* (Detroit, Michigan: Wayne State University Press, 2017), p. 63.
56 Hammond, Dorothy. "Magic: A Problem in Semantics," in *American Anthropologist*, vol. 72 (1971), pp. 1348-1356.
57 Lesses, Rebecca. *Ritual Practices to Gain Power: Angels, Incantations, and Revelation in Early Jewish Mysticism*. Harvard Theological Studies 44. (Harrisburg, PA: Trinity Press International, 1998).
58 Segol, Marla. *Word and Image in Medieval Kabbalah: The Texts, Commentaries, and Diagrams of the Sefer Yetzirah* (New York: Palgrave Macmillan, 2012), p. 100.
59 Idel, Moshe. *Golem! Jewish Magical and Mystical Traditions on the Artificial Anthropoid* (Albany, NY: SUNY Press, 1990); Idel, Moshe, "The Golem in Jewish Magic and Mysticism," in *Golem! Danger, Deliverance, and Art*, ed. Emily D. Bilski (Albany, New York: SUNY Press 1988), pp. 15-35.
60 Isbell, Charles D. *Corpus of the Aramaic Incantation Bowls* (Eugene, OR: Wipf and Stock Publishers, 1975).
61 Hayman, Peter. "Was God a Magician? Sefer Yesira and Jewish Magic," in *The Journal of Jewish Studies*, vol. 41 no. 2, p. 226-227.
62 Abram, David and Jensen, Derrick. "David Abram Interview." https://wildethics.org/essay/david-abram-interviewed-by-derrick-jensen/ Accessed May 18, 2020.
63 Kaplan, Aryeh. *Sefer Yetzirah: The Book of Creation in Theory and Practice* (Boston: Weiser Books, 1997). p. xi.
64 Michaelson, Jay. *Enlightenment by Trial and Error: Ten Years on the Slippery Slopes of Jewish Spirituality, Postmodern Buddhism, and Other Modern Heresies* (Teaneck, NJ: Ben Yehuda Press, 2019); Thich Nhat Hanh, *Peace is Every Step: The Path of Mindfulness in Everyday Life* (New York: Bantam, 1992).
65 See Gruenwald, Itamar. *Apocalyptic and Merkavah Mysticism* (Leiden: Brill, 2014).
66 Shulman, David. "Is There an Indian Connection to *Sefer Yetzirah*?" in *Aleph*, vol. 2 (2000), pp. 191-199.
67 Meroz, Ronit. "Between *Sefer Yetzirah* and Wisdom Literature," in *Journal for the Study of Religions and Ideologies*, vol. 6 no. 18, (Winter 2007), p. 127.
68 Liebes, Yehuda. *The Ars Poetica of the Sefer Yetzirah* (Tel Aviv: Schocken, 2000), p. 9.
69 Kaplan, Aryeh. *Sefer Yetzirah: The Book of Creation in Theory and Practice* (Boston: Weiser Books, 1997), p. 2.

70 Kaplan, Aryeh. *Sefer Yetzirah: The Book of Creation in Theory and Practice* (Boston: Red Wheel/Weiser, 1997), p. 46.
71 Segol, Marla. *Word and Image in Medieval Kabbalah: The Texts, Commentaries, and Diagrams of the Sefer Yetzirah* (New York: Palgrave Macmillan, 2012), pp. 37, 43.
72 Meroz, Ronit. "Between *Sefer Yetzirah* and Wisdom Literature," in *Journal for the Study of Religions and Ideologies*, vol. 6 no. 18, (Winter 2007), p. 106.
73 *Sefer Yetzirah* 3:3
74 Work-Makinnae, Dawn. "The Rhineland Deae Matronae: Collective Female Deity in Germanic Europe," in *Goddesses in World Culture*, ed. Patricia Monaghan (Santa Barbara, CA: Praeger, 2011).
75 Hayman, Peter. *Sefer Yesira: Edition, Translation, and Text-Critical Commentary* (Tubingen, Germany: Mohr Siebeck, 2004), p. 117.
76 Hayman, Peter. *Sefer Yesira: Edition, Translation, and Text-Critical Commentary* (Tubingen, Germany: Mohr Siebeck, 2004), p. 116.
77 Zohar I, 1a and elsewhere.
78 Zohar III, 249a-b.
79 Hawley, John Stratton. *Devi: The Goddesses of India* (New Delhi, India: Aleph Book Company, 2017), pp. 49-76.
80 Bek-Pedersen, Karen. *The Norns in Old Norse Mythology* (Edinburgh, Scotland: Dunedin Academic Press, 2013), section 2.2.3.
81 See Washington, Teresa N., *Our Mothers, Our Powers, Our Texts: Manifestations of Aje in Africana Literature* (Oya's Tornado, 2005), p. 13-55.
82 Irigaray, Luce, *This Sex Which Is Not One* (Ithaca, NY: Cornell University Press, 1985), p. 31.
83 Ibid., p. 120.
84 There are a variety of expanded versions of 1:9, many with more masculine-sounding language. For example, a number of versions add: "His Throne is established of old." Others add: "Blessed and twice blessed is His name." Assuming that the briefest text is the original, perhaps later Jewish copyists or commentators were not so comfortable with the feminine ring of the language and tried to change it by adding more masculine phrases.
85 Liebes, Yehuda. *The Ars Poetica of the Sefer Yetzirah* (Tel Aviv: Schocken, 2000), p. 142.
86 Barad, Karen. "Transmaterialities: Trans*/Matter/Realities and Queer Political Imaginings," in *GLQ: A Journal of Lesbian and Gay Studies*, vol. 21, no. 2-3, p. 390.
87 See, for example, Genesis 1:24, where a creature is called a *nefesh chaya*, a living being, Genesis 2:7 where Adam is called a *nefesh chaya*, Leviticus 2:1, where a person is called a *nefesh*, or the famous phrase "a life for a life" (Deut. 9:21) which in Hebrew is *nefesh tachat nefesh*.

Endnotes to Visualization Practice

1 Babylonian Talmud, Avodah Zarah 18a
2 Hellner-Eshed, Melila. *A River Flows from Eden: The Language of Mystical Experience in the Zohar* (Palo Alto, CA: Stanford University Press, 2009), p. 76.
3 Fine, Lawrence, "The Art of Metoposcopy: A Study in Isaac Luria's Charismatic Knowledge," in *AJS Review*, vol. 11 no. 1 (Spring 1986), pp. 79-101.
4 Vital, Hayyim (ed. Morris Faierstein), *Jewish Mystical Autobiographies*, (Mahwah, NJ: Paulist Press, 1999), cf. pp. 44-45, 114-117, 138-143.
5 Garb, Jonathan. *Shamanic Trance in Modern Kabbalah* (Chicago: University of Chicago Press, 2011).
6 Michaelson, Jay, *God in Your Body* (Woodstock, VT: Jewish Lights, 2009); Firestone, Tirzah, *The Receiving: Reclaiming Jewish Women's Wisdom* (San Francisco: HarperOne, 2004); Novick, Leah, *On the Wings of Shekhinah: Rediscovering Judaism's Divine Feminine* (New York: Quest Books, 2008); Roth, Jeff, *Jewish Meditation Practices for Everyday Life: Awakening Your Heart, Connecting with God* (Woodstock, VT: Jewish Lights, 2009).
7 Shainberg, Catherine, *Kabbalah and the Power of Dreaming* (Rochester, VT: Inner Traditions, 2005). Also see: schoolofimages.com.
8 Kaplan, Aryeh, *Jewish Meditation: A Practical Guide* (New York: Schocken, 1995).
9 Hammond, Dorothy. "Magic: A Problem in Semantics," in *American Anthropologist*, vol. 72 (1971), pp. 1348-1356.
10 Some, Malidoma Patrice. *Of Water and Spirit: Ritual, Magic and Initiation in the Life of an African Shaman* (New York: Tarcher-Pulham, 1994), p. 181-190.

Endnotes to Chapter 1

1. Some scholars believe the number thirty-two has been inserted here by an editor to harmonize the (originally separate) narrative about the ten dimensions with the narrative about the twenty-two letters. Since the number thirty-two is never again mentioned in the book, this theory is entirely plausible.
2. Proverbs 8:22-23, 27-28, 30-32
3. Ackerman, Susan. *Under Every Green Tree: Popular Religion in Sixth Century Judah* (Leiden: Brill 2018).
4. Proverbs 8:15, 34-35
5. Proverbs 8:2
6. For example, see Midrash Tanhuma, Bereishit 1.
7. John 1:1; I Corinthians 1:24b; Bulgakov, Sergei, *Sophia: The Wisdom of God: An Outline of Sophiology* (Hudson, NY: Lindisfarme Press, 1993).
8. MacRae, George. "The Jewish Background of the Gnostic Sophia Myth," in *Novum Testamentum*, vol. 12 no. 2 (April 1970), pp. 86-101.
9. Matt, Daniel. *The Essential Kabbalah: The Heart of Jewish Mysticism* (San Francisco: Harper-Collins, 2006).
10. Meroz, Ronit. "Between *Sefer Yetzirah* and Wisdom Literature: Three Binitarian Approaches in *Sefer Yetzirah*." in *Journal for the Study of Religions and Ideologies*, vol. 6, no. 18 (Winter 2007), pp. 102-142.
11. Even in the one text where the *sefirot* are described as bowing before God's throne, they are multiple.
12. Meroz, Ronit. "Between *Sefer Yetzirah* and Wisdom Literature: Three Binitarian Approaches in *Sefer Yetzirah*." in *Journal for the Study of Religions and Ideologies*, vol. 6, no. 18 (Winter 2007), p. 102.
13. Genesis 1:2
14. Hayyim Vital, *Sefer Etz Chayyim*, Chapter 2.
15. Segol, Marla. *Word and Image in Medieval Kabbalah: The Texts, Commentaries, and Diagrams of the Sefer Yetzirah* (New York: Palgrave MacMillan, 2012), p. 40.
16. Diamond, James A. "YHWH: The God that Is vs. The God that Becomes," https://www.thetorah.com/article/yhwh-the-god-that-is-vs-the-god-that-becomes. Accessed Sept. 21, 2019.
17. Kaplan, Aryeh. *Sefer Yetzirah: The Book of Creation in Theory and Practice* (Boston: Red Wheel/Weiser, 1997), p. 5.
18. Hayman, Peter. *Sefer Yesira: Edition, Translation, and Text-Critical Commentary* (Tubingen, Germany: Mohr Siebeck, 2004), p. 60.
19. Liebes, Yehuda. *The Ars Poetica of the Sefer Yetzirah* (Tel Aviv: Schocken, 2000), p. 35.
20. See note 87 to the Introduction.

21 Kaplan, Aryeh. *Sefer Yetzirah: The Book of Creation in Theory and Practice* (Boston: Weiser Books, 1997), p. 19-20.
22 Liebes, Yehuda. *The Ars Poetica of the Sefer Yetzirah* (Tel Aviv: Schocken, 2000), p. 22.
23 Stroumsa, Sarah. "Wondrous Paths: The Isma'ili Context of Saadya's 'Commentary on Sefer Yesira," in *Bochumer Philosophisches Jahrbuch fur Antike und Mittelalter*, vol. 18:1 (2015), p. 74-90.
24 Babylonian Talmud, Rosh haShanah 16b
25 Abram, David. *The Spell of the Sensuous: Perception and Language in a More-Than-Human World* (Vintage, 1997), Chapter 1.
26 Hayman, Peter. *Sefer Yesira: Edition, Translation, and Text-Critical Commentary* (Tubingen, Germany: Mohr Siebeck, 2004), p. 65.
27 Hayman notes the extreme variation among manuscripts in the text of 1:2. (Hayman, Peter. *Sefer Yesira: Edition, Translation, and Text-Critical Commentary* (Tubingen, Germany: Mohr Siebeck, 2004), p. 65.) Here, I use the variant text found in the Short Recension, in the Parma manuscript, and treat this section as a kind of road map or table of contents, detailing the categories into which the divinely engraved channels are sorted.
28 In later kabbalah, *sefirot* comes to mean the ten emanations of the divine.
29 Gershom Scholem, *Origins of the Kabbalah* (Berlin: Walter de Gruyter and Co., 1962), p. 26.
30 Liebes, Yehuda. *The Ars Poetica of the Sefer Yetzirah* (Tel Aviv: Schocken, 2000), pp. 12-15.
31 Scholem has no explanation for why the word "engrave" would be used in relationship to the ten counting numbers. Cf. Busi, Giulio. "Engraved, Hewed, Sealed: *Sefirot* and Divine Writing in the *Sefer Yetzirah*," in *Jerusalem Studies in Jewish Thought*, vol. 20 (2005), p. 5.
32 Busi, Giulio. "Engraved, Hewed, Sealed: *Sefirot* and Divine Writing in the *Sefer Yetzirah*," in *Jerusalem Studies in Jewish Thought*, vol. 20 (2005), pp. 1-11.
33 Saadya Gaon, *Commentaire sur le Sefer Yesira ou Livre de la Creation par le Gaon Saadya de Fayyoum* (trans. and ed. M. Lambert, Paris, 1891, trans. into English by Scott Thompson and Dominique Marson, San Francisco, 1985).
34 Pirkei Avot 5:6
35 Midrash Tanhuma, Bereishit 1
36 Job 26:7
37 Kaplan, Aryeh. *Sefer Yetzirah: The Book of Creation in Theory and Practice* (Boston: Red Wheel/Weiser, 1997), p. 32.
38 Dr. Nathaniel Berman pointed this out to me in a conversation in May 2019.
39 Scholem, Gershom. *Origins of the Kabbalah* (Berlin: Walter de Gruyter and Co., 1962), p. 28.

40 The word *yesodot* can mean elements, as in the four elements earth, water, air, and fire. That is, the elements are the basic foundations of all substances. The *sefirot* and letters in *Sefer Yetzirah* often have the function of elements.
41 Hayman, Peter. "Some Observations on Sefer Yesira: The Temple at the Center of the Universe," in *Journal of Jewish Studies*, vol. 37 no. 2, p. 180.
42 Gen. 17:10-14; Liebes, Yehuda. *The Ars Poetica of the Sefer Yetzirah* (Tel Aviv: Schocken, 2000), p. 30.
43 Ibid., p. 57.
44 Babylonian Talmud, Sanhedrin 100a, Menachot 90a.
45 Liebes, Yehuda. *The Ars Poetica of the Sefer Yetzirah* (Tel Aviv: Schocken, 2000), p. 12-15.
46 Saadya Gaon, *Commentaire sur le Sefer Yesira ou Livre de la Creation par le Gaon Saadya de Fayyoum* (trans. and ed. M. Lambert, Paris, 1891, trans. into English by Scott Thompson and Dominique Marson, San Francisco, 1985).
47 Dan, Joseph, *The Ancient Jewish Mysticism* (Tel Aviv: MOD Books, 1989), p. 54-55; Scholem, Gershom, *Major Trends in Jewish Mysticism* (New York: Schocken Books, 1946/1974), p. 40-79.
48 There is considerable debate about whether Gnosticism originated within Judaism or Christianity, but its sects have shown both influences. See Dan, Joseph, *The Ancient Jewish Mysticism* (Tel Aviv: MOD Books, 1989), pp. 54-55.
49 Dan, Joseph. *The Ancient Jewish Mysticism* (Tel Aviv: MOD Books, 1989), p. 45.
50 Proverbs 8:12, 14
51 Bennema, Cornelis. *The Power of Saving Wisdom: An Investigation of Spirit and Wisdom in Relation to the Soteriology of the Fourth Gospel* (Eugene, OR: Wipf and Stock, 2007), p. 75.
52 Scholem, Gershom. *The Kabbalah* (New York: Plume, 1978), p. 9.
53 Philo, *Questions and Answers on Genesis*, http://www.earlyjewishwritings.com/text/philo/book8.htm Accessed Sept. 27, 2018.
54 Wadsworth, Christopher. *The Holy Bible in the Authorized Version* (London: Rivingtons, 1876), comment on Judges 5:16-19.
55 "and looked down one as far as I could," from Frost, Robert. "The Road Not Taken" in *Mountain Interval* (New York: Henry Holt, 1916).
56 Babylonian Talmud, Gittin 89b
57 Kaplan, Aryeh. *Sefer Yetzirah: The Book of Creation in Theory and Practice* (Boston: Weiser Books, 1997), p. 38.
58 Hayman, Peter. *Sefer Yesira: Edition, Translation, and Text-Critical Commentary* (Tubingen, Germany: Mohr Siebeck, 2004), p. 70.

59 However, Hayman holds this to be an error in the manuscript (Hayman, p. 71).
60 A koan told of Yamaoka Tesshu (1836-1888). Quoted in Nolan, Hamilton, "Zen Koans Explained: Nothing Exists." https://gawker.com/zen-koans-explained-nothing-exists-1537931448 Accessed Oct. 28, 2019.
61 Quoted in Brill, Alan, "Rabbi Aryeh Kaplan—Creating 20th Century Jewish Meditation." https://kavvanah.wordpress.com/2018/10/09/rabbi-aryeh-kaplan-creating-20th-century-jewish-meditation/ Accessed Oct. 10, 2018.
62 Zornberg, Avivah Gottlieb. *The Murmuring Deep: Reflections on the Biblical Unconscious* (New York: Schocken Books, 2009), pp. xiii, xxix.
63 It is also possible to read the text as "sit the Creator on His place" which is somewhat less evocative, but in my view the implications are the same.
64 Michaelson, Jay. *Jewish Enlightenment* (Teaneck, NJ: Ben Yehuda Press, 2019), p. 39.
65 Matt, Daniel. *The Essential Kabbalah: The Heart of Jewish Mysticism* (San Francisco: Harper-Collins, 2006).
66 Liebes, Yehuda. *The Ars Poetica of the Sefer Yetzirah* (Tel Aviv: Schocken, 2000), p. 65.
67 Jastrow, Marcus. *Dictionary of the Targumim, the Talmud Bavli and Yerushalmi, and the Midrashic Literature* (Peabody, Massachusetts: Hendrickson Publishers, 2005), p. 830.
68 Ecclesiastes 1:13
69 Liebes, Yehuda. *The Ars Poetica of the Sefer Yetzirah* (Tel Aviv: Schocken, 2000), p. 55.
70 Genesis Rabbah 39:7
71 Weiss, Tzahi. *Sefer Yetzirah and Its Contexts: Other Jewish Voices* (University of Pennsylvania Press, 2018), pp. 74-75, 109.
72 See Deut. 12:5 and elsewhere. Liebes, Yehuda. *The Ars Poetica of the Sefer Yetzirah* (Tel Aviv: Schocken, 2000), p. 196.
73 Ezekiel 1:13-14
74 Kaplan, Aryeh. *Sefer Yetzirah: The Book of Creation in Theory and Practice* (Boston: Red Wheel/Weiser, 1997), p. 39.
75 Proverbs 8:22
76 Proverbs 8:24
77 Exodus 3:1-6; Exodus 19:18; Genesis 15:18
78 Isaiah 6:5-7
79 Interestingly, in Exodus Rabbah 1:26 there is a midrash (legend) in which Moses burns his mouth on a coal as an infant, causing him to have a speech impediment. This midrash seems to be based on the same connection between prophet, mouth, and coal.

80 See Deuteronomy 6:4. For the monotheistic reading, see Maimonides, *Mishneh Torah, Hilchot Kriat Shema* 1:2 and 1:4. For the mystical reading, see for example Zohar III, 263a, where the Shema describes the unification of many divine aspects, and the writings of Shneur Zalman of Liadi (*Shaar haYichud vehaEmunah* III), who says "the spirit that flows to each thing from the mouth of God is the only thing that removes it constantly from nothingness and brings it into being."
81 This observation comes from Judd Matlin, who mentioned this insight during a class in May 2019 at the Rowe Center in Rowe, MA.
82 Liebes, Yehuda. *The Ars Poetica of the Sefer Yetzirah* (Tel Aviv: Schocken, 2000), p. 155.
83 The related word *emek* is most commonly used for valley.
84 Babylonian Talmud, Megillah 3b, 6a
85 Ronit Meroz divides *Sefer Yetzirah* into three authors: the Covenant Account (characterized by language about covenant), the Depth Account (characterized by the word *omek* or depth), and the Sealing Account, which focuses on the 22 letters and describes "sealing" the universe. Meroz sees our current section as the centerpiece of the Depth account. (Meroz, Ronit. "Between Sefer Yetzirah and Wisdom Literature," *Journal for the Study of Religions and Ideologies*, vol. 6 no. 18 (Winter 2007), pp. 101-142.)
86 Jastrow, Marcus. *Dictionary of the Targumim, The Talmud Babli and Yerushalmi, and the Midrashic Literature* (Hendrickson Publishers, 2005), p. 1053.
87 This image of the house founded on hollow depths echoes the earlier passage in which we hear "stand each thing on its absence." The image may be related to the legend that there were hollow tunnels beneath the Temple, known as the *shittim* or foundations.
88 Meroz, Ronit. "Between Sefer Yetzirah and Wisdom Literature," *Journal for the Study of Religions and Ideologies*, vol. 6 no. 18 (Winter 2007), p. 112.
89 Silverstein, Kathryn. "Deep Desires: Spatiotemporal Erotica in Hebrew Priestess Re/Writing and the Question of Essentialism." Unpublished paper, presented at the Kohenet Hebrew Priestess Institute, Isabella Freedman Jewish Retreat Center, Falls Village, CT, March 2017, p. 5.
90 Ibid., p. 10.
91 Keller, Catherine. *Face of the Deep: A Theology of Becoming* (New York, NY: Routledge, 2003), p. 164.
92 Kaplan, Aryeh. *Sefer Yetzirah: The Book of Creation in Theory and Practice* (Boston: Red Wheel/Weiser, 1997), pp. 48-49.
93 Hayman, Peter. "Was God a Magician? Sefer Yetzirah and Jewish Magic," *Journal of Jewish Studies*, vol. 41.2 (1990), p. 234.
94 Meroz, Ronit. "Between Sefer Yetzirah and Wisdom Literature," *Journal for the Study of Religions and Ideologies*, vol. 6 no. 18 (Winter 2007), pp. 112-113.

95 Liebes, Yehuda. *The Ars Poetica of the Sefer Yetzirah* (Tel Aviv: Schocken, 2000), p. 37.
96 Babylonian Talmud, Sukkah 49a
97 Liebes, Yehuda. *The Ars Poetica of the Sefer Yetzirah* (Tel Aviv: Schocken, 2000), p. 182.
98 Campbell, Joseph. *The Power of Myth* (Norwell, MA: Anchor, 1991), p. 89.
99 Ezekiel 1:14
100 Barad, Karen. "Transmaterialities: Trans*/Matter/Realities and Queer Political Imaginings," in GLQ: A Journal of Lesbian and Gay Studies, vol. 21, no. 2-3, pp. 387-422.
101 Ibid.
102 Meroz, Ronit. "Between Sefer Yetzirah and Wisdom Literature," *Journal for the Study of Religions and Ideologies*, vol. 6 no. 18, (Winter 2007), p. 120.
103 Liebes, Yehuda. *The Ars Poetica of the Sefer Yetzirah* (Tel Aviv: Schocken, 2000), p. 154.
104 Meroz, Ronit. "Between Sefer Yetzirah and Wisdom Literature," *Journal for the Study of Religions and Ideologies*, vol. 6 no. 18, (Winter 2007), p. 126.
105 Isaiah 66:15; Jeremiah 4:13
106 Genesis 2:7
107 Aryeh Kaplan also notes this image of the glassblower: Kaplan, Aryeh. *Sefer Yetzirah: The Book of Creation in Theory and Practice* (Boston: Red Wheel/Weiser, 1997), p. 69.
108 Some kabbalists later identified this first sefirah with the Zohar's first sefirah: Keter, the manifestation of the divine will to create, does seem similar to *Ruach Elohim Chayyim* in that it is the beginning of God's creative process. Other kabbalists identify Divine Breath with the sefirah of Chochmah, which is also closely associated with the act of creation (Kaplan, Aryeh. *Sefer Yetzirah: The Book of Creation in Theory and Practice* (Boston: Red Wheel/Weiser, 1997), pp. 68, 358.)
109 Unterman, Alan and Horowitz, Rivka, "Ruach haKodesh," in *Encyclopedia Judaica* (Jerusalem: Judaica Multimedia/Keter, 1997), CD-ROM edition.
110 Babylonian Talmud, Berachot 55a
111 Hayman, Peter, *Sefer Yesira: Edition, Translation, and Text-Critical Commentary* (Tubingen, Germany: Mohr Siebeck, 2004), pp. 80-81.
112 This language is not lost on the later kabbalists. They frequently identify this second *sefirah* of "breath" with *Malkhut*—the tenth *sefirah*, associated with the divine feminine—or with Binah, the second *sefirah*, the cosmic Divine Mother. (Kaplan, Aryeh. *Sefer Yetzirah: The Book of Creation in Theory and Practice* (Boston: Red Wheel/Weiser, 1997), p. 359, note 189.)
113 Zechariah 2:10. The four winds also appear in Daniel 7:2 and 11:4.
114 Genesis 2:10-14
115 Babylonian Talmud, Berachot 13b. Also see Taanit 3b, Avodah Zarah 10b.

116 Yehuda Liebes draws similar conclusions (Liebes, Yehuda. *The Ars Poetica of the Sefer Yetzirah* (Tel Aviv: Schocken, 2000), pp. 35-36.)
117 The later kabbalah understood the third sefirah in *Sefer Yetzirah* (water) according to their own notions of the *sefirot*. Citing numerous kabbalistic sources, Kaplan understands the third elemental sefirah, water, to be identical with Chochmah, the sefirah called Wisdom—a masculine creative principle (Kaplan, Aryeh. *Sefer Yetzirah: The Book of Creation in Theory and Practice* (Boston: Weiser Books, 1997), p. 73, p. 360, note 199). However, in the classical kabbalah, water is most clearly associated with *chesed* or lovingkindness, or with *malkhut* (which is sometimes referred to as the "sea")..
118 Dillard, Annie. *The Abundance: Narrative Essays Old and New* (Ecco, 2016).
119 Genesis 1:2
120 Gruenwald, Itamar. "Some Critical Notes on the First Part of Sefer Yetzira," in *Revue des Etudes Juives*, vol. 132, (1973) p. 498. While this theory could be plausible, Hayman points out that if the text here used to be much briefer, there are no witnesses to that fact, as there are no manuscripts with such a simple version. (Hayman, Peter, *Sefer Yesira: Edition, Translation, and Text-Critical Commentary* (Tubingen, Germany: Mohr Siebeck, 2004), pp. 86-87.
121 Some variant texts have "form" a garden. (Hayman, Peter, *Sefer Yesira: Edition, Translation, and Text-Critical Commentary* (Tubingen, Germany: Mohr Siebeck, 2004), p. 85.)
122 Hayman suggests that the passage describes no "floor" to creation, but I think the garden can be construed to be the floor. See Hayman, Peter. *Sefer Yesira: Edition, Translation, and Text-Critical Commentary* (Tubingen, Germany: Mohr Siebeck, 2004), p. 87.
123 Jastrow, Marcus. *Dictionary of the Targumim, The Talmud Babli and Yerushalmi, and the Midrashic Literature* (Hendrickson Publishers, 2005), p. 990.
124 Grant, Andrew. "Entanglement: Gravity's Long-Distance Connection," in *ScienceNews: Magazine of the Society for Science and the Public*, Oct. 17, 2015. https://www.sciencenews.org/article/entanglement-gravitys-long-distance-connection Accessed Oct. 22, 2018.
125 Jastrow, Marcus. *Dictionary of the Targumim, The Talmud Babli and Yerushalmi, and the Midrashic Literature* (Hendrickson Publishers, 2005), p. 814.
126 *Sefer Yetzirah* 1:3, 1:7, 3:3
127 Hayman, Peter. "Was God a Magician? Sefer Yesira and Jewish Magic," in *The Journal of Jewish Studies*, vol. 41 no. 2, pp. 226-227.
128 Liebes, Yehuda. *The Ars Poetica of the Sefer Yetzirah* (Tel Aviv: Schocken, 2000), p. 177.

129 Hayman, Peter. "Some Observations on Sefer Yesira: The Temple at the Center of the Universe," in the *Journal of Jewish Studies*, vol. 37 no. 2, pp. 176-182.
130 I Chronicles 9:24
131 Hayman, Peter. "Some Observations on Sefer Yesira: The Temple at the Center of the Universe," in the *Journal of Jewish Studies*, vol. 37 no. 2, p. 180; Josephus, *Antiquities of the Jews*, 8:96; Yadin, Yigael. *Megillat haMikdash/The Temple Scroll: The Hidden Law of the Dead Sea Sect* (New York: Random House, 1985), vol. 1, p. 193.
132 Genesis Rabbah 10:3
133 Ibid., p. 179.
134 Levenson, Jon D. *Creation and the Persistence of Evil* (Princeton, NJ: Princeton University Press, 1994), p. 17.
135 Hayman, Peter. "Was God a Magician? Sefer Yesira and Jewish Magic," in *The Journal of Jewish Studies*, vol. 41 no. 2, pp. 225-237.
136 Isbell, Charles D. *Corpus of the Aramaic Incantation Bowls* (Eugene, OR: Wipf and Stock Publishers, 1975), p. 27.
137 The practice was not exclusive to Jews but was practiced often by Jews, with both Jewish and non-Jewish clients. The bowls were produced in the sixth to eighth centuries, during the time *Sefer Yetzirah* was likely written.
138 Shani, Ayelett. "Bewitched: What Makes a Jewish Sorceress?" *HaAretz*, Dec. 6, 2013. https://www.haaretz.com/.premium-what-makes-a-jewish-sorceress-1.5297200 Accessed Sept. 18, 2019.
139 Levene, Dan. "Curse or Blessing: What's in the Magic Bowl?" Presented during the Ian Karten Lecture, University of Southampton, 2002. Published in Parkes Institute Pamphlet, 2002.
140 http://www.britishmuseum.org/research/collection_online/collection_object_details.aspx?objectId=1402667&partId=1
141 Duling, D.C. "Testament of Solomon: 1st to 3rd Centuries A.D." in *Old Testament Pseudepigrepha*, Vol. 1, ed. James H. Charlesworth (Peabody, MA: Hendrickson Publishers, 1983), p. 948.
142 Faraj, A.H., and Moriggi, Marco. "Two Incantation Bowls from the Iraq Museum," *Orientalia*, vo. 74 no. 1 (2005), p. 79.
143 Isbell, Charles D. *Corpus of the Aramaic Incantation Bowls* (Eugene, OR: Wipf and Stock Publishers, 1975), p. 78 (Text 26).
144 Hunter, Erica C.D. "Incantation Bowls: A Mesopotamian Phenomenon?" in *Orientalia*, vol. 65, no. 3 (1996), p. 223.
145 Ibid., p. 220-233.
146 Moriggi, Marco. *A Corpus of Syriac Incantation Bowls: Syriac Magical Texts from Late-Antique Mesopotamia* (Leiden: Brill, 2014), p. 48.
147 Isbell, Charles D. *Corpus of the Aramaic Incantation Bowls* (Eugene, OR: Wipf and Stock Publishers, 1975), p. 32 (Text 7).

148 Hunter, Erica C.D. "Incantation Bowls: A Mesopotamian Phenomenon?" in *Orientalia*, vol. 65, no. 3 (1996), p. 223; Moriggi, Marco. *A Corpus of Syriac Incantation Bowls: Syriac Magical Texts from Late-Antique Mesopotamia* (Leiden: Brill, 2014), p. 48.
149 Babylonian Talmud, Sukkah 53b
150 Jerusalem Talmud, Sanhedrin 29b.
151 Babylonian Talmud, Sukkah 49b
152 Tillich, Paul, 'The Demonic: A Contribution to the Interpretation of History", (1926, trans. Elsa L. Tamley), in *The Interpretation of History* (New York: Scribner, 1936), p. 85.
153 Weiss, Tzahi. *Sefer Yetzirah and Its Contexts: Other Jewish Voices* (Philadelphia: University of Pennsylvania Press, 2018), pp. 55-56.
154 Ibid., pp. 72-75.
155 Ibid., pp. 51-52.
156 Regarding *Yud Heh Vav*, Scholem understands this first combination of the divine name to spell *Yaho*, a divine name cognate to *Iao*, a secret divine name used by the Gnostic writer Valentinus. In the Pistis Sophia the name *Iao* is associated with the four directions of the world. Scholem understands *Yud Heh Vav* to be related to this Gnostic formulation of the Divine name that seals the world's boundaries. (Scholem, Gershom. *Origins of the Kabbalah* (Berlin: Walter de Gruyter and Co., 1962), p. 32.)
157 The Baghdad manuscript is Hayman's manuscript Z.
158 Weiss, Tzahi. *Sefer Yetzirah and Its Contexts: Other Jewish Voices* (Philadelphia: University of Pennsylvania Press, 2018), pp. 24-25, 33, 52.
159 Ibid., p. 33.

Endnotes to Chapter 2

1. As with many of the sections of *Sefer Yetzirah*, there is some controversy around the placement of this first passage of Chapter 2. Hayman observes that in many manuscripts of *Sefer Yetzirah*, this paragraph (2:1) appears in the middle of Chapter 1 rather than at the beginning of Chapter 2. However, in the Short Recension the paragraph appears here, at the beginning of Chapter 2, and Hayman thinks this is its proper placement. (Hayman, Peter. *Sefer Yesira: Edition, Translation, and Text-Critical Commentary* (Tubingen, Germany: Mohr Siebeck, 2004), pp. 92-94.)
2. Weiss, Tzahi. *Sefer Yesirah and Its Contexts: Other Jewish Voices* (Philadelphia: University of Pennsylvania Press, 2017), p. 66.
3. Ibid.
4. Liebes and Hayman translate this differently as "twenty-two letters are the foundation." (Hayman, *Sefer Yesira*, pp. 92-93; Liebes, p. 16).
5. Hayman, Peter. *Sefer Yesira: Edition, Translation, and Text-Critical Commentary* (Tubingen, Germany: Mohr Siebeck, 2004), p. 79.
6. Weiss, Tzahi, *Sefer Yesirah and Its Contexts: Other Jewish Voices* (Philadelphia, PA: University of Pennsylvania Press, 2018), p. 19.
7. Genesis 3:8; Genesis 2:7; Numbers 12:8
8. Hayman, Peter. *Sefer Yesira: Edition, Translation, and Text-Critical Commentary* (Tubingen, Germany: Mohr Siebeck, 2004), p. 97.
9. Gruenwald, Itamar (1973). "Some Critical Notes on the First Part of Sefer Yetzira," in *Revue des Etudes Juives*, vol. 132, p. 476 note 2.
10. Scholem, Gershom. "Yezirah, Sefer," in *Encyclopedia Judaica*, vol. 16 (1971), p. 784.
11. Hayman, Peter. *Sefer Yesira: Edition, Translation, and Text-Critical Commentary* (Tubingen, Germany: Mohr Siebeck, 2004), p. 97.
12. Ibid., pp. 92-93.
13. Ibid., p. 95.
14. Liebes, Yehuda. *The Ars Poetica of the Sefer Yetzirah* (Tel Aviv: Schocken, 2000), pp. 236-237.
15. Shulman, David. "Is There an Indian Connection to *Sefer Yetzirah*?" in *Aleph*, vol. 2 (2000), pp. 191-199.
16. Upanishad Aitareya Aranyaka Upanishad, third *adyaya*, ninth *khanda*.
17. Ibid., fourth *adyaya*, first *khanda*.
18. There is an interesting parallel here with the Talmudic understanding of the *bat kol* or divine voice, which is a manifestation of prophetic spirit that speaks to humans and is feminine. (Babylonian Talmud, Berachot 61b, Sanhedrin 11a, Megillah 29a, and elsewhere).
19. Rig Veda 10.125

20 In many manuscripts, this passage also mentions the two hundred thirty-one gates. Some variations of the text say two hundred twenty-one, though this is an error that seems to have crept in during the copying process (Hayman, *Sefer Yesira*, p. 99).
21 See, for example, Kaplan, Aryeh. *Sefer Yetzirah: The Book of Creation in Theory and Practice* (Boston: Weiser Books, 1997), p. 111; Segol, Marla, *Word and Image in Medieval Kabbalah: The Texts, Commentaries, and Diagrams of the Sefer Yetzirah* (New York: Palgrave MacMillan, 2012), p. 96.
22 Ibid. I discovered this image after developing the ideal of a double wheel on my own and was delighted to find confirmation in a medieval commentary.
23 Babylonian Talmud, Berachot 2b.
24 Babylonian Talmud, Berachot 31a
25 In alternate texts, this phrase reads "if good, then higher than delight, if evil, lower than plague." (Hayman, Peter, *Sefer Yesira: Edition, Translation, and Text-Critical Commentary* (Tubingen, Germany: Mohr Siebeck, 2004), pp. 98-100.)
26 Liebes, Yehuda. *The Ars Poetica of the Sefer Yetzirah* (Tel Aviv: Schocken, 2000), p. 147.
27 From the root *mem-vav-reish*, meaning "to change." (Brown, F., Driver, S. and Briggs, C. *The Brown-Driver-Briggs Hebrew and English Lexicon* (Peabody, MA: Hendrickson Publishers, 2000), p. 558. See Jeremiah 2:11 for another use of the word *heimir* to mean "exchange."
28 Leviticus 19:36
29 Brown, F., Driver, S. and Briggs, C. *The Brown-Driver-Briggs Hebrew and English Lexicon* (Peabody, MA: Hendrickson Publishers, 2000), p. 1053.
30 Hearn, Lian. *Emperor of the Eight Islands: The Tale of Shikanoko Book I* (Farrar, Strauss, and Giroux, 2016).
31 Hur, Nam-lin. *Prayer and Play in Late Tokugawa Japan* (Harvard University Press, 2000), p. 84.
32 Exodus 25:3; Lev. 27:3, 27:16
33 Lev. 25:25
34 Hayman includes this phrase and what follows it in his earliest recoverable version in brackets. While the evidence is not conclusive, Hayman considers whether this section (beginning with "*Aleph* with them all") may not be from the earliest version of *Sefer Yetzirah*, but might be a later gloss or explanation of God's "weighing and exchanging" of the letters. If this is so, it would be hard to conclude exactly what practice was originally meant by "weighing and exchanging" letters. (Hayman, Peter. *Sefer Yesira: Edition, Translation, and Text-Critical Commentary* (Tubingen, Germany: Mohr Siebeck, 2004), pp. 50, 103-104). Jewish readers of the passage understood the practice to mean "*Aleph* with them all and them

all with *Aleph*, *Bet* with them all and them all with *Bet*" and it became a central Jewish meditation practice used by Abraham Abulafia and many others. (cf. Kaplan, Aryeh. *Meditation and Kabbalah* (Boston: Weiser Books, 1989), pp. 107-110.)

35 Honigsberg, David. "Rava's Golem," in *Journal of the Fantastic in Arts*, vol. 7 no. 2/3 (26/27), pp. 137-145; Kaplan, Aryeh. *Sefer Yetzirah: The Book of Creation in Theory and Practice* (Boston: Weiser Books, 1997), pp. 113, 117.
36 Kaplan, Aryeh. *Sefer Yetzirah: The Book of Creation in Theory and Practice* (Boston: Weiser Books, 1997), pp. 113, 117.
37 Hayman, Peter. *Sefer Yesira: Edition, Translation, and Text-Critical Commentary* (Tubingen, Germany: Mohr Siebeck, 2004), p. 103.
38 Ibid., p. 100.
39 Proverbs 8:3
40 Weiss, Tzahi. *Sefer Yesirah and its Contexts: Other Jewish Voices* (Philadelphia: University of Pennsylvania Press, 2017), p. 64.
41 Weiss, Tzahi, *Sefer Yesirah and Its Contexts: Other Jewish Voices* (Philadelphia, PA: University of Pennsylvania Press, 2018), p. 64-65.
42 Liebes, Yehuda. *The Ars Poetica of the Sefer Yetzirah* (Tel Aviv: Schocken, 2000), p. 162.
43 Hayman, Peter. *Sefer Yesira: Edition, Translation, and Text-Critical Commentary* (Tubingen, Germany: Mohr Siebeck, 2004), pp. 104-105.
44 Ibid.
45 Ibid. See Babylonian Talmud, Chagiga 12a, and Genesis Rabbah 4:7
46 Exodus 13:21-22. Private conversation with Batya Diamond, Feb. 28, 2019.
47 I Kings 7:23
48 Proverbs 9:1
49 Sappho, fragment 9, in Barnard, Mary, *Sappho: A New Translation* (Oakland, CA: University of California Press, 1958).
50 Babylonian Talmud, Hagiga 17a, Rosh haShanah 4b, Yoma 80a

Endnotes to Chapter 3

1. Liebes, Yehuda. *The Ars Poetica of the Sefer Yetzirah* (Tel Aviv: Schocken, 2000), p. 17. The *Shin* stands for "fire" because it is the last letter of the word *eish*, fire—the first letter, *aleph*, is already taken by *avir* or air.
2. Frymer-Kensky, Tikvah. "Biblical Cosmology," in M. P. O'Connor and D. N. Freedman, *Backgrounds for the Bible*, (University Park, PA: Eisenbrauns, 1987), p. 233.
3. Meroz, Ronit. "Between *Sefer Yetzirah* and Wisdom Literature," *Journal for the Study of Religions and Ideologies*, vol. 6 no. 18 (Winter 2007), p. 116.
4. Shulman, David. "Is There an Indian Connection to *Sefer Yetzirah*?" in *Aleph*, vol. 2 (2000), p. 197.
5. Zornberg, Avivah Gottlieb. *The Murmuring Deep: Reflections on the Biblical Unconscious* (New York: Schocken Books, 2009), introduction.
6. Rosh-Pinnah, Eliyahu. "The *Sefer Yetzirah* and the Original Tetragrammaton," in *The Jewish Quarterly Review*, vol. 57 (1966-1967), p. 219.
7. Idel, Moshe, "The Golem in Jewish Magic and Mysticism," in *Golem! Danger, Deliverance, and Art*, ed. Emily D. Bilski (New York, 1988), pp. 15-35; Idel, Moshe. *Golem! Jewish Magical and Mystical Traditions on the Artificial Anthropoid* (Albany, NY, 1990).
8. Kaplan, Aryeh. *Sefer Yetzirah: The Book of Creation in Theory and Practice* (Boston: Weiser Books, 1997), p. 140.
9. Liebes, Yehuda. *The Ars Poetica of the Sefer Yetzirah* (Tel Aviv: Schocken, 2000), p. 26.
10. Jastrow, Marcus. *Dictionary of the Targumim, The Talmud Babli and Yerushalmi, and the Midrashic Literature* (Peabody, MA: Hendrickson Publishers, 2005), pp. 397, 428-429.
11. This plays out in the later kabbalah through the opposite forces of *chesed* (love/generosity) and *gevurah* (judgment/severity/limitation).
12. This is very similar to the Talmudic image of the three books of the righteous, the wicked, and the in-between (Babylonian Talmud, Rosh haShanah 16b). The image here may in some way be echoing this notion of three categories/books of individuals.
13. Kaplan, Aryeh. *Sefer Yetzirah: The Book of Creation in Theory and Practice* (Boston: Weiser Books, 1997), p. 140.
14. Jastrow, Marcus. *Dictionary of the Targumim, The Talmud Babli and Yerushalmi, and the Midrashic Literature* (Peabody, MA: Hendrickson Publishers, 2005), p. 672.
15. Hayman, Peter. *Sefer Yesira: Edition, Translation, and Text-Critical Commentary* (Tubingen, Germany: Mohr Siebeck, 2004), p. 114.
16. Cerf, Moran. "Neuroscientists Have Identified How Exactly a Deep Breath Changes Your Mind," Quarizy, Nov. 19, 2017, https://qz.com/

quartzy/1132986/neuroscientists-have-identified-how-exactly-a-deep-breath-changes-your-mind/ Accessed Nov. 18, 2018. The article cites research by Dr. Jose Herrero and Dr. Ashesh Mehta at NorthShore University Hospital.
17 Zohar II, 99a
18 Gordon, Cyrus H. "Aramaic Incantation Bowls," in *Orientalia* (Nova Series), vol. 10 (1941), p.120.
19 Isbell, Charles D. *Corpus of the Aramaic Incantation Bowls* (Eugene, OR: Wipf and Stock, 1975), pp. 48-49.
20 Kaplan, Aryeh. *Sefer Yetzirah: The Book of Creation in Theory and Practice* (Boston: Weiser Books, 1997), pp. 153-155.
21 This point about the language being "wrapped in male and female" was made by Rabbi Dianne Cohler-Esses during a lecture I gave at Congregation Romemu on March 23, 2019.
22 Cf. Zohar II, 63b, in which the Shema prayer is understood as a bringing together of differently gendered divine aspects.
23 Brown, F., Driver, S. and Briggs, C. *The Brown-Driver-Briggs Hebrew and English Lexicon* (Peabody, MA: Hendrickson Publishers, 2000), p. 367.
24 Cf. Cook, Edward. An Aramaic Incantation Bowl from Khafaje," in *Bulletin of the American Schools of Oriental Research*, vol. 285 (Feb. 1992), pp. 79-81; Gordon, Cyrus H. "Aramaic Incantation Bowls," in *Orientalia* (Nova Series), vol. 10 (1941), p. 120; Levene, Dan. "Curse or Blessing: What's in the Magic Bowl?" Presented during the Ian Karten Lecture, University of Southampton, 2002. Published in Parkes Institute Pamphlet, 2002.
25 This distinction between *machtam* and *mechutam* was pointed out to me by Rabbi Jeff Hoffman in a conversation on email, Oct. 17, 2019.
26 *Mechutam*, like *mechutal*, would have contained a *vav*, while *machtam* would not.
27 Isaiah 7:10
28 Genesis 1:11
29 Genesis 1:20
30 In fact, kabbalists identified the *Aleph, Mem,* and *Shin* with the three horizontal rows of the kabbalistic Tree of Life (Kaplan, p. 151).
31 Cavill, David. "God of Fire: A Study of Theophany and Pentateuch Fire Imagery." Unpublished Senior Project, Academy for Jewish Religion (Yonkers, NY, March 2017).
32 Gen. 3:24
33 Gen. 19:24
34 Exodus 19:18
35 Exodus 3:2-4; Exodus 14:21
36 Judges 13:20
37 Cf. Babylonian Talmud, Chagiga 14b; Berachot 6b; Eruvin 63a.

38 The Jewish philosopher Saadya Gaon, a commentator on the *Sefer Yetzirah*, also described the divine throne as composed of fire (Saadya Gaon, Book of Beliefs and Opinions 2:10).
39 Jonah 2:3
40 Job 38:17
41 Frymer-Kensky, Tikvah. "Biblical Cosmology," in M. P. O'Connor and D. N. Freedman, *Backgrounds for the Bible*, (University Park, PA: Eisenbrauns, 1987). p. 233; Vawter, Bruce, "A Note on the 'Waters Beneath the Earth,'" in *Catholic Bible Quarterly*, vol. 22 (1960), pp. 71-73.
42 Job 26:10; Proverbs 8:27
43 Abram, David. *The Spell of the Sensuous: Perception and Language in a More-Than-Human World* (Visalia, CA: Vintage, 1997), pp. 225-263.
44 Gold, Shefa. *The Magic of Hebrew Chant: Healing the Spirit, Transforming the Mind, Deepening Love* (Jewish Lights, 2013), pp. 6, 10.
45 Zornberg, Avivah. *The Murmuring Deep: Reflections on the Biblical Unconscious* (New York: Schocken Books, 2009), p. xx.
46 Ibid., p. xxi.
47 Hayman, Peter. *Sefer Yesira: Edition, Translation, and Text-Critical Commentary* (Tubingen, Germany: Mohr Siebeck, 2004), p. 116.
48 Kaplan, Aryeh. *Sefer Yetzirah: The Book of Creation in Theory and Practice* (Boston: Weiser Books, 1997), p. 80.
49 Hayman, Peter. *Sefer Yesira: Edition, Translation, and Text-Critical Commentary* (Tubingen, Germany: Mohr Siebeck, 2004), p. 159.
50 Kaplan, Aryeh. *Sefer Yetzirah: The Book of Creation in Theory and Practice* (Boston: Weiser Books, 1997), pp. 85-87, 143.
51 Matt, Daniel. *The Essential Kabbalah: The Heart of Jewish Mysticism* (San Francisco: Harper-Collins, 2006), pp. 73-83.
52 Hayman, Peter. *Sefer Yesira: Edition, Translation, and Text-Critical Commentary* (Tubingen, Germany: Mohr Siebeck, 2004), p. 120.
53 This is not, incidentally, true of the ten *sefirot*; in 1:7 each of the *sefirot* manifests in only one of the three "books."
54 Genesis 47:18 or Deut. 10:6; Jastrow, Marcus. *Dictionary of the Targumim, The Talmud Babli and Yerushalmi, and the Midrashic Literature* (Peabody, MA: Hendrickson Publishers, 2005), pp. 220-221.
55 Psalm 136:6
56 Psalm 23:5
57 Hayman, Peter. *Sefer Yesira: Edition, Translation, and Text-Critical Commentary* (Tubingen, Germany: Mohr Siebeck, 2004), p. 118.
58 Ibid.
59 Ibid., p. 121.
60 Hunter, Erica C.D. "Incantation Bowls: A Mesopotamian Phenomenon?" in *Orientalia*, vol. 65, no. 3 (1996), pp. 220-233.

Endnotes to Chapter 3

61 Moriggi, Marco. *A Corpus of Syriac Incantation Bowls: Syriac Magical Texts from Late-Antique Mesopotamia* (Brill, 2014), p. 48.
62 Psalms 104:1; Genesis 35:18
63 Genesis 1:24, Genesis 2:7, Leviticus 2:1, Deut. 9:21
64 Numbers 6:6
65 Babylonian Talmud, Berachot 61b
66 Babylonian Talmud, Sanhedrin 37a
67 Scholem, Gershom. *Kabbalah* (New York: New American Library, 1974), p. 161. Also see, for example, the discussion of *nefesh* in Chapter 1 of Hayyim Vital's Shaar haGilgulim (Gate of Reincarnations).
68 Genesis 1:27
69 Hayman, Peter. *Sefer Yesira: Edition, Translation, and Text-Critical Commentary* (Tubingen, Germany: Mohr Siebeck, 2004), pp. 121-122.
70 Ibid., p. 121.
71 Babylonian Talmud, Yoma 54a
72 Babylonian Talmud, Menachot 29b
73 For example, see Genesis 25:23-24 and Job 31:16
74 Deut. 7:13
75 The final form of the *Mem* is a rounded square that looks even more like a well, womb, or cave.
76 Underwood, Emily. "Your gut is directly connected to your brain, by a newly discovered neuron circuit," *Science* (Sept. 20, 2018). https://www.sciencemag.org/news/2018/09/your-gut-directly-connected-your-brain-newly-discovered-neuron-circuit Accessed Nov. 29, 2018.
77 Jeremiah 31:20
78 HeartMath Institute, *Science of the Heart, Vol. 1* (1993-2001): "Exploring the Role of the Heart in Human Performance: An Overview of Research Conducted by the HeartMath Institute," https://www.heartmath.org/resources/downloads/science-of-the-heart/ Accessed Oct. 19, 2019.
79 Cavill, David. "God of Fire: A Study of Theophany and Pentateuch Fire Imagery." Unpublished Senior Project, Academy for Jewish Religion (Yonkers, NY, March 2017).

Endnotes to Chapter 4

1. Hayman notes that the Long Recension contains a paragraph linking Bet to life/death, *Gimel* to peace/war, etc. as one would expect from our passage. (Hayman, Peter. *Sefer Yesira: Edition, Translation, and Text-Critical Commentary* (Tubingen, Germany: Mohr Siebeck, 2004), p. 143). In Hayman's earliest recoverable manuscript, grace and seed switch: grace comes before seed in the first part of the passage, but after seed in the second. This makes it hard to definitively associate these qualities with particular letters. (Ibid., p. 50.)
2. Kaplan, Aryeh. *Sefer Yetzirah: The Book of Creation in Theory and Practice* (Boston: Weiser Books, 1997), pp. 174-176.
3. Hayman, Peter. *Sefer Yesira: Edition, Translation, and Text-Critical Commentary* (Tubingen, Germany: Mohr Siebeck, 2004), pp. 127-128. Note that the order of the states is consistent in 4:1 from manuscript to manuscript, though some manuscripts switch "grace" and "wealth."
4. Ferraro, Jennifer and Bolat, Latif. *Quarreling with God: Mystic Rebel Poems of the Dervishes of Turkey* (White Cloud Press, 2007), p. 22.
5. Sappho, "Prayer to Our Lady of Paphos," in Barnard, Mary, *Sappho: A New Translation* (Oakland, CA: University of California Press, 1958), p. 39.
6. The lower seven *sefirot* are: *chesed*/grace, *gevurah*/limitation, *tiferet*/harmony, *netzach*/persistence, *hod*/beauty, *yesod*/foundation, and *malkhut*/sovereignty. Kaplan notes two prominent kabbalists' lists of the correspondences and neither is completely convincing: one version associates *hod* with sovereignty (although *hod*, which is glory, beauty, or surrender, is often understood to mean something like the opposite of sovereignty) and another associates *yesod* with peace, though *yesod* generally is associated with sexuality and would go better with seed. (Kaplan, Aryeh. *Sefer Yetzirah: The Book of Creation in Theory and Practice* (Boston: Weiser Books, 1997), p. 164.
7. Kaplan, Aryeh. *Sefer Yetzirah: The Book of Creation in Theory and Practice* (Boston: Weiser Books, 1997), p. 149.
8. Weiss, Tzahi. *Sefer Yesirah and Its Contexts: Other Jewish Voices* (Philadelphia, PA: University of Pennsylvania Press, 2018), p. 69.
9. Aryeh Kaplan suggests that the two forms of the *Reish* were known to the Jewish Mazya community in Tiberias in the 10th century (Kaplan, p. 160). Tzahi Weiss writes that a parallel Greek idea pairs the seven planets with the seven vowels; *Sefer Yetzirah* may have adapted this idea and used seven double letters instead of vowels (Weiss, Tzahi. *Sefer Yesirah and Its Contexts: Other Jewish Voices* (Philadelphia, PA: University of Pennsylvania Press, 2018), p. 21).
10. Lev. 27:10

Endnotes to Chapter 4

11 Jastrow, Marcus. *Dictionary of the Targumim, the Talmud Babli and Yerushalmi, and the Midrashic Literature* (Peabody, Massachusetts: Hendrickson Publishers, 2005), p. 1676.
12 Proverbs 6:3
13 Proverbs 8:2
14 Proverbs 14:1
15 It is fascinating that *Sefer Yetzirah* never uses the Hebrew phrase *beit hamikdash*, which would be the most direct reference to the Temple. Instead is uses phrases like *ma'on kodsho* (His holy dwelling) and *heichal hakodesh* (the holy shrine)—which are clear references to the Temple but do not use its proper name. It is as if the text doesn't want to be accused of too directly altering the meaning of the Temple to signify the cosmos.
16 Weiss, Tzahi. *Sefer Yesirah and Its Contexts: Other Jewish Voices* (Philadelphia, PA: University of Pennsylvania Press, 2018), p. 19.
17 Meroz, Ronit. "Between *Sefer Yetzirah* and Wisdom Literature," *Journal for the Study of Religions and Ideologies*, vol. 6 no. 18 (Winter 2007), p. 124.
18 Hayman suggests there is some possibility this phrase ("and it bears them all") is not original to the book, but it does appear in most manuscripts. (Hayman, p. 133).
19 Meroz, Ronit. "Between *Sefer Yetzirah* and Wisdom Literature," *Journal for the Study of Religions and Ideologies*, vol. 6 no. 18 (Winter 2007), p. 112.
20 Ibid., p. 110.
21 Hunter, Erica C.D. "Incantation Bowls: A Mesopotamian Phenomenon?" in Orientalia, vol. 65, no. 3 (1996), pp. 220-233.
22 Babylonian Talmud, Berachot 59b
23 Weiss, Tzahi. *Sefer Yesirah and Its Contexts: Other Jewish Voices* (Philadelphia, PA: University of Pennsylvania Press, 2018), p. 21.
24 Hayman, Peter. *Sefer Yesira: Edition, Translation, and Text-Critical Commentary* (Tubingen, Germany: Mohr Siebeck, 2004), pp. 136-137.
25 Ibid., pp. 137-138.
26 Hayyim Vital, Sefer Etz Hayyim 1:1
27 Babylonian Talmud, Berachot 60b. This prayer also appears near the beginning of the traditional Jewish morning prayer service, and is recited by traditional Jews when they come out of the bathroom.
28 See *Sefer Yetzirah* 2:5 in this translation.
29 According to Segol, what comes before this passage is theory, and what comes afterward is practice. This distinction does not entirely hold up, since some things before this passage appear to be practice, but it is an interesting comment on the centrality of the passage about the stones. (Segol, Marla. "Genre as Argument in the *Sefer Yetzirah*: A New Look at Its Literary Structure," in *Journal of the American Academy of Religion*, vol. 79 no. 4 (2011), p. 979.)

30 We should note that the paragraph has no tagline—no restatement of "seven doubles"—and therefore stands out from the rest of the chapter. According to Hayman's reading, it is possible that in earlier versions of *Sefer Yetzirah*, this paragraph concluded chapter 4.
31 Hayman, Peter. *Sefer Yesira: Edition, Translation, and Text-Critical Commentary* (Tubingen, Germany: Mohr Siebeck, 2004), pp. 138-139.
32 There are a number of textual differences between Chapters 3 and 4. In 3:10-12, "God made *Aleph* rule over breath, and tied a crown to it... and sealed with it..." In 4:5-6, God crowns the letters, but does not name the elemental quality they rule over, such as life, peace, seed, etc. Kaplan notes this as well. (Kaplan, Aryeh. *Sefer Yetzirah: The Book of Creation in Theory and Practice* (Boston: Weiser Books, 1997), pp. 174-178.) The text in Chapter 4 also does not use the word "seal." Perhaps a later rabbinic writer or editor was not at ease with the language of sealing—which, as we have said, is magical language. Instead, we have the language of "combined one thing with another, and formed with it...." The phrase "combined one thing with another" does not appear in all manuscripts, and Hayman believes it is a later addition (Hayman, Peter. *Sefer Yesira: Edition, Translation, and Text-Critical Commentary* (Tubingen, Germany: Mohr Siebeck, 2004), p. 139).
33 Lorelai Kude, personal communication, Jan. 15, 2019.
34 Hayman, Peter. *Sefer Yesira: Edition, Translation, and Text-Critical Commentary* (Tubingen, Germany: Mohr Siebeck, 2004), pp. 138-139.
35 Babylonian Talmud, Shabbat 156a
36 Ibid.
37 Kude, Lorelai, "Yesh Mazal l'Yisrael: Astrology and Identity in Jewish Culture" (Master's Thesis, Graduate Theological Union, March 2018).
38 This passage is not in the Short Recension, but it is in the Saadyan recension. Hayman includes it in his "earliest recoverable version" in brackets, noting that although it is not definite that this passage is from the earliest recoverable version, it is likely that it is from the earliest recoverable version given that its content is consistent with *Sefer Yetzirah* as a whole.
39 Deut. 4:26; 30:19, 31:28
40 Barad, Karen (1999), "Agential realism: feminist interventions in understanding scientific practices (1998)", in Biagioli, Mario, *The Science Studies Reader* (New York, New York: Routledge), pp. 1–11; Barad, Karen (2007). *Meeting the Universe Halfway: Quantum Physics and the Entanglement of Matter and Meaning* (Durham, North Carolina: Duke University Press, 2007).

Endnotes to Chapter 5

1. Liebes, Yehuda. *The Ars Poetica of the Sefer Yetzirah* (Tel Aviv: Schocken, 2000), p. 18.
2. Hayman notes very few manuscript variations in the order of the faculties. (Hayman, Peter. *Sefer Yesira: Edition, Translation, and Text-Critical Commentary* (Tubingen, Germany: Mohr Siebeck, 2004), p. 147.) In the Long and Saadyan recensions cited by Hayman, *Heh* and *Vav* correspond to sight and hearing, and so forth. However, Aryeh Kaplan's text lists the faculties in a different order, with different letter correspondences: *Heh* with speech, *Vav* with thought, *Zayin* with movement, etc. (Kaplan, Aryeh. *Sefer Yetzirah: The Book of Creation in Theory and Practice* (Boston: Weiser Books, 1997), pp. 215-218). Many contemporary practitioners who work with Sefer Yetzirah use Kaplan's correspondences. See, for example, Ribner, Melinda. *Kabbalah Month by Month: A Year of Spiritual Practice and Personal Transformation* (San Francisco, CA: Jossey-Bass, 2002).
3. Pirkei Avot 3:15
4. Brown-Driver-Briggs, p. 919.
5. Jastrow, Marcus. *Dictionary of the Targumim, The Talmud Babli and Yerushalmi, and the Midrashic Literature* (Peabody, MA: Hendrickson Publishers, 2005), p. 1456.
6. Schachter, S. and Singer, J. "Cognitive, social, and physiological determinants of emotional state," in *Psychological Review*, vol. 69 no. 5 (1962), pp. 379-399.
7. Jastrow, Marcus. *Dictionary of the Targumim, The Talmud Babli and Yerushalmi, and the Midrashic Literature* (Peabody, MA: Hendrickson Publishers, 2005), p. 366.
8. For a discussion of *hirhur* as a rabbinic term for sexual fantasy and sinful thoughts, see Naiweld, Ron. "Purity of Body, Purity of Self: Hirhur in Rabbinic Literature," in *Judaisme Ancien* (2014), pp. 209-235. For a discussion of *hirhurim* as anxious thoughts, see Zornberg, Avivah Gottlieb, *Genesis: The Beginning of Desire* (New York: Schocken, 1995), pp. 93-95.
9. Genesis 20, Genesis 28:10-19, Genesis 37:1-11, Genesis 40-41, I Kings 3, and Daniel 4, for example.
10. Babylonian Talmud, Berachot 57b. Berachot 55a-57b extensively discusses dreams as prophetic intimations.
11. Jastrow, Marcus. *Dictionary of the Targumim, The Talmud Babli and Yerushalmi, and the Midrashic Literature* (Peabody, MA: Hendrickson Publishers, 2005), p. 70.
12. Hayman, Peter. *Sefer Yesira: Edition, Translation, and Text-Critical Commentary* (Tubingen, Germany: Mohr Siebeck, 2004), pp. 149-150.
13. Exodus 19:12

14 Exodus 23:31, Joshua 1:4
15 Jeremiah 31:17
16 Babylonian Talmud, Shabbat 156b
17 Babylonian Talmud, Shabbat 75a
18 Goodenough, E.R. *Jewish Symbols in the Greco-Roman Period* (Princeton, NJ: Princeton University Press, 1988), pp. 167-218.
19 Goldman, Bernard. *The Sacred Portal: A Primary Symbol in Ancient Judaic Art* (Lanham, MD: University Publication Association, 1986), p. 64.
20 Segol, Marla. *Word and Image in Medieval Kabbalah: The Texts, Commentaries, and Diagrams of the Sefer Yetzirah* (New York: Palgrave MacMillan, 2012), p. 103.
21 Ibid., p. 101.
22 Ibid., p. 103.
23 Jastrow, Marcus. *Dictionary of the Targumim, The Talmud Babli and Yerushalmi, and the Midrashic Literature* (Peabody, MA: Hendrickson Publishers, 2005), p. 798.
24 Ibid.
25 The list of the constellations, months, and organs included here is from one of these later layers of *Sefer Yetzirah*, and can be found in both the Short and Long Recensions. (Hayman, Peter. *Sefer Yesira: Edition, Translation, and Text-Critical Commentary* (Tubingen, Germany: Mohr Siebeck, 2004), pp. 154-155.)
26 Maimonides, *Mishneh Torah*, Laws of Blessings 10:18; Pirkei deRabbi Eliezer 6:3, 7:5. Also see Midrash Tanhuma Buber, Bereishit 13:2.
27 Jerusalem Talmud, Rosh haShanah 1:2.
28 Neusner, Jacob. "Astrology in Ancient Judaism," in *Astronomy in Ancient Judaism* (eds. A. Avery-Peck and W.S. Green), *The Encyclopedia of Judaism, V, Supplement Two* (Leiden: The Netherlands/Boston, Brill 2004), pp. 20-31.
29 Kaplan, Aryeh. *Sefer Yetzirah: The Book of Creation in Theory and Practice* (Boston: Weiser Books, 1997), pp. 199-200; Ribner, Melinda, *Kabbalah Month by Month: A Year of Spiritual Practice and Personal Transformation* San Francisco, CA: Jossey-Bass, 2002).
30 Jastrow, Marcus. *Dictionary of the Targumim, The Talmud Babli and Yerushalmi, and the Midrashic Literature* (Peabody, MA: Hendrickson Publishers, 2005), pp. 356, 1344, 1307.
31 Kaplan, Aryeh. *Sefer Yetzirah: The Book of Creation in Theory and Practice* (Boston: Weiser Books, 1997), p. 214.
32 Genesis 1:21, 2:19, 9:10-16
33 Seidenberg, David. *Kabbalah and Ecology: God's Image in the More-than-Human World* (Cambridge University Press, 2016).
34 Seidenberg, David. *Kabbalah and Ecology: God's Image in the More-than-Human World* (Cambridge University Press, 2016), p. 211.

Endnotes to Chapter 5

35 This particular version is from the Saadyan Recension. See Hayman, Peter. *Sefer Yesira: Edition, Translation, and Text-Critical Commentary* (Tubingen, Germany: Mohr Siebeck, 2004), p. 160.
36 Kaplan, Aryeh. *Sefer Yetzirah: The Book of Creation in Theory and Practice* (Boston: Weiser Books, 1997), pp. 214-218.
37 Lorelai Kude, private communication, Jan. 15, 2018.
38 Zohar I, 119b-120a; Zohar I, 154b-155a
39 Tikkunei Zohar 147b; *Reishit Chochmah* 2:8 (Elijah ben Moses de Vidas).

Endnotes to Chapter 6

1. Marla Segol notes that the beginning and the end of the book reflect one another. She suggests that *Sefer Yetzirah* has a ring structure: it begins with an invocation, proceeds to a central point, and works its way back toward the start (Segol, Marla. *Word and Image in Medieval Kabbalah: The Texts, Commentaries, and Diagrams of the Sefer Yetzirah* (New York: Palgrave MacMillan, 2012), pp. 49-61.)
2. Hayman ultimately includes the passage because of its presence in the Saadyan Recension. However, it is not clear where to place the paragraph, since Saadya Gaon places it earlier, in Chapter 3. (Hayman, Peter. *Sefer Yesira: Edition, Translation, and Text-Critical Commentary* (Tubingen, Germany: Mohr Siebeck, 2004), pp. 51, 171.) Following the Vilna Gaon's version, Kaplan places it later, as the penultimate passage of the book. This in some way makes the most sense, as the passage is clearly meant as an ending. (Kaplan, Aryeh. *Sefer Yetzirah: The Book of Creation in Theory and Practice* (Boston: Weiser Books, 1997), p. 254.)
3. Hayman, Peter. *Sefer Yesira: Edition, Translation, and Text-Critical Commentary* (Tubingen, Germany: Mohr Siebeck, 2004), pp. 168-169.
4. Ibid., p. 171.
5. Ibid., pp. 168-169.
6. Ibid., pp. 175-176.
7. Numbers 28:19
8. Genesis 21:28
9. Deuteronomy 32:8
10. Abram, David, *The Spell of the Sensuous: Perception and Language in a More-Than-Human World* (Visalia, CA: Vintage, 1997), pp. 183-184.
11. Isaiah 8:2
12. Deuteronomy 30:19; 32:1
13. Deuteronomy 19:15
14. Ruth 4:10
15. Roberts, Elizabeth F.S. "Ritual Humility in Modern Laboratories, or, Why Ecuadorian IVF Practitioners Pray," in Sax, William, Quack, Johannes, and Weinhold, Jan. (ed). *The Problem of Ritual Efficacy* (Oxford: Oxford University Press, 2010) pp. 131-168.
16. Exodus 38:21
17. Hayman, Peter. *Sefer Yesira: Edition, Translation, and Text-Critical Commentary* (Tubingen, Germany: Mohr Siebeck, 2004), pp. 176-177.
18. Kaplan, Aryeh. *Sefer Yetzirah: The Book of Creation in Theory and Practice* (Boston: Weiser Books, 1997), pp. 231-232.

19 Job 26:13; Kaplan, Aryeh. *Sefer Yetzirah: The Book of Creation in Theory and Practice* (Boston: Weiser Books, 1997), p. 233. The Hebrew term for Pole Serpent is *Nachash Bareach*.
20 Kude, Lorelai. "Yesh Mazal l'Yisrael: Astrology and Identity in Jewish Culture" (Master's Thesis, Graduate Theological Union, March 2018), p. 50.
21 Ibid.
22 Scharf, Andrew. *The Universe of Shabbetai Donnolo* (Warminster, England: Aris and Phillips, 1976), p. 11.
23 Gaon, Saadia. *Commentaire sur le Sefer Yetzirah*, trans. Mayer Lambert (Lagresse: Verdier, 2001), p. 73.
24 Kaplan, Aryeh. *Sefer Yetzirah: The Book of Creation in Theory and Practice* (Boston: Weiser Books, 1997), p. 236, quoting the Vilna Gaon on Tikunei Zohar 49 (89b).
25 Segol, Marla. *Word and Image in Medieval Kabbalah: The Texts, Commentaries, and Diagrams of the Sefer Yetzirah* (New York: Palgrave MacMillan, 2012), p. 62.
26 Kaplan, Aryeh. *Sefer Yetzirah: The Book of Creation in Theory and Practice* (Boston: Weiser Books, 1997), pp. 232-233.
27 Enuma Elish. See Dalley, Stephanie, *Myths from Mesopotamia* (Oxford: Oxford University Press, 1987), p. 328.
28 Genesis 1:21; Psalms 104:26; Job 40:25
29 Genesis 1:6
30 Segol, Marla. *Word and Image in Medieval Kabbalah: The Texts, Commentaries, and Diagrams of the Sefer Yetzirah* (New York: Palgrave MacMillan, 2012), p. 62.
31 Attanasio, A. A. *The Serpent and the Grail* (San Francisco, CA: HarperPrism, 1999), p. 20.
32 Brown, F., Driver, S. and Briggs, C. *The Brown-Driver-Briggs Hebrew and English Lexicon* (Peabody, MA: Hendrickson Publishers, 2000), p. 166.
33 Mancuso, Piergabriele. *Shabbetai Donnolo's Sefer Hakhmoni, Studies in Jewish History and Culture* (Leyden, Netherlands: Brill, 2010), p. 348.
34 Ezekiel 10:2, 13
35 Ezekiel 1:21
36 Pirkei Avot 4:1
37 Babylonian Talmud, Berachot 54a
38 St. John of the Cross, "La Noche Oscura del Alma," from Sarmiento, Edward. "A Study of the Poem 'Noche Oscura del Alma' of St. John of the Cross," *New Blackfriars*, vol. 72, no. 849 (May 1991), pp. 230-239.
39 Kaplan, p. 242.
40 Meroz, Ronit, "Between Sefer Yetzirah and Wisdom Literature," *Journal for the Study of Religions and Ideologies*, vol. 6 no. 18 (Winter 2007), p. 114. Meroz, who understands *Sefer Yetzirah* as a weaving of three source texts, sees this

concern with opposites as characteristic of what she calls the "Depth Account."

41 Kohler, Kaufmann and Ginzburg, Louis. "Sefer Yezirah," in *Jewish Encyclopedia* (1906). http://www.jewishencyclopedia.com/articles/15084-yezirah-sefer Accessed Feb. 5, 2019.

42 Kohler, Kaufmann and Ginzburg, Louis. "Sefer Yezirah," in *Jewish Encyclopedia* (1906). http://www.jewishencyclopedia.com/articles/15084-yezirah-sefer Accessed Feb. 5, 2019.

43 Genesis Rabbah 12:6

44 Kaplan, Aryeh. *Sefer Yetzirah: The Book of Creation in Theory and Practice* (Boston: Weiser Books, 1997), p. 247.

45 Hayman, Peter. *Sefer Yesira: Edition, Translation, and Text-Critical Commentary* (Tubingen, Germany: Mohr Siebeck, 2004), p. 51.

46 The manuscript tradition concerning this passage is extremely difficult, with significant divergence between the Short Recension and the Saadyan Recension (Hayman, Peter. *Sefer Yesira: Edition, Translation, and Text-Critical Commentary* (Tubingen, Germany: Mohr Siebeck, 2004), p. 180-181). There are also a variety of locations for this paragraph—some manuscripts place it in Chapter 4 rather than Chapter 6 (Meroz, Ronit, "Between Sefer Yetzirah and Wisdom Literature," *Journal for the Study of Religions and Ideologies*, vol. 6 no. 18 (Winter 2007), p. 118; Hayman, pp. 180-181).

47 Hayman, Peter. *Sefer Yesira: Edition, Translation, and Text-Critical Commentary* (Tubingen, Germany: Mohr Siebeck, 2004), pp. 180-181.

48 Hayman names these passages 48a and 48b, and notes a complex history in which they appear in various places in Chapter 3, 4, or 6; are sometimes together and sometimes apart; and are sometimes combined with other passages. Hayman believes them to be separate passages, and believes that they both belong near the end of the book. However, they make more sense when read together, and so the current translation has put them together. (Hayman, Peter. *Sefer Yesira: Edition, Translation, and Text-Critical Commentary* (Tubingen, Germany: Mohr Siebeck, 2004), pp. 30-31, 155-156, 180-181.

49 Hayman, Peter. *Sefer Yesira: Edition, Translation, and Text-Critical Commentary* (Tubingen, Germany: Mohr Siebeck, 2004), p. 191.

50 Babylonian Talmud, Makkot 23a; Niddah 66a, Horayot 13b, and elsewhere.

51 See, for example, Babylonian Talmud, Gittin 68a-b; Song of Songs Rabbah 3:8.

52 II Chronicles 3:1; Mekhilta deRabbi Yishmael 14:15

53 The respective Hebrew verbs are *heivin, ba,* and *tzipah*.

54 See Idel, Moshe, "The Golem in Jewish Magic and Mysticism," in *Golem! Danger, Deliverance, and Art*, ed. Emily D. Bilski (Albany, New York: SUNY

Press 1988), p. 15-35; Kude, Lorelai. "Yesh Mazal l'Yisrael: Astrology and Identity in Jewish Culture," (Master's Thesis, Graduate Theological Union, March 2018).

55 Sharon Blackie, interviewed by Rodger Kamenetz during the Dreamwork Summit, Oct. 29, 2019, sponsored by The Shift Network. https://thedreamworksummit.com/

56 Liebes, Yehuda. *The Ars Poetica of the Sefer Yetzirah* (Tel Aviv: Schocken, 2000), p. 73.

57 Exodus 19:18, Exodus 40:34

58 In some manuscripts, the phrase about friendship alters to "called him his friend" rather than "made him his friend." (Hayman pp. 184-185.)

59 Hayman, Peter. *Sefer Yesira: Edition, Translation, and Text-Critical Commentary* (Tubingen, Germany: Mohr Siebeck, 2004), p. 185.

60 See Meroz, Ronit. "Between Sefer Yetzirah and Wisdom Literature," *Journal for the Study of Religions and Ideologies*, vol. 6 no. 18 (Winter 2007), p. 120.

61 Isaiah 45:17.

62 Genesis 13:15; Exodus 14:13; 12:24; Deut. 12:28; I Sam. 20:42

63 Sefer Yetzirah 4:4

Endnotes to Appendix III

1. Kaplan, Aryeh. *Sefer Yetzirah: The Book of Creation in Theory and Practice* (Boston: Weiser Books, 1997), p. 113.
2. Hayman, Peter. *Sefer Yesira: Edition, Translation, and Text-Critical Commentary* (Tubingen, Germany: Mohr Siebeck, 2004), p. 100.
3. Kaplan, Aryeh. *Sefer Yetzirah: The Book of Creation in Theory and Practice* (Boston: Weiser Books, 1997), p. 111.
4. Kaplan's instruction is to visualize the earth, then "carve each letter out of the ground and stand each one up, making a circle of letters surrounding him like a wall." Then, one visualizes a line between the two letters one is combining. Ibid., p. 109.
5. Segol, Marla. *Word and Image in Medieval Kabbalah: The Texts, Commentaries, and Diagrams of the Sefer Yetzirah* (New York: Palgrave MacMillan, 2012). I discovered this image after I'd already imagined the configuration on my own—I was delighted to find confirmation in a medieval commentary.
6. Cited in Kaplan, Aryeh. *Meditation and Kabbalah* (Boston: Weiser Books, 1989), p. 96.
7. However, one could pick a different system: for example, cycling through all of the Hebrew vowels (ah, eh, ei, ee, o, oo) during the course of the recitation.

References

Abram, David. *The Spell of the Sensuous: Perception and Language in a More-Than-Human World* (Visalia, CA: Vintage, 1997).

Abram, David and Jensen, Derrick, "David Abram Interview." Accessed May 22, 2020. https://wildethics.org/essay/david-abram-interviewed-by-derrick-jensen/

Ackerman, Susan. *Under Every Green Tree: Popular Religion in Sixth Century Judah* (Atlanta, GA: Scholars Press, 1992).

Alexander, Bobby. *Victor Turner Revisited: Ritual as Social Change* (Riga, Latvia: Scholars Press, 1991).

Attanasio, A. A. *The Serpent and the Grail* (New York: HarperPrism, 1999).

Barad, Karen., "Agential realism: feminist interventions in understanding scientific practices," in Biagioli, Mario, *The Science Studies Reader* (New York: Routledge), 1–11.

———. *Meeting the Universe Halfway: Quantum Physics and the Entanglement of Matter and Meaning* (Durham, NC: Duke University Press, 2007).

———. "Transmaterialities: Trans*/Matter/Realities and Queer Political Imaginings," in *GLQ: A Journal of Lesbian and Gay Studies*, vol. 21, no. 2-3, 387-422.

Barnard, Mary. *Sappho: A New Translation* (Oakland, CA: University of California Press, 1958).

Bek-Pedersen, Karen. *The Norns in Old Norse Mythology* (Edinburgh, Scotland: Dunedin Academic Press, 2013).

Bennema, Cornelis. *The Power of Saving Wisdom: An Investigation of Spirit and Wisdom in Relation to the Soteriology of the Fourth Gospel* (Eugene, OR: Wipf and Stock, 2007).

Blackie, Sharon. Interview with Rodger Kamenetz during the Dreamwork Summit, Oct. 29, 2019, sponsored by The Shift Network. https://thedreamworksummit.com/

Brill, Alan. "Rabbi Aryeh Kaplan—Creating 20th Century Jewish Meditation." Accessed Oct. 10, 2018. https://kavvanah.wordpress.com/2018/10/09/rabbi-aryeh-kaplan-creating-20th-century-jewish-meditation/

Brown, F., Driver, S. and Briggs, C. *The Brown-Driver-Briggs Hebrew and English Lexicon* (Peabody, MA: Hendrickson Publishers, 2000). Reprinted from the 1906 edition.

Bulgakov, Sergei. *Sophia: The Wisdom of God: An Outline of Sophiology* (Hudson, NY: Lindisfarne Press, 1993).

Busi, Giulio. "Engraved, Hewed, Sealed: Sefirot and Divine Writing in the Sefer Yetzirah," in *Jerusalem Studies in Jewish Thought*, vol. 20 (2005), 1*-11*.

Campbell, Joseph. *The Power of Myth* (Norwell, MA: Anchor, 1991).

Cavill, David. "God of Fire: A Study of Theophany and Pentateuch Fire Imagery." Unpublished Senior Project, Academy for Jewish Religion, Yonkers, NY (March 2017).

Cerf, Moran. "Neuroscientists Have Identified How Exactly a Deep Breath Changes Your Mind," *Quartzy*. Nov. 19, 2017. Accessed Nov. 18, 2018. https://qz.com/quartzy/1132986/neuroscientists-have-identified-how-exactly-a-deep-breath-changes-your-mind/.

Cook, Edward. "An Aramaic Incantation Bowl from Khafaje," in *Bulletin of the American Schools of Oriental Research*, vol. 285 (Feb. 1992), 79-81.

Dalley, Stephanie. *Myths from Mesopotamia* (Oxford: Oxford University Press, 1987).

Dan, Joseph. *The Ancient Jewish Mysticism* (Tel Aviv: MOD Books, 1989).

Diamond, James A. "YHWH: The God that Is vs. The God that Becomes." Accessed Sept. 21, 2019. https://www.thetorah.com/article/yhwh-the-god-that-is-vs-the-god-that-becomes/

Dillard, Annie. *The Abundance: Narrative Essays Old and New* (New York: Ecco, 2016).

Douglas, Mary. *Purity and Danger: An Analysis of Concepts of Pollution and Taboo* (London: Routledge, 2002).

Duling, D.C. "Testament of Solomon: 1st to 3rd Centuries A.D." in *Old Testament Pseudepigrepha*, Vol. 1, ed. James H. Charlesworth (Peabody, MA: Hendrickson Publishers, 1983).

Durkheim, Emile. *The Elementary Forms of the Religious Life* (Oxford: Oxford World's Classics, 1912).

Elior, Rachel. *The Three Temples: On the Emergence of Jewish Mysticism* (Oxford: The Littman Library of Jewish Civilization, 2004).

Faraj, A.H., and Moriggi, Marco. "Two Incantation Bowls from the Iraq Museum," *Orientalia*, vo. 74 no. 1 (2005), 71-82.

Ferraro, Jennifer and Bolat, Latif. *Quarreling with God: Mystic Rebel Poems of the Dervishes of Turkey* (Ashland, OR: White Cloud Press, 2007).

Fine, Lawrence. "The Art of Metoposcopy: A Study in Isaac Luria's Charismatic Knowledge," in *AJS Review*, vol. 11 no. 1 (Spring 1986), 79-101.

Firestone, Tirzah. *The Receiving: Reclaiming Jewish Women's Wisdom* (San Francisco: HarperOne, 2004).

Frost, Robert. "The Road Not Taken" in *Mountain Interval* (New York: Henry Holt, 1916).

Frymer-Kensky, Tikvah. "Biblical Cosmology," in M. P. O'Connor and D. N. Freedman, *Backgrounds for the Bible*, (University Park, PA: Eisenbrauns, 1987).

Gaon, Saadia. *Commentaire sur le Sefer Yetzirah*, trans. Mayer Lambert (Paris: Verdier, 2001).

Garb, Jonathan. *Shamanic Trance in Modern Kabbalah* (Chicago: University of Chicago Press, 2011).

Gold, Shefa. *The Magic of Hebrew Chant: Healing the Spirit, Transforming the Mind, Deepening Love* (Woodstock, VT: Jewish Lights Publishing, 2013).

Goldman, Bernard. *The Sacred Portal: A Primary Symbol in Ancient Judaic Art* (Lanham, MD: University Publication Association, 1986).

Goodenough, E. R. *Jewish Symbols in the Greco-Roman Period* (Princeton, NJ: Princeton University Press, 1988), 167-218.

Gordon, Cyrus H. "Aramaic Incantation Bowls," in *Orientalia* (Nova Series), vol. 10 (1941), 116-141.

Grant, Andrew. "Entanglement: Gravity's Long-Distance Connection," in *ScienceNews: Magazine of the Society for Science and the Public*, Oct. 17, 2015. Accessed Oct. 22, 2018. https://www.sciencenews.org/article/entanglement-gravitys-long-distance-connection.

Gruenwald, Itamar. "Some Critical Notes on the First Part of Sefer Yetzira," in *Revue des Etudes Juives*, vol. 132 (1973), 475-512.

Hammond, Dorothy. "Magic: A Problem in Semantics," in *American Anthropologist*, vol. 72 (1971), 1348-1356.

Harari, Yuval. *Jewish Magic before the Age of Kabbalah* (Detroit: Wayne State University Press, 2017).

Hawley, John Stratton. *Devi: The Goddesses of India* (New Delhi, India: Aleph Book Company, 2017).

Hayman, A. Peter. *Sefer Yesira: Edition, Translation, and Text-Critical Commentary* (Tubingen, Germany: Mohr Siebeck, 2004).

———. "Some Observations on Sefer Yesira: The Temple at the Center of the Universe," in *The Journal of Jewish Studies*, vol. 37 no. 2, 176-182.

———. "Was God a Magician? Sefer Yesira and Jewish Magic," in *The Journal of Jewish Studies*, vol. 41 no. 2, 226-227.

Hearn, Lian. *Emperor of the Eight Islands: The Tale of Shikanoko Book I* (New York: Farrar, Straus, and Giroux, 2016).

HeartMath Institute, Science of the Heart, Vol. 1 (1993-2001): "Exploring the Role of the Heart in Human Performance: An Overview of Research

Conducted by the HeartMath Institute," Accessed Oct. 19, 2019. https://www.heartmath.org/resources/downloads/science-of-the-heart/.

Hellner-Eshed, Melila. *A River Flows from Eden: The Language of Mystical Experience in the Zohar* (Stanford, CT: Stanford University Press, 2009).

Honigsberg, David. "Rava's Golem," in Journal of the Fantastic in Arts, vol. 7 no. 2/3 (26/27), 137-145.

Honko, Lauri. "The Problem of Defining Myth," in *Sacred Narrative: Readings in the Theory of Myth*, ed. Alan Dundes (Berkeley: University of California Press, 1984).

Hunter, Erica C.D. "Incantation Bowls: A Mesopotamian Phenomenon?" in *Orientalia*, vol. 65, no. 3 (1996), 220-233.

Hur, Nam-lin. *Prayer and Play in Late Tokugawa Japan* (Cambridge, MA: Harvard University Press, 2000).

Idel, Moshe. *Golem! Jewish Magical and Mystical Traditions on the Artificial Anthropoid* (Albany, NY: SUNY Press, 1990).

———. "The Golem in Jewish Magic and Mysticism," in *Golem! Danger, Deliverance, and Art*, ed. Emily D. Bilski (Albany, NY: SUNY Press, 1988), 15-35.

———. *Studies in Ecstatic Kabbalah* (Albany, NY: SUNY Press, 1988).

Irigaray, Luce, *This Sex Which Is Not One* (Ithaca, NY: Cornell University Press, 1985).

Isbell, Charles D. *Corpus of the Aramaic Incantation Bowls* (Eugene, OR: Wipf and Stock Publishers, 1975).

Jastrow, Marcus. *Dictionary of the Targumim, The Talmud Babli and Yerushalmi, and the Midrashic Literature* (Peabody, MA: Hendrickson Publishers, 2005).

Kaplan, Aryeh. *Meditation and Kabbalah* (Boston: Weiser Books, 1989).

———. *Sefer Yetzirah: The Book of Creation in Theory and Practice* (Boston: Weiser Books, 1997).

Keller, Catherine. *Face of the Deep: A Theology of Becoming* (New York: Routledge, 2003).

Kohler, Kaufmann and Ginzburg, Louis. "Sefer Yezirah," in *Jewish Encyclopedia* (1906). Accessed Feb. 5, 2019. http://www.jewishencyclopedia.com/articles/15084-yezirah-sefer.

Kude, Lorelai. "Yesh Mazal l'Yisrael: Astrology and Identity in Jewish Culture," (Master's Thesis, Graduate Theological Union, March 2018).

Langerman, Y. Tzvi. "On the Beginning of Hebrew Scientific Literature and on Studying History through "Maqbilot" (Parallels)," in *Aleph*, no. 2 (2002), p. 169-189.

Lesses, Rebecca. *Ritual Practices to Gain Power: Angels, Incantations, and Revelation in Early Jewish Mysticism*, (Harvard Theological Studies 44). (Harrisburg, PA: Trinity Press International, 1998).

Levene, Dan. "Curse or Blessing: What's in the Magic Bowl?" Presented during the Ian Karten Lecture, University of Southampton, 2002. Published in Parkes Institute Pamphlet, 2002.

Levenson, Jon D. *Creation and the Persistence of Evil* (Princeton, NJ: Princeton University Press, 1994).

Liebes, Yehuda. *The Ars Poetica of the Sefer Yetzirah* (Tel Aviv: Schocken, 2000).

Lobel, Andrea. *Under a Censored Sky: Astronomy and Rabbinic Authority in the Talmud Bavli and Related Literature* (Dissertation, Concordia University, Montreal, Quebec, 2015).

MacRae, George. "The Jewish Background of the Gnostic Sophia Myth," *Novum Testamentum*, vol. 12 no. 2 (April 1970), 86-101.

Mancuso, Piergabriele. *Shabbetai Donnolo's Sefer Hakhmoni, Studies in Jewish History and Culture* (Leiden, The Netherlands: Brill, 2010).

Matt, Daniel. *The Essential Kabbalah: The Heart of Jewish Mysticism* (San Francisco: Harper-Collins, 2006).

Meroz, Ronit. "Between Sefer Yetzirah and Wisdom Literature," *Journal for the Study of Religions and Ideologies*, vol. 6 no. 18 (Winter 2007), 101-142.

Michaelson, Jay. *Evolving Dharma: Meditation, Buddhism, and the Next Generation of Enlightenment* (Berkeley, CA: North Atlantic Books, 2013).

———. *Enlightenment by Trial and Error* (Teaneck, NJ: Ben Yehuda Press, 2019).

Moriggi, Marco. *A Corpus of Syriac Incantation Bowls: Syriac Magical Texts from Late-Antique Mesopotamia* (Leiden, The Netherlands: Brill, 2014).

Neusner, Jacob. "Astrology in Ancient Judaism, Astronomy in Ancient Judaism" (eds. A. Avery-Peck and W.S. Green), *The Encyclopedia of Judaism*, V, Supplement Two (Leiden, The Netherlands/Boston: Brill, 2004).

Nolan, Hamilton. "Zen Koans Explained: Nothing Exists." Accessed Oct. 28, 2019. https://gawker.com/zen-koans-explained-nothing-exists-1537931448.

Philo, *Questions and Answers on Genesis*. Accessed Sept. 27, 2018. http://www.earlyjewishwritings.com/text/philo/book8.html

Pines, Shlomo. "Points of Similarity between the Exposition of the Doctrine of the Sefirot in the Sefer Yezira and a Text of the Pseudo-Clementine Homilies: The Implications of this Resemblance," in *Proceedings of the Israel Academy of Sciences and Humanities*, vol. 7 no. 3 (Jerusalem, 1989).

Ribner, Melinda. *Kabbalah Month by Month: A Year of Spiritual Practice and Personal Transformation* (San Francisco: Jossey-Bass, 2002).

Rosh-Pinnah, Eliyahu. "The Sefer Yetzirah and the Original Tetragrammaton," in *The Jewish Quarterly Review*, vol. 57 (1966-1967), 212-225.

Schachter, S. and Singer, J. "Cognitive, social, and physiological determinants of emotional state," in *Psychological Review*, vol. 69 no. 5 (1962), 379-399.

Sarmiento, Edward. "A Study of the Poem 'Noche Oscura del Alma' of St. John of the Cross," *New Blackfriars*, vol. 72, no. 849 (May 1991), 230-239.

Sax, William, Quack, Johannes, and Weinhold, Jan. (ed). *The Problem of Ritual Efficacy* (Oxford: Oxford University Press, 2010).

Scharf, Andrew. *The Universe of Shabbetai Donnolo* (Warminster, England: Aris and Phillips, 1976).

Schilling, Lachelle. "Desierto Divino: Messages from the Earth." https://feminismandreligion.com/2017/02/17/desierto-divino-messages-from-the-earth-by-lachelle-schilling/

Scholem, Gershom. *Kabbalah* (New York: New American Library, 1974).

———, *On The Kabbalah and its Symbolism* (New York: Schocken Books, 1941).

———. *Origins of the Kabbalah* (Berlin: Walter de Gruyter and Co., 1962).

———. "Yezirah, Sefer," in *Encyclopedia Judaica* vol. 16 (1971), 782-788.

Segol, Marla. "Genre as Argument in the Sefer Yetzirah: A New Look at Its Literary Structure," in *Journal of the American Academy of Religion*, vol. 79 no. 4 (2011), 961-990.

———. *Word and Image in Medieval Kabbalah: The Texts, Commentaries, and Diagrams of the Sefer Yetzirah* (New York: Palgrave Macmillan, 2012).

Seidenberg, David. *Kabbalah and Ecology: God's Image in the More-than-Human World* (Cambridge University Press, 2016).

Shani, Ayelett, "Bewitched: What makes a Jewish Sorceress?" HaAretz, Dec. 6, 2013. https://www.haaretz.com/.premium-what-makes-a-jewish-sorceress-1.5297200.

Shulman, David. "Is There an Indian Connection to Sefer Yetzirah?" in *Aleph*, vol. 2 (2000), 191-199.

Silverstein, Kathryn. "Deep Desires: Spatiotemporal Erotica in Hebrew Priestess Re/Writing and the Question of Essentialism." Unpublished paper, presented at the Kohenet Hebrew Priestess Institute, Isabella Freedman Jewish Retreat Center, Falls Village, CT, March 2017.

Some, Malidoma Patrice. *Of Water and Spirit: Ritual, Magic and Initiation in the Life of an African Shaman* (New York: Tarcher-Pulham, 1994).

Stroumsa, Sarah. "Wondrous Paths: The Isma'ili Context of Saadya's 'Commentary on Sefer Yesira,'" in *Bochumer Philosophisches Jahrbuch fur Antike und Mittelalter*, vol. 18, no. 1 (2015), 74-90.

Thích Nhất Hạnh. *Peace is Every Step: The Path of Mindfulness in Everyday Life* (London: Bantam, 1992).

Tillich, Paul, "The Demonic: A Contribution to the Interpretation of History," (1926, trans. Elsa L. Tamley), in *The Interpretation of History* (New York: Scribner, 1936).

Turner, Victor. *The Forest of Symbols: Aspects of Ndembu Ritual* (Ithaca, NY: Cornell University Press, 1967).

Underwood, Emily. "Your gut is directly connected to your brain, by a newly discovered neuron circuit," *Science*, Sept. 20, 2018. Accessed Nov. 29, 2018. https://www.sciencemag.org/news/2018/09/your-gut-directly-connected-your-brain-newly-discovered-neuron-circuit.

Unterman, Alan and Horowitz, Rivka, "Ruach haKodesh," in *Encyclopedia Judaica* (Jerusalem: Judaica Multimedia/Keter, 1997), CD-ROM edition.

Vawter, Bruce, "A Note on the 'Waters Beneath the Earth,'" in *Catholic Bible Quarterly*, vol. 22 (1960), 71-73.

Vital, Hayyim (ed. Morris Faierstein). *Jewish Mystical Autobiographies* (Mahwah, NJ: Paulist Press, 1999).

Wadsworth, Christopher. *The Holy Bible in the Authorized Version* (London: Rivingtons, 1876).

Washington, Teresa N., *Our Mothers, Our Powers, Our Texts: Manifestations of Aje in Africana Literature* (Oya's Tornado, 2005), 13-55.

Weinstock, I. *Levarer haNusach shel Sefer Yetzirah*, Temirin I (Jerusalem: Mossad haRav Kook, 1972), 9-71.

Weiss, Tzahi. *Sefer Yesirah and Its Contexts: Other Jewish Voices* (Philadelphia, PA: University of Pennsylvania Press, 2018).

Wolfson, Elliot. "Text, Context, Pretext: A Review Essay of Yehudah Liebes," in *Studies in Hellenistic Judaism*, vol. 16 (2004), 218-228.

Work-Makinnae, Dawn. "The Rhineland Deae Matronae: Collective Female Deity in Germanic Europe," in *Goddesses in World Culture*, ed. Patricia Monaghan (Santa Barbara, CA: Praeger, 2011).

Yadin, Yigael. *Megillat haMikdash/The Temple Scroll: The Hidden Law of the Dead Sea Sect* (New York: Random House, 1985).

Zornberg, Avivah Gottlieb. *The Murmuring Deep: Reflections on the Biblical Unconscious* (New York: Schocken Books, 2009).

Ancient and Medieval Texts Cited

Babylonian Talmud
Bible
Elijah ben Moses de Vidas, *Reishit Chochmah*
Enuma Elish
Hayyim Vital, *Sefer Etz Chayyim*
Hayyim Vital, *Shaar haGilgulim*
Jerusalem Talmud
Josephus, *Antiquities of the Jews*
Maimonides, *Mishneh Torah*
Mekhilta deRabbi Ishmael
Midrash Rabbah
Midrash Tadshe
Midrash Tanhuma
New Testament
Pirkei deRabbi Eliezer
Rig Veda
Saadya Gaon, *Book of Beliefs and Opinions*
Shneur Zalman of Liadi, *Shaar haYichud vehaEmunah* (Gate of Unity and Faith)
Upanishads
Zohar

www.ingramcontent.com/pod-product-compliance
Lightning Source LLC
Chambersburg PA
CBHW050547160426
43199CB00015B/2564